D1744370

A History of
THE END
of the World

A History of THE END of the World

Yuri Rubinsky
Ian Wiseman

An Invisible Book

QUILL

New York   1982

Copyright © 1982 by
BGMRW Holdings, Inc.

Created, designed, and prepared for publication by
Invisible Books.

All rights reserved. No part
of this book may be reproduced or utilized in any form
or by any means, electronic
or mechanical, including
photocopying, recording or
by any information storage
or retrieval system, without
permission in writing from
the Publisher. Inquiries
should be addressed to
William Morrow and Com-
pany, Inc. 105 Madison
Avenue, New York, N. Y.
10016.

Printed in the United States
of America

First Quill Edition
1 2 3 4 5 6 7 8 9 10

**Library of Congress Cata-
loging in Publication Data**
Rubinsky, Yuri.
  A history of the end of the
    world.
  Includes index.
  1. End of the world.
  2. History—Philosophy.
I. Wiseman, Ian. II. Title.
[CB161.R8 1982b] 001.9 82-7568
ISBN 0-688-01392-9 AACR2
ISBN 0-688-01388-0 (pbk.)

Invocation

O for Mr Peabody's Way-Bac machine to send us hurtling back through time with a lightness of spirit, with an ability to laugh, with the power to remember that history is the joint creation of people angry, courageous, determined, dreaming, foolish, funny, hearing voices, impractical, in mobs, insecure, inspired, jealous, lazy, lustful, powerful, seeing visions, self-righteous, strong, stubborn, stupid, tired, zealous, right or wrong. Let us not forget that their stories grow directly into ours, that they—makers of history just as we are—are more like us than unlike.

There is very little in history as powerful as an idea, and nothing as convincing as an idea whose time is come. The time seems always to be right for the idea that the world is coming to an end.

Roberto d'Asturias, 1941

We believe whatever we want to believe.
Demosthenes, 348 BC
Quoted by Hal Lindsay in
The Late Great Planet Earth

Philip Roth: Do you think the destruction of the world is coming soon?
Milan Kundera: That depends on what you mean by the word "soon".
Roth: Tomorrow or the day after.
Kundera: The feeling that the world is rushing to ruin is an ancient one.
Roth: So then we have nothing to worry about.
Kundera: On the contrary. If a fear has been present in the human mind for ages there must be something to it.

Quoted in Milan Kundera,
The Book of Laughter & Forgetting

Table of Contents

Chapter One...
4032 BC to the 800s AD:
The world's major religions and great mythic sources illuminate for us our place as mortals on a mortal earth. The Old Testament prophets turn the garden of Eden into the paradise that will accompany the End of the World. All we need is someone to lead us there.

Chapter Two...
30 AD to 1000:
Christ is born and talks mostly about the Kingdom of Heaven. Visionaries, theologians and oracles reshape his view of the End, bringing it down to earth and expecting it to arrive later this afternoon.

Chapter Three...
1000 AD to 1492:
By the year 1000, everyone is in on the fun. Messiahs appear frequently and always gather followers. Humanity, particularly the unhappy and the poor, realizes that radical action can move the End closer. Action such as fighting the Crusades or discovering America.

Chapter Four...
1492 to the 1890s:
The Americas get to live through the first of the man-induced Ends. Europeans discover themselves to be as deadly as the plague, as efficient as a flood. The native tribes and nations discover what the Europeans already know: all they can hope for in times of distress is the possibility of paradise. They figure God won't let white people in.

Chapter Five...
The 1760s to the present:
Meanwhile, back in the old world, the popularity of visionaries and doomsayers, quacks, cults and serious religions never wanes. Soon they're in the Americas too. As major changes shake up the world's beliefs, the End remains constant and pure, but diversifies. Paradise grows even more alluring.

Chapter Six...
The 1760s to the present:
The Industrial Revolution directs our imaginations to the Ends of the World brought about by technology. Science picks up where industry left off, inventing—for the first time—the End that might really be final. Science fiction is born and reminds us, on the one hand, that we can precipitate our own End and, at the same time, that forces loose in the universe are of such a scale that we may never know what hit us.

An Introduction

World, This Is The End.
End, The World

Written expressly for the lay person who wants a straightforward account of a complex subject, this book is the recounting of all those optimistic times when mankind anticipated and described the End. Throughout history people have labelled esoteric aspects of the End as millennialism, millenarianism, post-, pre- and amillennialism, apocalypticism, chiliasm and various otherisms. Wherever possible this book replaces these terms with the pure, dangerous idea of the End of the World.

For the truth of the matter—and it has ever been thus—is that whatever End we imagine, we are all jointly responsible for the continuing existence of this big ball we call the earth. In the old days the collective sins of enough sinners or the collective holiness of enough faithful could precipitate the End. Today the collective politics of a handful of politicians or the collective science of a handful of scientists can do the same.

For most of its history, the study of the End of the World is interwoven with religious study. But the End is not simply a part of religious faith; it is the End that gives reason and purpose to all that has gone before.

Conversely, it is also true that everyone who preaches or prophesies an End, or any philosophic or religious system that formulates an orderly view of the End, is simultaneously attempting to make sense of life, discovering where life is most vulnerable and in what ways most fragile.

Every End teaches mortality. One reads about the End to be reminded of our gift, which is the earth, which is life.

The End and Hope

In his last column in *Harper's*, before stepping down as the magazine's editor in December 1981, Lewis Lapham wrote:

"The next twenty years bid fair to present mankind with both the brightest opportunity and the gravest peril that the human community has had to confront in the five thousand years of its written history. The rewards of success bear comparison with the biblical hope of millennium; the penalties for failure correspond to the biblical presentiments of catastrophe. We all will need our wits about us; none of us can afford to dismiss lightly any theorem, commentary, or hypothesis arising from the wellsprings of hope, rather than the pit of fear."

We Call It By Name

By coming to the world the End becomes less abstract. It is a point of intersection, the only moment since Creation when the temporal age meets the eternal. As we (mankind, acting together in myth) have always done for the Creation, we give the End physical attributes to make it comprehensible. We perceive the End as a living organic creature, the collective creation of a humanity that is afraid of it, but that can change or tame it, that sidles up to it coyly or calls on it to destroy our enemies.

In the End we find solace and power, we are comforted or made afraid. We sense in-tuitively and individually that to understand our place in relentless time, we must understand our relation to a beginning and an end. Every End in these pages is someone's attempt to find the End we can believe in, the one we can dare or hope to happen. And because of what these ends tell us about ourselves, our comfort, our fear and our imaginations, they help us believe in the present.

So Far We've Always Muddled Through

At its core, this book is the history of the idea of the End of the World. Its early chronology based on the apocalyptic beliefs of religious systems, this book is often the story of charismatic leaders thrown into spectacular relief against a backdrop of out-of-focus societies. Later the History of the End becomes the story of technology threatening our mortality, and humanity finding an outlet in fiction.

As far as possible, this History is in a chronological order; clearly the past influences the present. There are striking similarities among End beliefs; we can account for them by assuming they share biblical and earlier sources or by imagining that such powerful parallels suggest origins in a universal collective unconscious.

Most remarkable of the shared beliefs is mankind's insistence on survival. No matter what people have thought, we have always survived, or intended to survive, the End of the World.

In almost every End thus far imagined, humanity has insisted on redemption, on a creation with every destruction, on the presence of a handful of survivors, on a continuous renewal of life. Until the detached scientific predictions of the twentieth century, no End had been final.

To Help You Understand History: An Experiment You Can Try

With any sort of indelible or at least semi-permanent marker or paint, write your name on a fence or the side of an abandoned building, anywhere appropriate for graffiti but not a place that you normally frequent. After your name, write a date roughly six months after the date of your act of vandalism.

As you write, it can only be considered prophecy. A passerby will either say "How silly" or assume that the writer wrote the wrong year. "Funny", he or she will say, "the paint looks quite fresh. You would think it had been written today. Perhaps the writer intends to come back here on that day."

A month later, after the paint fades a bit, the inscription will be less meaningful. It will transmit no information whatsoever to fresh viewers. "Curious", he or she may say, "I could have sworn that this fence wasn't yet built on the date of that scribble. Oh, my mistake; that date hasn't come yet."

A few days before the recorded date, passersby will be confused. "Is it really the 21st already?" they will ask, and be relieved to hear that the author must have been mistaken. "Maybe he was drunk," they will suggest; "his handwriting is certainly messy enough."

On the date itself, you have a choice: you can visit the site, thereby fulfilling your own prediction, or you can avoid it at all costs. For the sake of the experiment, we would encourage the second course of action.

A passerby sees the faded, peeling graffito with the date. "That must have been written just earlier today," he or she comments to an uninterested friend. "Rotten paint. It already looks like it was written weeks ago. People should spend the extra dollars for quality."

A week later the inscription is history. Someone runs into you at a party. "I see where you were down at the corner of such-and-such last week scrawling your name in big letters on a fence."

"Yes", you say, "I was."

At that moment you begin to sense that the truth of prophecy is sometimes hard to track down, that the truth of history is a matter of opinion and secrets that we'll never crack, never could crack. And, still on the subject of history....

The Cynical View: An Experiment the Authors Could Have Tried

History is no more than the continual piling up of occasionally credible sources and posterity's collective willingness to agree on the truth of those sources.

The following explanation is exaggeration. One could imagine that if a copy of this book survives a few generations to end up in a reference library, later readers will have little choice but to take seriously this piece of fiction:

The late 1960s was a period of widespread panic. Hundreds of thousands of young people flocked to North America's west coast, particularly to California, where, they insisted, in a newly structured Christian society they would be able to survive the imminent End of the World.

One could pretend the era fulfilled the prophecies of the Irish monk William Butler Yeats who had predicted that after roughly twenty centuries, the Antichrist—a "rough beast its hour come round at last"—would pave the way for the Second Coming.

Just as the early Christians had done under the Roman Empire, these young people—dubbed "hippies" by their leaders and the media—refused to serve in the army because such service contradicted the instructions of Christ and refused to take part in normal societal obligations that to them were irrelevant given the nearness of the End.

Religious leaders of the rest of North American society were quick to condemn the apocalyptic visions of the hippies as being of Satan; they announced that the young peoples' hallucination-inducing chemicals—described by some partakers as "religious sacraments"—were, in fact, the work of the Antichrist.

The panic was thereby doubled: the hippies pointed to what they saw as the moral and spiritual bankruptcy of the rest of the world as a certain sign of the End, the "tribulation" and "wickedness" and "wars and rumors of war" predicted by Jesus in the Gospel of Matthew. The more staid Christians saw the very existence of the hippies as a sign of the end: as the Bible warned, the masses were following false prophets, blaspheming and insisting (as the Antichrist surely would) that their way was the true way.

The central point of this story is, of course, untrue. Many historical records are as shaky as this imaginative apocalyptic vision of the 1960s. It's only their age gives them the aura of authority.

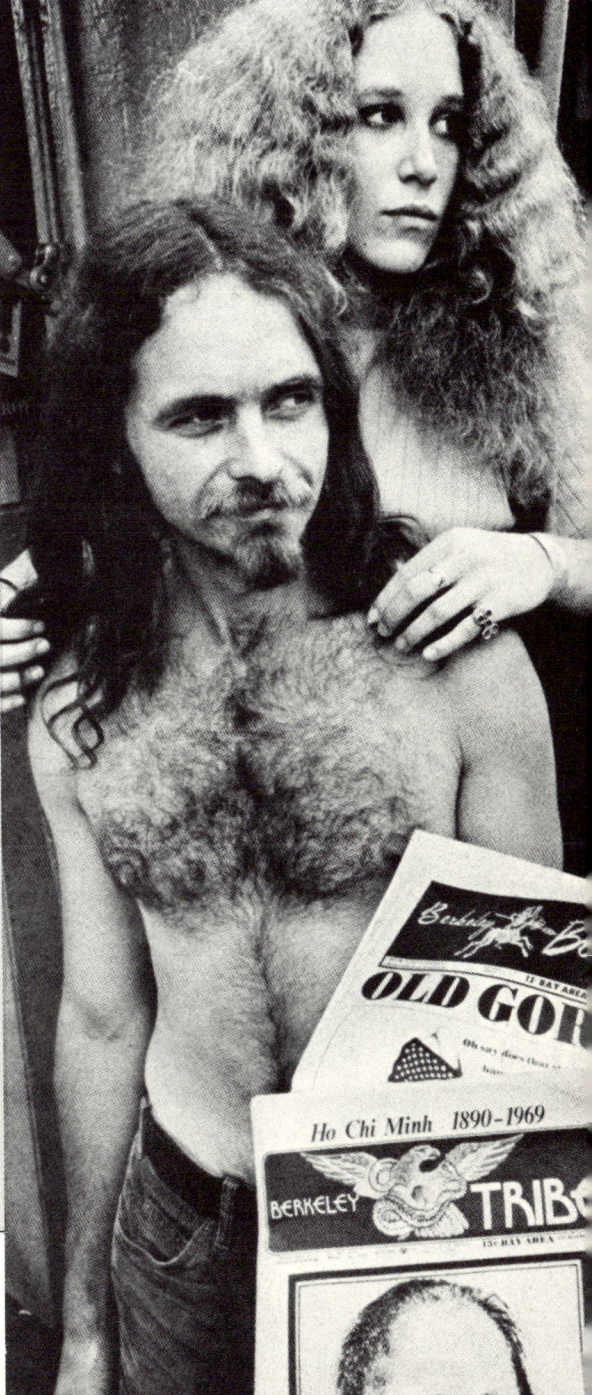

Religious Fervor?
Or Madness

Millennialist movements—usually brief flare-ups of people expecting good government, great happiness and prosperity—have been compared to hysteria epidemics and seen as eloquent examples of the madness of crowds. Some of the movements have been just that. Herein lies a great problem for believers and cynics alike.

How does one decide which movements are truly religious and which are simply insane? If God exists, and if he can appear through visions to humans, then there must be some means of distinguishing between bogus visitations and the genuine article. This problem has plagued the church since religion began.

Well-adjusted individuals, stable in all aspects of their lives, sometimes act very strangely indeed when they are acting in concert or in crowds. Many writers have noted this phenomenon but none has been able to solve its central mystery. Most of these sociologists, however, agree on one point: the crowd will not move as a collective unless the predisposition already exists in each individual. What this means, quite simply, is that given the right physical impetus or conditions, an individual can be made ready for a change.

The resulting change can be quite dramatic, including the discarding of all inhibitions. Think of the enthusiasm, the crazed dancing, the visions. Imagine a modern psychoanalyst studying the symptoms of Hung Hsiu-ch'uan of the Taiping Rebellion, or those of Mother Ann of the Shakers, or of Antonio Conselheiro of the Brazilian Canudos movement; imagine him analyzing a cargo cultist who describes his religious fervor as "head-he-go-round". Religion? Or madness?

Some millennialism, and some madness, has clearly come from situations of relative deprivation, usually when a poor people have come into contact with a richer people, technologically more advanced. The poor traditionally covet the wealth of the rich. As native lands were colonized by Europeans, particularly by missionaries who preached that the End was close, the poor took from the doctrines the most apocalyptic notions.

The madness theory, of course, cannot account for all the Ends that humanity created. But one must admit that the belief in the End comes from deep within us.

A Note Dated December 24,084AD, Found in the Rubble

The End of the World, when it finally came, was unconvincing. We were not warned by comets or sulphurous glowing on the northern horizons. There were no strange inexplicable fires or spontaneous crowds of looters or troops of horsemen foreshadowing our imminent annihilation.

There was only one sign, one subtle ominous signal: for some time man had forgotten to be concerned with his demise.

At the moment when we stopped imagining the End, we quietly loosed our hold on life.

Through the ages we lost our imaginative agility, our ability to sense in a present world the seed of its destruction—and recognizing that seed, to alert ourselves consciously or unconsciously, to the element it contained or implied which opposed or countered life.

We took our continued life for granted. We assumed inertia was an argument in favor of existence. We forgot that the apocalypse would be heralded by trumpets, comets, supernova, mass suicide and the rending of the heavens. And it was not.

The End of the World, when it finally came, was anti-climactic. It was very quiet, not multitudes in panic or a handful of children wailing. It was just one small voice, exhaling slowly, perhaps—and perhaps even now we exaggerate—perhaps sighing.

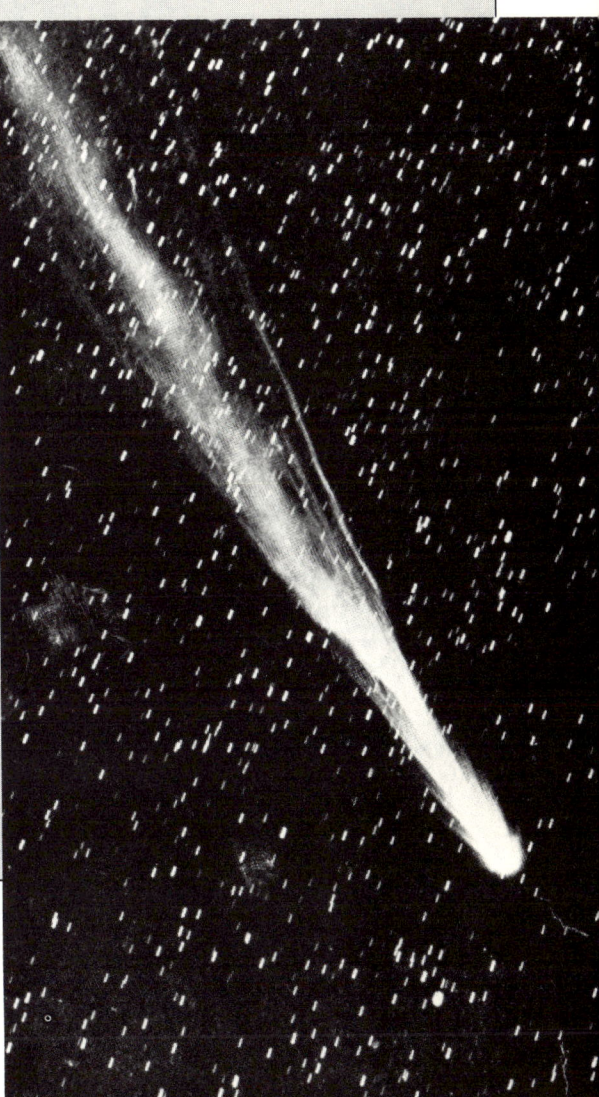

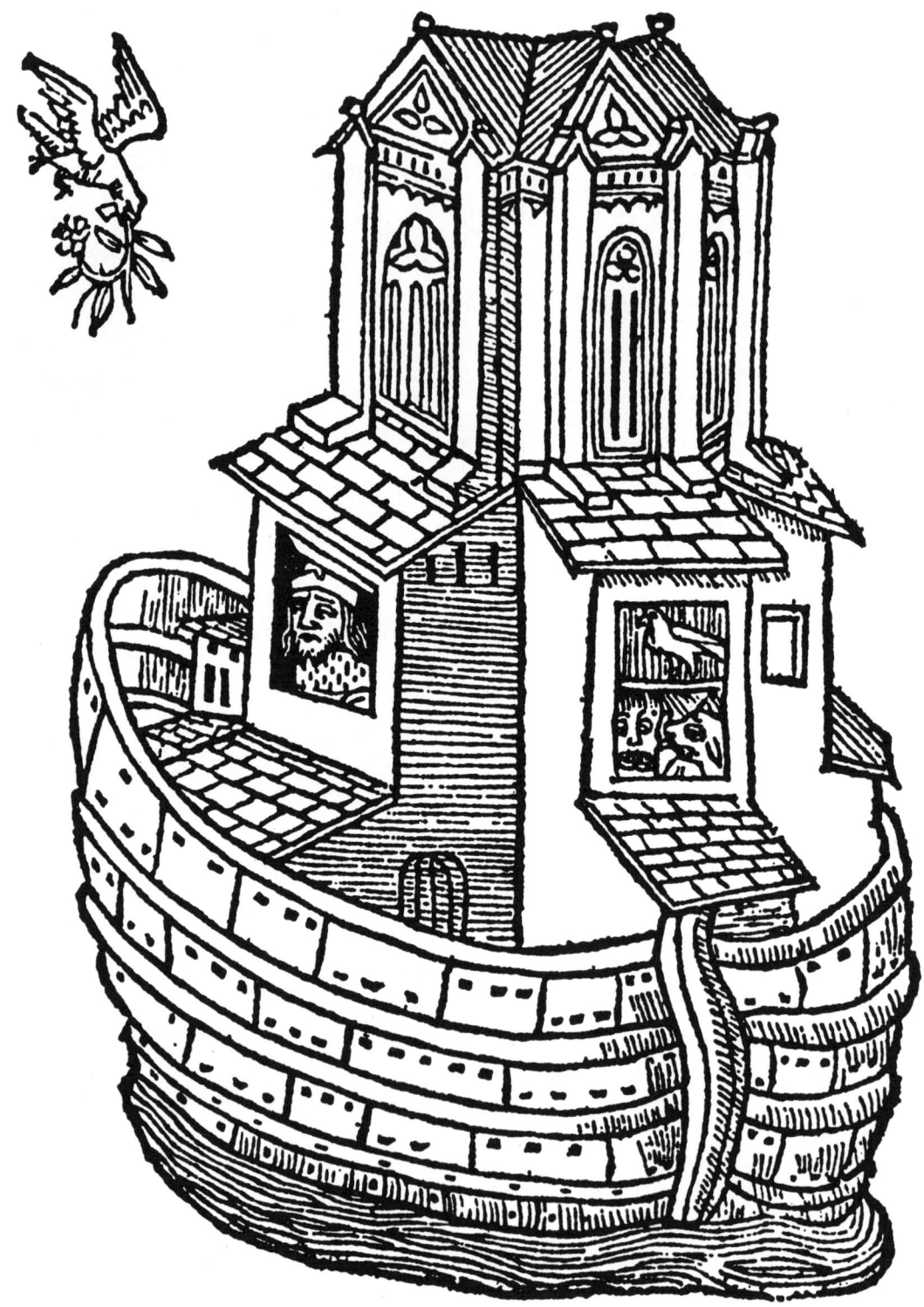

Chapter One

We Have Lived with the End for a Long, Long Time

The fact that there is an Old Testament is not, by itself, remarkable. There are other ancient chronicles, many of them equally concerned with the End of the World. This chapter presents a sampling of religious beliefs from throughout the pre-Christian and non-Christian world.

But the intention underlying the first books of the Bible gives the collection a particular importance. Their authors recorded events *as if they made sense together*. They did not simply record the passage of time, but decided, collectively, that events displayed a unity of some kind.

That unity, of course, follows from one central idea: there is an absolute spiritual and moral authority—in this book we call it God—that manifests itself in the lives of men and women, that has always done so, and that will continue to do so in accordance with its own plans, until such time as its purpose has been fulfilled.

Much of the growth of Western civilization, if not all of it, revolves around the attempts by men and women to understand God's purpose. This book records the moments in which we—humanity, acting collectively over centuries—found clues (or so we believed, each time) as to the purpose, our final destination as a people, as a world.

Men and women have always wanted to know where they came from, why they lived and what the world was all about. Inventing beginnings for themselves, they also invented ends.

This chapter recounts those ends in their earliest incarnations; these are ends pulled out of the chronology of history to introduce the spread of apocalypse across cultures and time. These are the ends that gave birth around the world to the next ends, that, slowly, gave us the Ends we live with today.

Eden and the End

Judeo-Christian perceptions and contexts have shaped this book. Accordingly, in the beginning, literally or allegorically, was Genesis and the garden of Eden.

Adam and Eve and the serpent left behind them the linear story-form of beginning, middle and end without which this book and its subject could not exist, and they introduce, in glorious detail, the concept of paradise: a garden worth striving for, worth hoping to re-attain. Without these two ideas there could have been no impetus for human progress.

In the face of all suffering, the hope of a better life ahead has given mankind reason to live. For most of history, that better life has been the one promised by God for the time of the Messiah's coming or Second Coming. It can manifest itself in one of two ways:

• It can be part of history and continuous with it, a state of perfection and fulfillment that grows out of our spiritual development; or

• It can cut off history, replacing the temporal order of human events with a new creation.

The most important aspect of the argument of continuous history is its implication that mankind can achieve perfection. Certainly Ends have been imagined and written whose purpose is to frighten mankind into better behavior; they take for granted our ability to improve if we so wished.

However, in a God-ordained End in which a new order suddenly replaces the old, mankind has to *deserve* the perfection that either accompanies or comprises the End. (In the Old Testament, Isaiah recounts the words of God: "For behold I create new heavens and a new earth; and the former things shall not be remembered or come into mind.")

The word "paradise" is an old Persian word describing a walled garden. Ancient Semitic and earlier Sumerian myths locate a sinless man in a garden paradise from which he is banished. During the centuries before Christ, a more sophisticated version of the quest for paradise appeared: perhaps the deserving might find it after death.

In medieval times many people felt the garden of Eden still existed, on earth, and could be rediscovered. The search continued; as late as the Renaissance it was a major impetus in the boom of exploration and discovery.

Meanwhile, prophecies were accumulating that made it clear that there would be a paradise-like kingdom on earth, ushered in by a great and just Messiah—and the righteous dead would be raised to share in it with the living.

Over time, these hopes grew less and less tangible, and paradise retreated to heaven, where it waits to this day.

There have been outbursts of enthusiasm for a heaven on earth, however, and many medieval visionaries actually saw a paradise of the New Jerusalem descending to earth. Its features included the river of life, miraculous life-giving trees and freedom from pain and death.

Very interesting. Details of the physical properties of the paradise at the End come directly from the garden of Eden.

Gilgamesh Meets the Survivor of the Flood

Genesis, the first book of the Bible, establishes images that recur throughout the History of the End. Perhaps the most important is the idea that the End will not be final, that God will have compassion for some of his creation and save a handful of the blessed. But the story doesn't really originate there.

In the 1850s a group of British archaelogists excavating at Nineveh, one of the buried cities of Mesopotamia, discovered what they believed to be an account of Noah's flood. What they had uncovered were the tablets containing the Babylonian *Epic of Gilgamesh*, a story whose origins can be traced back more than two thousand years before the birth of Christ.

Halfway through the tale, Gilgamesh, after losing his closest friend, ponders the meaning of mortality. He sets off in search of Utnapishtim, an old man who has acquired eternal life. The old man tells Gilgamesh the story of a great flood.

Forewarned by Ea, a friendly and thoughtful god, the old man built a great boat with seven decks, the top one an acre in size. In it he put a great furnace, with 50,000 gallons of coal and 25,000 of asphalt. It took a huge work force seven days to complete the vessel.

Soon after, the storm began. The old man took his family and the workers into his ark, along with domestic and wild animals. The flood came suddenly and violently, submerging even the mountains. The storm, inclement enough to send even the gods cringing into the safest reaches of heaven, broke on the seventh day.

For six more days the great ship lay anchored at the top of Mount Nisir, the only visible land. On the seventh Utnapishtim set a dove free, then a swallow and finally a raven. The first two returned but the raven found food.

The old man set the rest of the animals loose and offered a sacrifice to the gods for sparing him. The gods, relieved that they had not gone too far, responded by giving him and his wife eternal life.

Then they led him away and gave him a place to live on terra firma, at the mouth of the rivers. Gilgamesh, like readers to this day, was impressed and suitably humbled.

The old man's story, however, is not necessarily the source for Noah's adventures.

The Many Stories of Noah, the Flood We Share

The Epic of Gilgamesh is a rewrite. Utnapish-tim's adventures seem to have been based on an earlier Sumerian story in which En-lil, the chief god, decided to destroy mankind. A pious king, Ziusudra, is instructed by another god, En-ki, to build a huge boat to save himself. Afterward Ziusudra is given immortality.

The earliest datable tablets (copied by a scribe in 1692 BC) are of a slightly different version of the story: the god's names are the same but the king is Atram-hasis. En-ki, unable to betray the god's secrets to a mortal, whispered them to the reed wall of the king's house, saying "destroy the house, build a ship, despise goods and keep the soul alive". Atram-hasis managed to save his family and the "beasts of the fields" from the wrath of the gods.

From these beginnings grew up the great wealth of stories that tell of Noah. The two slightly contradictory accounts in Genesis are the most authoritative; other versions, in writings that didn't become part of the Bible, filled in gaps and details and created a whole folklore of flood. In the days of Noah, only ten generations after Adam and Eve, people believed the earth was thick and flat, a disc resting upon the waters. The sky was a huge and solid dome with the stars attached and the weather stored up behind.

There were giants on earth in those days, offspring of marriages between the sons of God and the daughters of men. Life expectancy was great: Enoch lived 365 years (considered the perfect age—one year for each day of a full year), his son Methuselah, 969 years and his son Lamech, 777 years. Lamech had a son, Noah.

According to the *Book of Enoch*, one of the better known non-biblical old writings, shortly after Noah's birth Lamech told Methuselah that his son was like an angel, his eyes like the rays of the sun, his "countenance glorious", so perfect a child that he was born circumcised. Methuselah warned Lamech to keep secret his son's real name to escape the evil of magicians; accordingly Noah was called Mena-chem until after the flood.

Putting together the stories from many of

the Noahic sources, one arrives at a detailed but often contradictory version of the well-known myth.

Noah was about 500 when God warned him that he would send a flood to destroy mankind, for "all flesh had corrupted his way upon the earth" and "the earth was filled with violence". Noah planted a tree of gopher wood, had time to wait twenty years while it grew and used it for planking in the ark. He spent several decades building, following plans in an old book in a jewel-encrusted box that had been passed down from Adam. He warned his neighbours to mend their ways but they scoffed, and, being giants, told him if a flood came they would stop the water with their feet. He continued to build his boat, on high, dry land, far from the sea.

The ark was in three decks, animals below, birds on the middle deck, humans above. Men and women were kept separate, their quarters divided by the gigantic corpse of Adam. Pairs of animals appeared in such numbers that Noah couldn't take them all. He engaged in an orderly system of natural selection: he allowed on board all animals that lay down at the door, and turned away all animals that stood waiting. He took thirty-two species of bird and 365 reptiles. There is no record of the number of mammals. Noah tried to keep the flies out of the ark but the devil said if they didn't board, he would. Noah took them as the lesser of two evils. In some versions of the story, the devil hid in the shadow of Naamah, Noah's shrew of a wife, and thus came aboard. In others, the donkey was slow and Noah, impatient, yelled "Hurry, even though Satan be with you." The devil took this as an invitation and came on board. The griffons were skeptical and refused to enter the ark. The unicorn, according to much later stories, was dilly-dallying and missed the boat.

Huge cracks and crevices appeared in the earth's surface and the subterranean ocean welled up through the "fountains of the great deep". The waters were hot, having passed through hell; the giants burned the soles of their feet. God sealed the door of the ark,

21

plucked two of the stars fom the Pleiades and water spilled out of the heavens.

As the waters rose, seven hundred thousand terrified people surrounded the sealed boat and tried to break down the door. Noah's grandson Canaan escaped to a mountaintop but drowned nonetheless. The giant Og, king of Bashan, climbed atop the ark and there survived, fed through a hole in the roof.

A seasick lion bit Noah and lamed him for life. Rats became a problem but Noah rubbed the lion's nose and it sneezed forth a hungry cat. Noah then passed his hand over the elephant and it gave birth to a pig, which ate all the filth of the other animals.

The ark started leaking. In one version a snake managed to stop up a small hole with its tail. In another, the dog blocked a leak with its nose—this is why dogs' noses are cold and wet. In yet another, Noah's wife stopped up the leak with her elbow—and this is why women's elbows (so the story goes) are always cold.

The only illumination was Adam's book, its jewels shining in the dark. Some sources suggest the interior was lit by a glowing philospher's stone (the mysterious alchemical mineral that turns other metals into gold).

Finally after forty days (according to the major traditions) the rain stopped. The waters slowly subsided. Noah sent out a white raven to seek dry land; it instead found a floating corpse that it started to eat; since that time its feathers have been black. Noah later released a dove that returned with a leaf from a tree growing on the Mount of Olives.

The ark settled on a mountain top, later identified as Mount Ararat in the Caucasus. Because Noah was now lame—according to some stories—he was considered unfit to offer a thanksgiving sacrifice. Instead, his son Shem built an altar and performed the rite.

Life began anew, this time more civilized: Noah invented agricultural tools like the hoe and the plow. With some guidance from Satan,

he discovered the grape and planted a vineyard, fertilizing the soil with the blood of a lamb, a lion, an ape and a pig. This explains why when a man drinks, he first is as a lamb, bleating and simple, then roars bravely as a lion, then like the ape becomes foolish, and finishes by rolling in the mud. Noah, in fact, is recognized as the inventor of drunkenness. One day his curious son Ham watched as Noah drank too much wine, made love to his wife and passed out. For this, in an early form of racism, Ham was condemned to have black skin and other Negroid characteristics and was given dominion over Africa. The two good sons took a cloth and, walking backward so they wouldn't see their naked father, covered him as he lay in a drunken stupor. For this they were given Europe and Asia.

These are only a few of the many variations on the tale of Noah. As interesting as the details are, they are important only as evidence of the way the flood has captured the imagination of mankind for so long and with such a strong sense of the physical realities of the event. When chroniclers describe an End of the World, either retrospectively as in the case of Noah, or in prediction, they are always concerned with the physical details. No less today than in ancient times.

The Fish and the Flood

Like some 200 other tribes and nations, the people of India also had a myth about one great flood that destroyed almost all human life.

Its hero was Manu. One morning he was brought his regular pan of water for washing and in it was a small fish that swam into his hands. That was surprise enough, but when the fish spoke to him, Manu knew that this was an extraordinary sign. He listened.

Take care of me, said the little creature, and I will save you from an enormous flood. Manu agreed and reared the fish, first in a jar and later in a small pond. When it was large enough to fend for itself, Manu released it into the sea.

The great fish spoke again, naming the year of the coming storm and advising its former keeper to build a ship. When the floods began to lift the vessel, Manu went aboard. The great fish returned, allowing the boat to be tied to its horn, and towed Manu rapidly to the highest mountain, where he tied the ship to a tree.

Later, as the waters gradually subsided, Manu slowly descended the mountain to discover that all the creatures of the land had been swept away. He alone remained.

No More Floods!

We survived the floods. For the first time in recorded history, the End of the World came and went.

Literature was given a series of powerful symbols for the wrath of God, images of judgement, devastation and waste, metaphors of great stormy waters to express tribulation. These symbols would reappear time and time again and become the common vocabulary of apocalypse.

But Noah's flood also left behind it the idea of God's everlasting covenant, a promise attested to by the rainbow, that "while the earth remaineth, seed time and harvest, and cold and heat, and summer and winter, and day and night shall not cease".

God admits in the eighth chapter of Genesis that "the imagination of man's heart is evil" but promises to never again curse the ground. He prepares the way for life free of the danger of a devastating end. For the next several millennia, the End of the World will be completely bound up with the idea of a hopeful, optimistic End that will fulfill God's plans for the planet.

In a nutshell, the promises escalate. After the flood, God simply says he will not destroy mankind again. Later, he promises a homeland and a place in history to the descendents of Abraham. When they undergo a great variety of perils and persecutions, he guarantees them revenge and a better life. The ultimate stage of that better life eventually comes to imply the End of this world and its replacement by another, happier one.

Greek Gods: the Good, the Bad And the Ugly

Like many ancient peoples, the ancient Greeks were polytheistic, believing in a great host of gods who would at times come to earth and mingle with the mortals. These idolized immortals were by turns playful, whimsical and spiteful and at all times larger than life. While they never quite succeeded in achieving the End of the World, they often threatened it, sometimes accidently and sometimes willfully.

From the very beginning the earth seemed close to its end. When Zeus made war on his father, Cronos, there was a great battle of rocks and thunderbolts. The earth shook and the oceans boiled; wild winds fanned fires that levelled the forests. When the dust and ash settled, Zeus had won and Cronos was banished to the underworld. As an aftereffect of this war, Atlas was doomed to carry the heavens on his shoulders so they would not fall and crush the earth.

A council of gods was formed and Zeus became the ruling deity in heaven. The troubles were just beginning. Prometheus, who had helped Zeus overcome his evil father, had meanwhile invented man and wanted to give him fire to sustain him. Zeus looked at these early men, decided they were not deserving of fire, and resolved to wipe out the entire race and replace it with a new one. Prometheus succeeded in protecting mankind and bringing it fire, but Zeus condemned him to eternal torment.

Zeus took his revenge on mankind, too, by presenting a gift: a woman named Pandora who had been schooled in guile, deceit and treachery by the gods who knew those arts best. No sooner had she been accepted on the earth than she opened a box that Prometheus had ordered kept shut. Out flew hatred, pestilence and famine in the forms of flying insects; out came murder and war, envy and revenge and a multitude of plagues to torture men's bodies. Then Pandora closed the lid. Mankind did not die immediately, but the seeds were sown, and we have not been a happy race since.

As if all this wasn't enough, another god—this time a goddess—was trying to bring the world to an end. Demeter, the goddess of earth, had a beautiful daughter whom Zeus lured away as a bride for the king of the underworld.

Demeter was spiteful in her mourning and vented her displeasure on humanity. All crops failed, no seeds germinated, no fruit grew and no flowers blossomed. All men would have perished had not Zeus, who had now made his peace with the human race, intervened.

Zeus remained a friend of the earth until the evils loosed by Pandora had become too widespread. Fraud, violence and war became the norm and, one by one, the gods retired to the heavens, refusing to set foot on the planet. Zeus called a council of the gods and proposed to destroy mankind and start anew with another race. The council considered burning the world, but they feared the blaze might accidently incinerate the heavens. Finally, they voted for a flood.

Prometheus heard of this plan and sought out his son, Deucalion, and Pyrrha, his wife, the most virtuous humans on earth. He advised them to build an ark.

Zeus precipitated his flood but the chosen couple escaped, floating up to the top of Mount Parnassus and weathering the nine-day deluge. When the waters subsided, Deucalion made a sacrifice to Zeus, who softened and granted him a wish. Deucalion wished for children. Zeus told the couple to toss some stones back over their shoulders. The stones were transformed into men and women.

In another myth, the gods came close to terminating the world by fire. It wasn't Zeus' doing this time, but Apollo's. He unwisely allowed his son to drive the chariot of the sun one day, and the horses, unaccustomed to the lighter load, spooked and bolted. First they swung too high, scorching the stars, and then too low, passing between the earth and the moon, igniting the clouds and the mountains. The earth caught on fire. The desert of Libya dried to the condition in which it exists today, and the Ethiopians became black for the first time. Zeus, realizing all was lost unless he took swift action, hurled a thunderbolt and killed the boy, setting the chariot back on its usual path.

Once again the world didn't end. Hope sprang, and continues to spring, eternal.

The Stoics and the Regenerating Fire

The Stoics were a group of Greek philosophers, popular from 300 BC to 200 AD, who believed in order, on both the personal and cosmic levels. The founder of the philosophy was a man named Zeno, born in Cyprus in the days when Aristotle was at the peak of his powers.

No coherent body of writings has survived—in fact, scholars refer to their literature as the Fragments—but enough remains to follow their thought on selected topics. One of those topics is the End of the World.

The earth in those days was at the center of, but separate from, the rest of the universe. The Stoics, therefore, while believing the universe was eternal, could easily imagine an End of the World. The world, moreover, possessed only four elements—fire, air, water and earth—of which fire was the most important, the one that would precipitate the end.

Long before it was fashionable, the Stoics believed the world was round. It was a ball of earth, covered by a layer of water, covered by a layer of air. And then, farther out where the air was rarefied, there was fire, the substance of the stars, and of God.

Zeno taught that the world, at recurring times, would be dissolved by fire, totally destroyed, only to be reborn out of the same flames. This great conflagration would purify the world, eliminating all evil and leaving future inhabitants prudent and wise.

The Stoics' god was not, however, cruel or vindictive. The philosophers believed that the creation, and the re-creation, of the world was his work, but they held that the End was an uncontrollable matter, brought about by the pervasiveness, and the unpredictability, of fire. It wasn't god's will, it was accidental.

And they were content that the flames, which could reconstitute a visually identical world, gave their god a unique chance to make minor alterations to man's occasionally backsliding character.

Virgil and the New Golden Age

About forty years before the birth of Christ, the Roman poet Virgil had a millennial vision. He foresaw a glorious new age, one that would come to pass in the lifetime of the child to whom he addressed his fourth *Eclogue*.

Virgil was a devoted admirer of the Emperor Augustus who, in time, became the poet's patron. There are those who believe they detect the insincerity of flattery and backscratching in Virgil's writings, particularly where he predicts a new golden age.

Whatever his motivation, the writer did have a vision. Life would become divine, men would mingle with gods, and it would be a time of great peace. The earth, untilled, would produce ivy and foxgloves, mixed beans and spices. The goats, uncalled, would return home with udders full of milk, unbothered by lions or serpents. (Serpents, in fact, would perish, along with poisonous plants.)

Eventually the people of the earth would stop trading, since every land would bear every fruit. Craftsmen would no longer have to dye wool, because the sheep themselves would attain magnificent colors. Every virtuous need would be provided for.

Virgil was wrong on most of the details but it is worth noting that Augustus, no doubt buoyed up by his friend's optimism, did bring peace, order and prosperity to the Roman world.

The Hindus and the Endless Ends

An end, even when it is the termination of existence, is not necessarily the absolute end. This is the key to understanding Hindu eschatology.

Hindu literature is old, dating from about 1400 BC, and varied. There is no central book, rather there is a collection of works, some philosophical and others mythical. And there are great variations in belief, stemming in part from the conviction that the soul is eternal, while the world is temporal and subject to recurring destruction.

It matters little where the story begins. One of the Hindu systems of time is that of the four ages: Krita, Treta, Dvapara and Kali. If we can see them metaphorically as four seasons, then today we would be in the winter of a year that is over four million actual years long.

The spring, Krita, the beginning of a cycle, the purest of times, is an idyllic state of perfection when shelter and food are magically provided by trees, and meditation is the highest virtue.

This utopia disintegrates through the ensuing ages, wisdom and religion are lost, and man becomes greedy and materialistic. Crime, fear and abortion are common. By the time of Kali, the wintry age of nobility has been replaced by wealth, scholarship by arrogance, virtue by power and marriage by pleasure. Social inequalities are divisive, and people die young.

Finally there is disease, drought and famine, followed by revolution and war, and the epoch-ending cataclysm. This takes the form of a total drought that removes all sustenance from the surface of the earth.

After every thousand of these seasonal cycles, the god Vishnu performs a more spectacular End: he drinks all the water on the planet and then dries the entire surface of the earth. He creates seven suns that ignite the world, burning all the vegetation and creating a global desert. Everything is consumed by fire. Then colossal clouds pour down rain, killing the fires and creating one huge ocean. When the storms subside, the seas come to rest.

Vishnu, too, comes to rest, in a long meditative sleep from which he will awaken to continue the cycle, to recreate the world.

Buddhism: Enlightened Men, Descended Gods

Buddhism is a religion like no other. It doesn't concern itself with the objective world, or the historically religious, and insists that men are as well off as any gods. There is no real law, no real church, no savior. There is only, to the believer, the way; and there is only, to the outsider, metaphysics.

Buddhism began in the sixth century BC in India, partially as a reaction against Hinduism, from which it borrowed the concepts of impermanence and reincarnation. There was an original Buddha, a gentleman named Siddharta Gautama, who grew discontent with the privileges of his noble birth and abandoned his wealth to search for fundamental truth. After many dead ends and much frustration and asceticism, he received (or achieved) a great enlightenment, a consciousness and knowledge that went beyond all intellectual process. He realized, moreover, that such enlightenment was attainable by anyone who could find the way. This was the beginning of Buddhism. A variety of possible ends appears in its literature. None of them seems central or particularly useful in understanding the religion.

Millennialist ideas recur from time to time. In one version a future Buddha, called Maitreya, will appear 30,000 years hence, announcing his final rebirth, breaking the great chain of reincarnation. All men will live in India, a new India made much larger by the partial drying up of the oceans. The earth will be covered with a rich, weedless grass that effortlessly produces a tasty rice, and all trees will bear leaves, flowers and fruit simultaneously. Maitreya will live for 60,000 years, and his students another 10,000.

In another version there is to be a union between the state law (of Japan) and Buddhist truth, bringing a new golden age. The moral law will be achieved by all men and even the great deities of old, Brahma and Indra, will descend to earth to participate in the celebrations.

Another school claims the original Buddha predicts an end to the eon—through not necessarily to the world—when the new Buddha arrives. Between his first appearance and his second, five disappearances will take place marking the end of religion. There will be the disappearance of the attainment, of proper conduct, of learning, of the outward form and of the relics. Then comes the new Buddha.

Buddhism went through a period of decay in India in the seventh century AD and, as Islam was knocking on the western door, Buddhism left by the eastern, moving first into Ceylon, Burma and Thailand, and later into China, Korea and Japan. It is in these areas that the religion remains strongest today.

Zoroaster Learns to Separate the Saved from the Damned

In the centuries immediately after Christ, Iran, then known as Persia, was not an Islamic nation. It was, in fact, a powerful empire—by the third century Iran and Rome controlled the entire known world—whose chief religion was Zoroastrianism. Frontier quarrels notwithstanding, the two empires were generally friendly, each having an ambassador in the other's court, and as a consequence, Zoroastrianism very nearly became the imperial religion of Rome, too. It was a popular religion throughout that empire, but ultimately the throne of the Caesars chose Christianity as its official religion. By the fourth century AD Zoroastrianism was fading quickly in the West.

If the emperors had chosen Zoroastrianism, the modern view of the End of the World would be only superficially different.

The authority in Zoroastrianism is Ahura Mazda, the god of light who spreads wisdom and virtue. Ahura's teachings on the subject of the End have a familiar ring, and one wonders who was influenced by whom.

A fierce winter was on its way, a winter to terminate all life, and Ahura Mazda spoke to Yima, commanding him to build a great enclosure. Into that place he must bring the seeds of men, animals, birds and blazing fires. When Yima asks how he should choose these seeds, he is instructed carefully. No humpbacks, no impotents, no lunatics, no liars and none who are jealous or leprous. In this early survival of the fittest, the fairest were picked.

On another occasion Zoroaster himself, the founder of the religion, wondering how the faithful and virtuous would be saved, asked Ahura about salvation. He was told there will be fifty-seven days of raising the dead, after which each man will be conscious of his sins. The good will be taken to heaven, the evil thrown into hell for three days. All the metals of the earth will then melt into great rivers, and all men must walk through them. To the saved the sensation will be of wading through warm milk; to the damned it will be like walking through scalding metal.

Each couple will be reunited, but no children will be born to them. The molten metal will have leveled the surface of the earth perfectly flat, filling the valleys just as it filled the cavities of hell. And for ever after, all life on earth will be immortal. No valleys, no sin, no death. Thus spake Ahura Mazda.

Iran remained Zoroastrian until the great Islamic invasions of the seventh century united the Arab world and, for a while, threatened to unite the entire globe.

Islam: When the Terror Descends

By the seventh century, Christianity was prospering, having conquered paganism and consolidated itself within the old Roman Empire. For the first time there appeared to be no serious religious or imperial threats. Then, seemingly out of nowhere, came the hordes of Islam. Arabia moved, without warning or precedent, into the forefront of history. It brought with it, and spread a vigorous conception of, the End.

The leader of this new movement was Mohammed, a divine messenger, an apostle of god. His followers, the previously disunited Arab tribes, were fervently devoted and militaristic and they spread Islam faster than any religion before or since. Within fifty years, they controlled a world extending from the Atlantic (including France, Spain and Portugal) to the steppes of central Asia (including parts of the USSR and India).

The word and law of their god, Allah, as written and recorded by Mohammed, is contained in the Koran, a perplexing and disjointed book. God is its narrator, and he often returns with new twists to recurring themes. One of them is the End of the World.

The Koran does not name a date for the End. Some scholars feel it may have, at one time, but like all holy books it has been revised and rewritten and today there remain only a few statements indicating the hour is close. Some of these, furthermore, are rhetorical or ambiguous: "The knowledge of it is with Allah alone, and how dost thou know whether it may not be near?"

If Mohammed was guarded in appointing a time, he was the opposite when it came to describing the final judgement. The sun will darken and the stars scatter; the mountains will be removed and the seas dried up; the heavens will be folded together, offering a view of paradise, and all souls (even those of animals) will be brought to judgement.

When the terror descends, says the Koran in another passage, the earth shall be rocked, the mountains crumbled and the dust scattered. The companions of the right, the virtuous and those who know the Koran, shall pass into heaven; while the companions of the left, the sinful and the disbelievers, shall be fettered and roasted in hell. The trumpet will blow a single blast, the earth will be crushed with a single blow, and the terror shall come to pass.

The Vikings:
Ends for a Cold Climate

Scholars disagree as to the origins of the Norsemen's rich and varied literature of the End. The early Vikings have a history dating at least one thousand years before the birth of Christ, but the literature can only be followed back to 800 AD, around the time when the first Christians appeared in Scandinavia, flogging their millennialism.

It matters little, in the long run, that we can't trace the ancestry of these Nordic myths. The stories, in all their color and innovation, have been passed down to the present.

The most famous is the story of Ragnarok, which roughly translates as "twilight of the gods". Following a time of great immorality, when all the Norse taboos are broken, there is the sound of a warning trumpet. A horde of giants appear, to do battle with the gods. The swords shine brighter than the sun and as the battle progresses the gods fall one by one. Finally, with the last glimmer of sunlight, in a recurrent Norse motif, the earth sinks into the sea.

In another myth, a millennialist story, Baldr, a young god, is troubled by nightmares. To protect him, his mother extracts oaths from all stones, plants and animals, but she forgets mistletoe. The other gods taunt him and one evil god, having discovered the mother's oversight, has Baldr killed by a spear of mistletoe. The gods grieve and ask the highest god to return Baldr to life. Their petition is granted, providing all things weep for his return. The evil god refuses to weep and, as a result, the Vikings are still awaiting Baldr's second coming.

The End of the World seems to have been a favorite theme for Norse storytellers, particularly in Iceland and Norway. In the myth of the Fimbulwinter, a terrible winter destroys all life except for one couple, who restart the world. In the myth of the world fire, the sun turns black and flames flick up to the sky. And finally, in one story a wolf swallows the sun, thereby chilling the entire world.

The Birth of Apocalypse and the Role of the Old Prophets

While Gilgamesh was recording his flood story in about 2000 BC, the ancient Egyptians were creating a wave of literature about the social state of their land under the Twelfth Dynasty. They denounced the evils and misgovernment in the land in many works; one of them, *The Vision of Neferrohu*, is the oldest piece of apocalyptic literature yet discovered. A difficult work to understand, it swings suddenly from extremely pessimistic and downright catastrophic views of its times to enthusiastic and optimistic descriptions of life restored to a fairer social order.

Some 1800 years later Egyptians felt themselves oppressed again, this time under their rulers, the Ptolemies, and under the Romans. Out of this period came more socially motivated apocalyptic writings, including *The Curses upon Egypt of the Sixth Year of Bocchoris* and *The Demotic Chronicle* (a story very similar to the Old Testament's Book of Daniel).

Other sources in the Middle East, notably Persian, Mesopotamian and Canaanite myths, were incorporating and developing traditions that would influence Hebrew prophetic and apocalyptic literature. As in Egypt, the Hebrew literature built upon the social and moral wrongs of its time and predicted an ensuing catastrophe, the Day of the Lord.

"Prophet" is a Greek word for someone who does not speak his or her own thoughts, but speaks in ecstasy or under divine influence. When the Old Testament was translated into Greek, "prophet" was used to stand for the Hebrew "navi", roughly: "one who utters a god-given message". By the eleventh century BC, Hebrew prophets were also beginning to discuss the future.

The Old Testament can be thought of as having three parts: the Pentateuch, the five books of early history and the law; eight books of prophets, including Jeremiah, Ezekiel and Isaiah; and the remaining "sacred writing" —called the Hagiographs—among them Daniel.

Around 1000 BC, bands of "nevi'im" devoted to Yahweh, the God of Israel, performed frenzied rituals of dancing and chanting in front of large enthusiastic crowds. One reads of great numbers of prophets; at first they were considered, along with priests and wise men, crucial to the governing of the nation and were kept in food and shelter by kings and a well-intentioned populace. (They later grew into such a public nuisance that the Book of Zechariah exhorts mothers and fathers to slay any son who wants to become a prophet.)

These hundreds of ancient prophets would probably have no major part in history were it not for the fact that from their ranks appeared several truly gifted moral leaders with great powers of spiritual insight. They came from all walks of life but each felt called by God to declare his word. Taking cues from Adam and Eve's banishment from the Garden and God's flood-necessitating anger, they became particularly interested in the effect of sin on the rising and waning of world empires.

Amos, a Judean shepherd and one of the earliest major prophets, lived around 760 BC. He introduced the idea that there would come a specific moment when God's wrath would explode. He called it the "Day of the Lord" and described it as a day of darkness. For him—and this was also a new idea at the time—all nations shared one God who would reward spiritually upright conduct, not simply fastidious observance of ritual. For the Israelites, most startling of his pronouncements was that God would punish them for their terrible sin and corruption by bringing devastation upon the entire nation.

Amos was succeeded by Hosea who put forward a more optimistic view of God's judgement. He and Isaiah, who followed him, built the foundation for the End of the World that has lasted to the present: an End that is not really final.

Hosea knew that the Israelites' sin would soon force God to destroy them, but he could not reconcile this with his equal certainty that God had a divine loving purpose for his people. The retribution and judgement must precede an ultimate salvation.

Around 700 BC the Assyrians invaded Israel. For the prophet Isaiah, they were the irresistible force of God's punishment. He imagined they would leave behind a handful of purified Israelites, a group of elect who would fulfill God's divine purpose.

Jeremiah began preaching in 626 BC. He

was young, came from a priestly family, and his views differed significantly from those of his predecessors: upright and God-fearing non-Israelites, he felt, could be part of God's final kingdom. In this he foreshadows the later apocalyptic prophets whose concern was not the nation of Israel, but the world.

A scribe named Baruch probably wrote much of the biographical narrative in the Book of Jeremiah. It was to him that Jeremiah dictated his prophecies in 604 BC, linking together, for the first time, the fate of Israel and the cosmos. The Day of the Lord would spread chaos across the land and make its cities "lie wasted and empty". The heavens would shudder with sheer horror. The disasters he predicted came to pass in 587 BC when Jerusalem fell and the Babylonians exiled the majority of Israelites.

Everything changed at that moment. What had seemed the indestructible essentials of religious faith had all been destroyed or taken away...the Temple at Jerusalem, the Promised Land and the kingship appointed by God.

One of the exiles was Ezekiel, a former priest of the Temple. He is considered the first of the prophets to become an "apocalyptist", to signal the change in leadership from men of action to writers. Ezekiel took ancient imagery—paradise, giants, cherubs, Noah and the flood, the genesis and chronicles of nations—and reworked it, combining it with images of his own—fiery wheels, dry bones, "creeping things and abominable beasts". In so doing, he created the vigorous standard form that apocalyptic writing would follow for several centuries.

Ezekiel's visions were spectactular. They burst the confines of words and grammar. The first ones predict and account for the fall of Jerusalem. Employing a mime of symbols, Ezekiel acted out a siege with a clay file and an iron pan. On another occasion he shaved off his beard and cut his hair. He stood in the center of the city and proceeded to burn one-third of it, strike at a third with a sword and scatter the rest to the wind.

All the while he was completely silent; at the end he cried "This is Jerusalem!"

In another remarkable vision, God set Ezekiel down in a valley filled with dry bones and instructed him to prophesy to them. The bones began to shake and to move together. Muscles grew on them, and then flesh, and then skin. Finally he prophesied to the winds and from the four directions breath was blown into the dead, that they might live again.

These bones, explained God, are all of the people of Israel who shall be resurrected and united under one king in their own land, a king from the house of David, who shall rule over them forever.

Ezekiel brings together almost all the elements that will be used by future prophets in their descriptions of the End of the World and the new order that will follow in its destructive wake. One major item in the collection: the rebuilt Holy Temple in the center of Jerusalem.

The latter part of Ezekiel describes the great Temple as God intends it. Holy waters flow from beneath it in a river which is constantly increasing in volume, bringing life to the whole country. (This image returns in St John's vision of the Temple in the New Testament Book of Revelation.)

Ezekiel while in exile was not alone in his apocalyptic preaching. Some fifteen chapters of the Book of Isaiah were written by an unknown writer usually called Deutero-Isaiah (from the Greek word "deuteros", second). Often referred to as the Apocalypse of Isaiah, this section contains some of the most beautiful writing in the Old Testament.

Deutero-Isaiah predicts the coming of John the Baptist and then of Jesus Christ. He says that the Messiah will come from the house of David and will be scourged and rejected. He will have a greater success amidst the Gentiles than the Jews but shall reign forever. The Day of the Lord, with its battles on earth and among the gods, will devastate all people. Afterward there will be a new covenant established between God and mankind, more complete than that of Moses, and accompanied by a new creation: God shall give land to Israel forever and "will make her wilderness like Eden, and her desert like the garden of the Lord". And the sun will never set again.

The Birth of the Idea of Ages of History

A set of verses ostensibly composed around 200 BC explains that the Assyrians, Medes, Persians and Macedonians had each held power in their turn. In a more-or-less contemporary Persian document, the *Zand-i Vohuman Yasn*, Zoroaster, using the analogy of a tree made of four metals, describes the same sequence and announces the end of the fourth kingdom with no suggestion of what is to follow.

The identical four-empire schema was announced around 165 BC by the Roman chronicler Aemilius Sura. He went further: Rome, he insisted, was the heir to the world dominion.

Being able to recognize distinct periods in the past always helps in predicting the future. Every conceivable pattern is a clue. These ancient writings found their way into the Old Testament Book of Daniel that gave us the Book of Revelation that begat Joachim of Fiore who constructed the most elaborate systems of patterns ever.

Daniel and the Future

Written for the most part sometime around 167 BC, half in Hebrew and half in Aramaic, the Book of Daniel incorporates traditional material with supposedly current events as well as prophecies and interpretations —including some prophecies that seem to have been updated as time went by.

There are very few important biblical figures who are introduced without a genealogy, with neither mother nor father. Daniel is one of them.

He is first described as a young man taken prisoner from Jerusalem by the armies of Nebuchadnezzar, king of Babylon. Through his successful interpretation of dreams foretelling the future, and his miraculous delivery by God from a den of lions, he becomes a powerful figure in the Babylonian government.

The first interpretation is quite remarkable. Nebuchadnezzar has had a disturbing dream that he has since forgotten. All the magicians, sorcerers and astrologers insist that no one can interpret a dream without having it described to them. Daniel manages to describe the dream:

The king saw a great statue, its head gold, its breast and arms silver, its belly and thighs brass, its legs of iron and its feet partly iron and partly clay. A stone grew out of the statue and broke it into a fine dust. The dust was carried off by the wind. The stone continued to grow until it became a great mountain that filled the whole earth.

Whoever wrote the Book of Daniel simply combined two notions (which were fairly popular in his day: the sequence of five kingdoms and the use of metals to represent four ages in world history.

Daniel explains that each part of the statue stands for a successive empire, Babylon being the head of gold. The stone represents a fifth empire, a kingdom established by God that shall stand forever and that is usually imagined to be a Jewish messianic kingdom that would subjugate all gentile empires.

The Book of Daniel goes on to create much of the vocabulary of apocalypse: Daniel's is the first complete, coherent, vivid account in history of how the world will end.

Daniel's author didn't realize his accomplishment. He thought he was describing only how the ancient empires of the Middle East would end. Neither he nor his contemporaries imagined that the world would go on much longer than a few centuries, four or five at the most. It was later generations that transposed his visions to a larger-scale world.

Daniel's Apocalyptic Visions

The beast that in New Testament times was to be known as the Antichrist began life in the Book of Daniel. He was simply the fourth of the beasts representing empires, depicted by the statue in another of Nebuchadnezzar's dreams.

In it Babylon is represented by a lion with eagle's wings and three fangs among its teeth. The second beast, like a bear, is the kingdom of Darius the Mede. Daniel says "it was given a man's heart" (which symbolizes its humane character in saving the Israelites from the Babylonians). A leopard with four heads stands for the Persian Empire with its succession of four kings.

The fourth beast is too "dreadful and terrible" to warrant likening to an animal. Ten-horned, it stands for the Greek Empire, which had had ten rulers before Antiochus IV Epiphanus who was governing at the time that this part of Daniel was composed. The Greek, as far as Daniel was concerned, would be the last earthly empire.

The last beast—that is, Antiochus—will rule for three and a half years, the symbol of evil—half of seven, the ancient traditional number of completeness (a full week) and perfection. During this period the beast will come to think of himself as a god and will wage war with the true saints. But, in the end, God will sit in judgement and give his empire to the saints forever.

In a separate vision, Daniel saw a ram with two horns. It was pushing toward the west, the north and the south. From the west came a he-goat with a great horn and destroyed the ram. The goat's horn was in turn broken in the four directions of the winds and from one of them appeared a little horn that grew greater and greater.

The ram stood for the empire of the Medes and Persians, the goat was the Greek Empire of Alexander the Great and the little horn was Antiochus IV Epiphanus.

Daniel asks how long Antiochus' empire will last and is told 2300 days. (Some historians feel that a later writer-editor amended the previous prediction when time proved it faulty, but with a disarming charm, left the incorrect prophecy in the text.) And then, he is told, "the sanctuary shall be cleansed".

The book goes on to present a long and elaborate apocalypse, again detailing the empire of Antiochus and again confused about the time of the persecution: one verse predicts 1150 days (three and a half years by the old lunar calendar), a later one 1290 and a third mentions 1335 days.

Daniel's repetition of its seemingly conflicting visions—a curious type of redundancy-with-variations—is a style that we will see again in the Book of Revelation. These apocalyptic scenarios make the point firmly that they are myth—they are not dogma and therefore, of necessity, hard and fast; instead, as allegories where history dovetails deftly with prophecy, their themes and lessons transcend the facts.

Daniel bequeaths three crucial characteristics to the End of the World:

• a lack of attention to historical truth in the face of a greater concern with moral truth;

• the use of the prophetic timetable—incorporated with a knowledge that dates may be updated and prophecy readjusted;

• and pseudonymity—Daniel is the first major apocalyptic work that we know was not written by its ascribed author. It is the first of many.

The Importance of Being Ancient

One curious feature of much apocalyptic writing was that no one signed his own name to the work. Admittedly, some was rewritten older material, but the centuries around the time of Christ were mildly sophisticated: people realized that the great age of the prophets was over. They knew that if brand new lessons and predictions seemed to come from earlier times and could be shown to have previously proven accurate, they would have greater authority.

Apocalyptic literature has never lost this odd characteristic. Historians have been able to date works from biblical days to the Renaissance by scrutinizing their predictions. The moment that clear and precise prophecy gives way to murky generalization is usually taken as the time of writing.

There is a built-in skepticism to this procedure: the clear implication is that historians don't believe that prophets are actually capable of detailed prediction.

The Apocryphal Apocalypses

There are many historical writings contemporary with the biblical books that were never accepted as part of the canon. They are called apocryphal, from the Greek word for "hidden" Their very existence tells us that people were so interested in writings about the End of the World that having just the canonical books wasn't enough.

The Book of Jubilees, like so many religious books, was probably written by more than one author. It pretends to have been written by Moses after a revelation during his forty days and forty nights on Mount Sinai. Often called the *Apocalypse of Moses*, the book retells the early stories and laws from Genesis and the first chapters of Exodus. It expects 1000 years of rule by a powerful and just deliverer, a Messiah. It gives no details about him.

Many important views on the End of the World appear first in *Jubilees*, blithely contradicting each other: Moses is commanded to record events of the weeks and jubilee periods until the end of time, but later verses instruct an angel to record the future leading only up to the rebuilding of the Temple. (Twenty centuries later these events are still considered to be nearly simultaneous.) Some verses seem to indicate that there will come a judgement

that will establish the kingdom of the Messiah. Others suggest that after the establishment of a temporary kingdom, there will be a day of judgement for both the human and superhuman worlds. But still other verses indicate that the kingdom will evolve slowly and there will thus never be a moment of judgement in the process.

All these ideas reappear over the next centuries. Even if the old apocryphal books are not read today, the early biblical authors were certainly familiar with them, quoted from them and built whole theologies on the details.

The authors of *Jubilees* refer back to a *Book of Enoch*. Tertullian, one of the major early Christian theologians, cites it as divine authority. Although no longer considered part of the canonical works, an extensive collection of Enoch writings was very popular between 200 BC and 300 AD.

Enoch was the great-grandfather of Noah. The Book of Genesis never mentions his death. Instead, in his 365th year, he "walked with God" and was never seen again. Later writers, their curiosity piqued by this detail, created an Enoch lore that includes the *Book of Watchers*, *the Book of Giants*, *the Astronomical Book*, *the Book of Dreams* and the *Epistle of Enoch*.

Enoch was led by two angels through the different levels of heaven. He saw the store-houses of the snow and the dew, learned of the movements of the sun, moon and stars and was reassured that at the End of the World destruction and doom await sinners and the righteous will have deserved bliss.

In a passage entitled "Parables", repeated reference is made to a "Son of Man", the embodiment of Israel's messianic hopes. If, as many biblical scholars think, this portion of the book predates the life and teachings of Jesus, then it represents a major development in the concept of the Messiah: it anticipates not a mere symbol (as Daniel had) but a more personal Son of Man, a man.

The Apocalypse of Baruch was composed some 200 or 300 years later, toward the middle of the second century AD, from at least half a dozen sources dating between 50 and 130 AD. It is therefore concurrent with much of the New Testament writing and particularly interesting because of its anti-Christian over-tones.

The book pretends to have been written by Baruch, Jeremiah's secretary, after Jerusalem's destruction in 587 BC.

According to the story, after the collapse of the Holy City, Baruch chanted a lamentation over the ruins. He fasted for seven days and then had a vision: evil will be avenged, and the destruction he has witnessed will hasten the day of judgement and the beginning of the new age.

Baruch explained that the Messiah would appear in time to destroy the last of the four world empires described by Daniel. He will come in the form of lightning and every nation shall be subjugated to Israel. Then will come the golden age when "disease will withdraw and anxiety and anguish and lamentation will pass from amongst men...." No one shall die. Revenge and envy and hatred will disappear. Asps and dragons will play with the little children. And women will have no pain during childbirth.

Waiting Out the End at Qumran

One day in 1947, a young Bedouin goatherd tracked a stray goat to a dry, barren wall of terraces and caves overlooking the northwest shore of the Dead Sea. The goat darted into a dark cave. Trying to flush it out, the boy tossed a stone inside. He heard the sharp sound of shattering pottery.

Inside eleven caves, archaeologists found clay jars containing hundreds of rolled scroll manuscripts, some of them 2000 years old, the very latest ones dating from 68 AD. The Romans had destroyed a religious community of Essenes at Qumran on their way to Jerusalem, where they had razed the Temple. Someone had hidden the community's library and the dry air had preserved it.

The commnity had been founded in the second century before Christ by "the Teacher of Righteousness", a man who preached that the world was about to end and only his disciples would be saved.

This End was imminent and a certainty.

The Teacher of Righteousness had this knowledge from a perfectly unimpeachable source: the library contained parts of every book of the Old Testament except Esther (the only book that never mentions God) as well as many other books of the same vintage that were destined not to become part of the Bible.

Context is everything. The Essenes had so many writings that were concerned with the End of the World that one could imagine believing that all of the Old Testament revolved around nothing but the Day of the Lord. It did not, of course, but there is no doubt that as the Israelites' troubles increased, they grew more and more concerned with prophecies of the End and the accompanying Messiah. They were establishing a pattern that has stayed with mankind for thousands of years: when we find ourselves in times of great duress, no matter how caused, we instinctively look for an individual who we hope will save us.

Chapter Two

We Do Not Abandon Hope Who Hope for the End of the World

In a history of the End of the World one cannot underestimate the importance of understanding how early Christianity grew. At first it adopted completely the Jewish obsession with an apocalyptic and redemptive End, but slowly it grew more concerned with "things of this world".

The tumultuous early history of the Christian Church gave way to several centuries of stability. These in turn came to an end by the early middle ages when people began to realize that their living conditions could be improved. Once again peoples' minds turned to the promise of a better life in a new kingdom after the end of the material world.

We Pause for a Brief Moment of Summary

At this point in history, the image of the End of the World that was to become an integral part of Western civilization for 2,000 years was primarily a localized Jewish phenomenon. It had several major features:

- A first sign of the beginning of the End would be a great battle between the powers of evil (Gog's armies) and the forces of righteousness, the nation of Israel.
- This would be followed by a Day of the Lord, the day of judgement and the manifestation on earth of God's wrath and then love.
- All the dispersed Jewish exiles would be gathered together.
- The dead would be resurrected in order that they might take part in the next stage, the reign of the Messiah.
- That reign, a kingdom established on earth, would bring with it a garden paradise with the rebuilt Temple at Jerusalem as its focal point.

So much of Jewish belief—not just on the subject of the End of the World—revolves around the Temple that Jews had to restructure their lives completely when it was destroyed by the Romans in 70 AD and they were dispersed around the world. A formal part of this restructuring was the convening of the Jewish Council at Jabneh about 90 AD. One of its accomplishments was the stripping of authority of many of the old writings and the final compilation of the Old Testament.

Jesus the Apocalyptic

No one recorded Jesus' teachings during his lifetime. For at least thirty-five years after his death his history was kept alive only by the spoken words of teachers and missionaries.

Each time someone told the old stories it was in a different context, emphasizing different anecdotes and arguments, trying to convince people with a wide diversity of backgrounds and beliefs. The stories adapted themselves.

But there is no doubt that the people who knew Jesus best—his apostles, their families and the close circle of the early church—had the overwhelming impression that the world would soon end.

They knew, for example, that Jesus had felt it important to be baptized by John the Baptist, certainly a man of apocalyptic vision, whose first appearance in the Bible is marked by his cry: "Repent, for the kingdom of heaven is at hand." And they knew that almost all of Jesus' parables and teachings were concerned with describing the Kingdom of Heaven.

Jesus did not elaborate on the details of the apocalypse. (The details grew primarily out of the Book of Revelation, the last chapter in the Bible, not written until around 90 AD.) But he made it clear that these were "the last days" and that his preaching indicated the way to salvation. He would be persecuted and killed, but he would be raised from the dead. The next time he came to earth would mark the days of the last judgement.

The Early Christian Church

After the resurrection, everyone went home, Jesus to heaven and his band of disciples back to Galilee. Although they had been shocked that the Son of God could be killed, his ascension showed them that he had been exalted to heavenly glory. Some were disappointed, having expected—in spite of his denials—a revolution that would overthrow the occupying Roman forces. Some feared further harassment and investigation. All of them mourned their departed master and despaired for the future of his teachings.

The disciples returned to their families at the Lake of Tiberias. A close group now, they lived and fished together. Slowly the shock wore off. They gathered the shattered remnants of Jesus' teachings, recounting and recreating the events of his life. They were leaderless and not really expecting much of themselves, but they were convinced that Jesus would return.

They decided that Jesus' resurrection was in fact the first sign of the beginning of the end, to be followed by the universal resurrection of the dead and the manifestation of God's kingdom.

They became conscious of themselves as a group. They prayed and fasted together. Sometimes one would have a vision and speak again with Jesus, or see him again walking on the water. On one of the feast days they gathered in Jerusalem to preach and pray. They were beginning to acquire a new reputation—of their own—and there were many strangers present anxious to see these disciples, strangers who had come from Rome, Egypt, Libya, Mesopotamia, from all over the Roman Empire to be in the Holy City for the festivities.

According to the Acts of the Apostles, the Holy Spirit moved among the group, tongues of fire appeared over the heads of the disciples and they spoke to each of the foreigners in his own language. Later reports state that 3000 people were converted and baptized that day.

The band grew bolder and bolder, preaching throughout Jerusalem and gaining a great following. They explained that they were a new church, the church of the final days, and that Jesus had told them to preach and to forgive sins, because the End of the World was approaching.

The most devout followers sold their belongings and shared all that they had. Several men, led by a teacher named Stephen, were appointed to organize the daily dispensing of food.

The group's unorthodox teachings soon attracted the attention and enmity of the Jewish religious authorities who began a relentless persecution of the Christians. Their first victim was the martyr Stephen, who was stoned. This event scattered the frightened followers outside the city of Jerusalem and, by choice or by design, the first Christian missionary period began.

One of the persecutors was a man named Saul who afterward converted to Christianity and changed his name to Paul. Jesus' instructions to him were that he was to preach to non-Jews, the many pagan sects living in the lands around the Mediterranean Sea. No one had considered converting pagans before.

Paul was the first great missionary. He was to take his understanding of recent events in the Holy Lands out to the world. Eventually much of that world would call itself Christian and share a vision of the final days.

What Was a Christian?
Authority I: Organization

After Christ's resurrection, the group of apostles and their families and friends had little—yet much—in common.

They had a systematic body of beliefs and code of laws and history that was the Jewish Holy Book, the Old Testament. Most important for them were its predictions of a Messiah and a Messianic age: they believed that the events that had been foretold had come to pass with the arrival of Jesus, the man they called the Messiah ("Christos" in Greek). They shared a knowledge of his life and teachings, and they also shared a hope—nay, a certainty—that he would come again very soon to bring about the last judgement and the End of the World.

The history of the Christian church's first few centuries can be characterized by the answers to two questions: what was the nature of its authority over its adherents, and where did that authority come from?

One calls oneself Christian either knowing or not knowing what the term means. One imagines one is following the teachings of Christ, and—as we learn from history—one can call oneself Christian even while misinterpreting those teachings. In reinterpreting the teachings—or even the intentions behind the teachings—someone may decide one has become heretical. But that someone has to have the right to decide. One of the surprising aspects of the church's early history is that the apostles and their spiritual descendants had to convince the world that they had the right to call the shots, often over questions of interpretations of the End of the World and its details.

After his death, Jesus' followers were confused and dispirited. Many of them, not just his disciples, had spent a great deal of time with him, but no one had ever had to lead the group before. They needed a sign from Jesus as to his will. They got one.

The resurrected Christ appeared to Peter and reminded him that he was "the rock upon which the Church would be built". He asked him three times to "feed my sheep" and with that simple ceremony Peter was reconfirmed in his authority over the group until the end, when Jesus would come again. He later appeared to the rest of the disciples and they too assumed roles of leadership. (When Peter had to leave Jerusalem, for example, James, called the "brother of Jesus", took over his authority in the Holy City.)

The apostles believed that they had been asked by Christ to carry on the building of his church, to do whatever they thought was necessary and make whatever decisions they had to, in his absence, with his authority. They began by slowly creating a structure based roughly on the efficient Roman imperial system that they knew so well.

Deacons were elected to look after the day-to-day needs of the Christians, many of whom had given all their possessions to the church. Elders were appointed to instruct and be the spiritual leaders of each community. Priests were chosen to conduct the ceremonies and the laity was given its particular instructions. The apostles, naturally, were the highest order in the system but, as they could not be present in all congregations, with the authority vested in them by the resurrected Jesus, they ordained bishops. The bishops' authority extended over several districts, the most important one being Rome, the capital city of the Empire, whose first bishop was Peter himself.

The line of authority was very straightforward: God had sent Jesus. Jesus had chosen the apostles, instructed them in the gospels and sent them out to build the church. They in turn had ordained the leaders of the individual Christian communities.

Some Christians were already a bit surprised that Christ hadn't returned within the first decade or so after his resurrection. They decided that the End had been deferred to allow more time to baptize more people before the last judgement.

If for some reason the world didn't end in their lifetimes, then the bishops would choose and consecrate their successors. This ensured a direct spiritual link between the officers of the church and God. Nothing could get out of hand.

Politics: Can the Law Be Changed before the End of the World?

Christianity grew out of Judaism, a religion with particularly strict rules of observance. Jesus took as gospel the Jewish Old Testament and obeyed the Law of Moses. When, for instance, he ate with his disciples, he always observed the Jewish laws pertaining to eating "clean" (or kosher) meats.

Then came the church's missionary period, and with it, years of converting Gentiles to the new faith. This led to a major split between the church fathers. Paul had always seen his role as being preacher to Gentiles. James, Peter and John (whom Paul called the three pillars of the church) felt that their first duty was to the Jews. They were supported in this by the Gospel of Matthew: "Go not into any way of the Gentiles, and enter not into any city of the Samaritans: but go rather to the lost sheep of the house of Israel...verily I say unto you, Ye shall not have gone through the cities of Israel, till the Son of man be come."

The gospel clearly said to missionaries: "Israel first". The early Christians understood that the Jews were the chosen people of God and should have the first chance to be saved. The End of the World was so close that there would simply not be enough time to save the souls of all the Gentiles as well.

Paul disagreed, and from the strength of his vision and the miracle of his conversion, James, Peter and John had to admit that Paul's mission to the Gentiles was also assigned to him by God.

But this was not the end of the argument. Paul said that Gentile Christians should not be bound to follow the laws established by Moses, that they need not be circumcised, that they need not keep the rules of kosher. And they would, despite these freedoms, be welcome in the Kingdom of Heaven.

The Jewish Christians were horrified. Centuries of their history as a nation, their captivities and their wanderings, and centuries of adherence to the strict discipline of God's laws had earned them their long-awaited apocalyptic "promises of Israel". How could these new, liberal Christians receive equal rewards on the day of judgement?

Paul insisted that the era of obedience to the old laws ended when Christ died. This was a new era, a time of dependence on one's spiritual self for knowledge of rules by which one should live.

The Jewish Christians could not agree. They felt themselves part of the continuing history of Israel, one step closer to the End that had been prophesied. Indeed, the Gospel of Matthew went on to condemn Paul's attitude to the laws: "Till heaven and earth pass away, one jot or one tittle shall in no wise pass away from the law, till all things be accomplished." That is to say: the laws hold until the End of the World.

(The Gospel of Matthew, by the way, was written after the Jews-or-Gentiles controversy. Accordingly there is some reason to assume that the quotation ascribed to Jesus really came from a later Jewish Christian.)

The church members managed to compromise. In 48 AD, in Jerusalem, they held the first Council of the Apostles. Paul and his companion Barnabas threatened to carry on their missionary work in their own manner. As far as they were concerned, they were appointed by God and didn't need the blessing of the church fathers.

They didn't have to carry out their threat. Instead the strictest followers of the Jewish law backed down. A letter was sent to the Gentile Christian communities suggesting only that they eat clean meats and abstain from adultery.

This was the young church's first act of authority and its first major policy decision. From then on, James, the leader of the strict Jewish Christians, concerned himself with converting more Jews to Christianity. Paul concentrated on converting Gentiles. History tells us that they never met again.

The Scientific Basis of Apocalyptic Visions

Serious medical and scientific investigation of states of ecstacy and trances, of automatic writing and speech, show that it is possible for some people to write, speak and even answer questions without exercising any conscious control over the content.

Most authorities believe that the content of visions (as with dreams) is the joint product of data lying around in the medium's brain and the psychological environment of the visionary in his or her normal, wakeful periods. This suggests that a king's favorite seer would intuitively produce positive revelations.

Investigators have not been able to show that test subjects acting as media have ever come up with a brand new idea, that is, one that they may not have received previously, either consciously or unconsciously. Certainly, however, test subjects have been able to put together a variety of old ideas in new and often startling combinations, sometimes producing ideas entirely beyond their normal conscious capacities. Historically, this fact alone has suggested that people speaking or writing in trances are being controlled by some greater power or spirit.

For most of human history, the belief was widespread that seizure by spirits was responsible not only for visions and dreams but for epilepsy, catalepsy and insanity. This has always meant that the sincerity of a visionary is considered above suspicion. The faith of anyone who believes in him or her may therefore appear to rest on a firm basis.

Authority II: Prophets

One learns from the New Testament that prophets took a role in the early church second only to that of apostles. The Spirit of the Lord, speaking through a visionary, had an undeniable authority over members of the church. For at least a century there were many prophets, and their contribution to Christian literature is great, particularly to the literature of apocalypse.

Anyone can have a vision. At the very least, anyone can claim to have had a vision. Some can do this eloquently, convincingly—and change peoples' perceptions of truth. Unless God gives a sign, no one but the prophet himself or herself would ever be able to judge the authenticity of the vision. Jesus warned against false prophets but did not leave behind him a foolproof system for distinguishing the false from the true. This omission led to some very difficult times for the early church and considerable dissension and rivalry.

Authority III: Scripture

While waiting for Jesus' imminent return and the ensuing judgement, Christians quite naturally developed a distaste, even scorn, for the popular beliefs of the people around them and for the trivial details of social and political life in the Roman Empire. None of this could possibly matter, they felt, since when the world ended these concerns would be replaced by the far more important questions of sin, soul and redemption.

With time, however, it became clear that God was delaying. The church would have to formulate a correct attitude to the society in which it was situated.It began to do this by creating and preserving a written record of the life and teachings of Jesus. The apostles were dying off and with them the last direct link to Christ. It became apparent that their stories—with all their adaptations and divergences—had to be preserved.

The earliest parts of what is now called the New Testament date from between 50 and 64 AD. They are Paul's letters to the young Christian communities. Then came the Gospel of Mark, written in Rome between 65 and 70 by Peter's interpreter and travelling companion. Matthew and Luke, dated between 80 and 100, are both based in part on Mark. It is generally assumed that the so-called Gospel of Matthew is in fact an anonymous compilation from various sources; it is considered that the Gospel of Luke, as well as the book entitled the Acts of the Apostles, were both written by the aged Luke, known as the Physician.

The Gospel of John may have been written by the same author as the three Epistles of John (approximately 90 AD). It is unlikely, however, that any of those were written by the visionary and prophet John who wrote the book known for many years as either the Apocalypse of John or the Revelation of St John the Divine and now called Revelation.

More than any other source, that mysterious, powerful and poetical book is responsible for the language and imagery of the ensuing nineteen centuries' conception of the End of the World.

But these books were by no means the only collections of sayings and writings circulating among the churches. One can easily imagine the procedure whereby a written gospel comes into existence: Someone (Mark and Luke are only the most famous examples) wants to record what he or she remembers of the apostles' teachings. Someone else (Paul and perhaps Peter and John are three examples) sends a letter to one of the new churches elaborating on the scriptures or on a point of history. Someone else has a vision and records it on paper. Inevitably copies are made of these documents and they gain a random circulation around the shores of the Mediterranean. Each church has a different set of writings, their origins cloudy, their diversity extraordinary.

In addition to the ones we know from the New Testament, these were some of those writings: The Gospel of Philip; the Gospel of Thomas; the Gospel of Truth; the Gospel of the Egyptians; the Gospel of Mary (Magdalene); the Secret Book of John; the Secret Book of James; the Apocalypse of Peter; the Apocalypse of Paul; The Wisdom of Jesus Christ; Tripartitie Tractate; the Apocalypse of Adam; Zostrianos; the Teachings of Silvanus; Thunder, Perfect Mind. These were part of a much larger collection of apocryphal (literally "secret") Gnostic gospels. Many were purged from the churches and, over time, destroyed. There was no record of them until the 1940s when a large collection was discovered in Egypt. Scholars have only recently been able to study them.

Of all the writings in circulation, only the gospels attributed to Matthew, Mark, Luke and John, as well as Paul's letters and a handful of other documents ostensibly written by the original church fathers, managed to gain popular acceptance in most of the churches. By 180 AD, this collection comprised an authorized, or canonical, New Testament, the sacred companion volume for the Old Testament and the accepted basis for knowledge and discipline in the new Church. Its sacredness assured that it could no longer be edited, altered or added to. It had become authority, fixed and unyielding.

What Does This New New Testament Say About the End?

•"The Kingdom of God is at hand." Matthew 10:7
•"He who endures to the end will be saved. And this gospel of the kingdom will be preached throughout the whole world...and then the end will come." (Matthew 24:13,14)
•"This generation will not pass away till all these things take place." (Mark 13:30)
•"...with the Lord one day is as a thousand years, and a thousand years is as one day. The Lord is not slow about his promise as some count slowness, but is forbearing toward you, not wishing that any should perish, but that all should reach repentance." (2 Peter 3:8,9)
•"We who are alive, who are left, shall be caught up together with them in the clouds to meet the Lord in the air...the day of the Lord will come like a thief in the night." (1 Thessalonians 4:17)

Clearly it includes four minor contradictions:
1 This is the time of the end.
2 This is not quite the end, but it will be very soon.
3 This is not the end, but sooner or later it will come.
4 Be prepared anyway.

Diversity: The Heresy of Hearsay

One should not be surprised to discover that within several decades after the death of Christ a great number of churches had sprung up with the name Christian. Many had been founded by Paul on his travels; he had spent a few days preaching in a town or village and had been convincing. When he moved on, he left behind recollections of a set of stories and lessons, a basic sense of the faith and faith itself.

Many churches had been founded by pilgrims who had come to Jerusalem for holy festivities, heard Christians preach and been converted. They returned to their homes with zeal and hope, but no detailed instruction, no formal understanding of what it was to be a Christian.

Urgency was in the air. The End of the World was at hand; it was important to transmit the basic information to as many receptive people as possible, quickly.

But one should also not be surprised, therefore, to discover how different the beliefs were throughout the churches. Some of the more extreme ideas flared up quickly into sects and odd churches. Most soon disappeared but left behind them records of their variations on the Christian themes. It is perhaps hard to believe they could all call themselves Christian.

Gnosticism and Its Contribution to the End of the World

Gnosticism predates Christianity. It seems to have grown out of ancient Persian and Zoroastrian religions at a time when these and other Eastern religions were converging onto the powerful Greek culture. The mingling of these traditions with the new Christianity gave rise to a disparate and convoluted set of beliefs, all of which are called Gnosticism. Their main tenets included a conception of both good and evil gods and a sophisticated notion of a definitive End of the World.

In the earliest times, the spirit of Light was imprisoned on earth by the powers of Darkness, divided into separate sparks of light, each trapped in a human body. The goal of the Gnostic (literally "one with knowledge") is to return to the world of Light through a process of redemption. The world and its history are the work of evil holding mankind back from the transcendent liberation that is otherwise in store for us.

Each soul travels upward toward what's left of the Light, the shattered and scattered divine substance. Slowly the Light, with the addition of the souls that are sparks of the light, becomes whole again. When all the souls are gathered in, the physical universe, now without light, will end.

The Gnostic Church naturally considered itself possessed of the true understanding of Christ's teachings. Gnostics for the most part (there were many sects and sub-sects) did not believe Jesus had been of flesh and blood or that he had suffered; he was a god disguised as a man, a savior-messenger who could reveal the secret knowledge that would conduct the soul out of this world.

They went on to explain that Christ's return to the earth was not to be interpreted as physical, but spiritual. The resurrection was a metaphor for the opportunity of all people to experience the spiritual triumph over death.

This interpretation—and the Gnostics were the first to construct it—would later have a great influence on St Augustine, and through him on the whole history of the church and of the End.

According to the Gnostics, the apostles' literalness had political overtones. They felt the apostles had used the fact of their having witnessed the resurrection to give them incontestable authority over the new church, including the right to choose their own successors. The Gnostics were horrified. Anyone, they said, can have a personal experience of God's truth, not just apostles and their select. Anyone can have a vision.

Today one is perhaps intrigued by the Gnostic subtleties. But for half a century many Christians were convinced that they were heretics, the first of the false prophets that the Bible warns against. They were certainly not the last people in this history to be so accused.

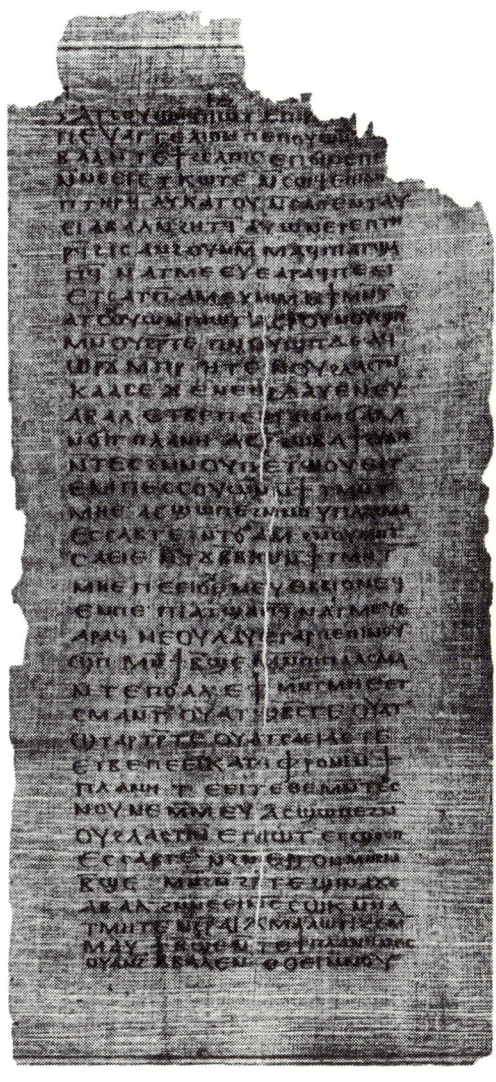

Introducing the Revelation of St John

The Book of Revelation is the only book in the Bible—indeed one of the first books in history—to be devoted to nothing but the End of the World. A strangely compelling work, probably written between 90 and 96 AD, it continues the traditions of three types of biblical and apocryphal writing: the epistle, the prophecy and the apocalypse.

The book is based on a set of visions given by God to John through the intermediary of an angel who shows the writer a set of visions of the future of the world, culminating with its End. John is to describe the visions to "the seven churchs of Asia", which is to say, to the entire church.

The imagery of the visions is neither realistic nor easy to interpret. The book uses many symbols (trumpets stand for divine voices, wings for mobility, horns for power, swords for the word of God, white robes for the world of glory, crowns for dominion) and numbers (the number seven, which had traditionally stood for fullness and perfection, appears fifty-four times; twelve, associated with the twelve tribes of Israel, appears twenty-three times, indicating their readiness for the End; 1000, which simply suggests a finite duration in years, is used six times.) Understanding Revelation is not a game for amateurs.

John attempts to inspire his persecuted fellow-Christians by explaining why they are having to endure oppression and how they will be rewarded.

One commentary points out that "the book shares one characteristic—a certain lack of coherence—with all other apocalyptic literature." This lack, and the book's heavy use of symbols, has been essential to its impact throughout the past nineteen centuries. No matter what we believe, in the ambiguities of Revelation we can always find support for our own salvation and the destruction of our enemies.

A Handy Outline to Revelation (For Reference During the Last Days)

Part I Hellos. John's introductory vision. (Chapter 1)

Part II Messages to the churches. (Chapters 2 and 3)

Part III What the future holds: (Chapters 4 to 22:5)

  1 The seven seals (4 to 8:1)
    a The vision of heaven (4)
    b The sealed book (5)
    c The six seals: four horsemen, martyrs and the wrath of God (6)
    d God's church protected and explained (7)
    e The opening of the seventh seal: silence (8:1)

  2 The seven trumpets (8:2 to 11)
    a The seven angels appear
    b The first four trumpets: super-natural calamities (8:7 to 12)
    c An eagle cries "Woe, woe, woe" (8:13)
    d The fifth and sixth trumpets: the bottomless pit and the destroying angels (9)
    e The angel with the open scroll, the two witnesses, the beast (10 to 11:13)
    f The seventh trumpet (11:14 to 19)

  3 The dragon (12 to 14:20)
    a Tries to destroy the woman's son (12:1 to 6)
    b Is defeated by Michael (12:7 to 12)
    c Pursues the woman (12:13 to 17)
    d Gives his authority to the beast (13:1 to 10)
    e A second beast appears (13:11 to 18)
    f The vision of the Lamb and the 144,000 (14:1 to 5)
    g The imminent judgement (14:6 to 20)

  4 The seven bowls (15:1 to 16)

  5 The judgement and the fall of Babylon (17 to 19:10)
    a The harlot and the beast (17)
    b The lament over the fall of Babylon (18)
    c The accompanying joy in heaven (19:1 to 10)

  6 The coming of Christ (19:11 to 22:5)
    a Victory over the two beasts (19:11 to 21)
    b The thousand year reign (20:1 to 10)
    c Victory over Satan (20:7 to 10)
    d The judgement (20:11 to 15)
    e All things are made new (21:1 to 8)
    f The description of the new Jerusalem (21:9 to 22:5)

Part IV Epilogue: Testimony and imminence of the End. (22:6 to the end)

Revelation: Just What Was Said to John

The Book of Revelation begins with a short vision in which Christ—"his eyes like a burning flame, his voice like the sound of the ocean and his face like the sun shining with all its force"—instructs John to tell the world what's to befall it. If one chooses to take the vision literally, it presents a remarkable scenario for the End.

The majority of Revelation is prophecy. It is in six parts and is set mostly in the court of heaven. God has entrusted the future of the world to the "Lamb", the only one worthy to break open the seven seals on the scroll that God holds. Surrounding God's throne are twenty-four elders and also present are four animals—one like a lion, one like a bull, one like a man, one like an eagle.

The Lamb breaks the first seal. Immediately John sees a white horse and its rider, a crowned armed conquerer. The next three seals are broken in turn. Three more horses appear with riders, a fiery red one (signifying the blood of wars), a black one (famine), and a pale sickly green horse whose rider is Death.

Christian commentators agree that the four horsemen represent Christ's sovereignty over the physical horrors of the world. God, through Christ, will manage to bring good out of all these evils.

The Lamb then breaks the fifth seal. Beneath the heavenly altar, John sees the souls of martyrs who cry out, asking when they will be avenged. They are given white robes and told to be patient until the completion of the roll of their brothers who were to be killed in Christ's services (as they themselves had been).

Commentators remind us that a seeking of vengeance wouldn't be in keeping with Christ's teaching. It is the martyrs who are looking for revenge, not John himself. The white robes symbolize their eventual victory and eternal heavenly existence. The time of this victory—the last judgement—will be determined by the "completeness" of their numbers, when God has determined that the final number of the elect has come to him.

A terrible earthquake accompanies the opening of the sixth seal. Stars fall from the sky. The sun turns black, the moon blood red. Mountains and islands are dislodged and people cry out in desperation. Conscious of their guilt, they beg the mountains to hide them from the wrath of God.

Before continuing with the seventh seal, John's vision turns to the church on earth, protected from the upcoming horrors. While four angels hold back the four winds (which are the destructive continuation of the works of the four horsemen), God's name appears on the foreheads of 144,000 of his servants. These servants, some of whom are presumably the martyrs referred to earlier, are the twelve tribes of Israel, with 12,000 from each tribe.

By the time Revelation was written, at least nine of the twelve tribes had disappeared. Few people held out any hope for their restoration. We can only assume that the 12 tribes here must stand for the vast array of Christian nations. The omission of the tribe of Dan from the list—it is replaced by Manasseh—later gave rise to predictions that the Antichrist would come from that tribe. (In Genesis 49, Jacob, as he lay dying, had predicted: "Dan shall be a serpent by the way, an adder in the path, that biteth the horse heels, so that his rider shall fall backward.")

John sees in front of the throne a vast multi-national, multi-tribal, multilingual multitude clothed in white robes. An elder explains that these are the people who have undergone the tribulation and have emerged victorious. Henceforward "they shall hunger no more . . . and God will wipe away every tear from their eyes."

The ambiguous relationship of the 144,000 elect to the multitude has caused much confusion over the centuries. Many people are convinced that this distinguishes between Jewish Christians and Gentile Christians or between martyrs and all other Christians or, and this is the most recent interpretation, between the 144,000 modern (often born-again) Christians, who will be taken from earth before the tribulation, and all the others, who will achieve true faith only after enduring terrible wars and the rule of the Antichrist.

The seventh seal is broken and there is complete silence for half an hour. Immediately afterward there is thunder, lightning and an earthquake.

Suspense builds toward the appearance of the seven angels who blow, in turn, the seven

trumpets. They call for repentance, signalling plagues and supernatural calamities.

The first trumpet brings hail and fire mingled with blood. One-third of the earth catches fire. The second trumpet brings a blazing mountain crashing into the sea, destroying a third of all sea-life. The next trumpet poisons one-third of the rivers and springs. The fourth one destroys a third of the light of the sun, moon and stars.

There is a momentary pause while an eagle, flying through the midst of heaven, cries, "Woe, woe, woe to those who dwell on earth."

The fifth trumpet introduces the demonic "fathomless pit". The pit releases a terrible

plague of locusts that torture mankind to the point where men "will long to die but death will elude them". These crowned half-human, half-monster winged creatures will have as their king an angel called Abaddon or, in Greek, Apollyon, the masculine form of "apoleia", destruction. (One should not be surprised in the early 1800s when various minor prophets insisted that this was N'Apollyon.)

With the sixth trumpet, 200 million horsemen attack, killing one-third of the earth's population. Out of the horses' mouths pour fire, smoke and sulphur. Their tails are like snakes. John learns that in spite of these horrors, the rest of mankind does not stop sinning, but continues to worship "demons and idols of gold and silver and bronze and stone and wood" and commit "murders, sorceries, fornication and theft".

The horsemen come from beyond "the great river Euphrates", the traditional home, in various revelations, of threatening pagan nations. (By the 1960s writers would be quick to point out that east of the Euphrates lies China, which had recently boasted that it could field an army of 200 million). The fire, smoke and sulphur that was once taken to signify a prophecy of the invention of gunpowder now has been understood to stand for the unleashing of the atomic bomb. Sulphur is, in fact, a component of gunpowder.

Just as the vision hesitated before the breaking of the seventh seal, it pauses to console and comfort Christendom before the last trumpet.

By the middle section of Revelation a gigantic mighty angel has been introduced, a rainbow over his head, clothed in clouds, his legs pillars of fire. He stands with one foot on the sea and the other on the land, holding a "little scroll open in his hand". His voice commands "the seven thunders", but John is expressly told not to reveal the angel's message.

The angel swears "that there should be no more delay" and gives John the scroll to eat. He does so.

John is told to measure the temple of God and the worshippers. He is told to not bother with "the court outside the temple . . . for it is given unto the Gentiles" who will trample the Holy City for forty-two months. God will then give power to two "witnesses" for 1,260 days. (Both these times signify three and a half years, the duration, according to Daniel, of the reign of the Antichrist.)

The witnesses, who later are killed by the Antichrist, are most likely Moses and Elijah. They are not mentioned by name and some have interpreted them to be Elijah and Enoch. For another three and a half years, the frolicking pagans to whom they "had been a torment" refuse to bury them. They will then rise from the dead and ascend to heaven. At that moment an earthquake will destroy a tenth of the city and kill 7,000 people. (Jerusalem when it was overrun by the Romans in 70 AD probably did have about 70,000 inhabitants. The vision is perhaps referring to this.) Suddenly all those still alive will be converted. The seventh trumpet sounds.

God has triumphed over the powers of evil and begins to reign. Heavenly voices proclaim that, "The kingdom of the world has become the kingdom of our lord and of his Christ, and he shall reign for ever and ever." (Utopias, this tells us, can be made real only in the Kingdom of God.) The twenty-four elders worship God, thanking him "who are and who wast"—the King James version of the Bible adds "and art to come", clearly superfluous at this unique moment in history when God no longer is "to come".

The Temple is suddenly thrown open with the Ark of the Covenant visible within. At the time of John's writing, the ark—a sacred chest signifying to the Jews God's presence among them—had long been lost, stolen or destroyed when the Babylonians captured Jerusalem in 586 BC. Many Jews believed that it had been hidden away in safety and would reappear in the Temple when Israel was restored or when the Messiah came.

The seventh trumpet triggers a long vision that is the story of the dragon, "the serpent of ancient times, who is called the devil and Satan". The figure of a pregnant woman appears. She is "clothed with the sun", has a crown of twelve stars upon her head and is crying out in the pains of labor. A huge red dragon with seven heads and ten horns descends from the sky, knocking down a third of the stars. It stands in front of the woman in order to devour instantly the newborn child. The male child, who is to rule "with a rod of iron" is snatched up to heaven, and the mother retreats to the safety of the desert for three and a half years.

War breaks out in heaven. The archangel Michael and his angels defeat the dragon. The losers end up on earth. The dragon begins to pursue the woman, but she is given two eagle's wings and escapes. A flood of water flows out of his mouth to drown her, but the earth opens up and swallows it. The frustrated Satan goes off to make war against the rest of her children—those who keep God's commandments and bear their witness to Jesus.

As John stands on the seashore—no longer in the court of heaven, but on earth, on Patmos—out of the sea rises a creature very much like the dragon, with seven heads and ten horns. With some characteristics of a leopard, others of a lion and a bear, the animal has one head that has healed after a mortal wound. This is the beast, Satan's agent on earth.

The beast rules over all the world for three and a half years, pouring out blasphemies against God and persecuting "the saints". Everyone on earth begins to worship both the dragon and the beast . . . all those, the Bible tells us, whose names are not written in the book of life.

With the exception of a handful of writers who apply the description of the beast to more modern times, almost all authorities agree that the creature stands for the Roman Empire, which was probably more dangerous for its religious pretensions than for its military might. The description of the healing after a mortal wound could refer to some specific event (such as the Empire coming back to life after the death of Julius Caesar; or the re-appearance of persecution under Domitian after the death of Nero) or simply to an anticipated quick growth of a cult following around the beast.

The beast, of course, is none other than the Antichrist. A second beast appears, "with two horns like a lamb" but speaking with the voice of the dragon. It performs miracles and brings to life a statue of the beast. It compels mankind to worship the Antichrist and brands their foreheads with the number 666. No one without a brand may buy or sell anything.

Later in the book this second creation is called the false prophet. It attempts to mimic the powers of good by coming as a lamb. In spite of several people's claims to the contrary, no one really knows what the number 666 means or where it comes from. Already by the second century no one seemed to understand the reference although several very complicated hypotheses have appeared. Curiously, some early manuscripts read 616 instead of 666.

John's vision shifts reassuringly from the beasts and the violence on earth to Jesus atop Mount Zion accompanied by 144,000 followers with his mark on their foreheads. This group is traditionally called the "remnant of Israel". (Greek Christian tradition was that Jesus' number was 888.) The group is listening to a powerful and beautiful song of waterfalls, thunder and harps, and only they can hear it. They are described as celibate men without guilt who follow the Lamb and have been "redeemed from mankind as first fruits to God".

Theologians hasten to point out that related passages describing the 144,000 elect make it clear they are not really celibate; they are the totality of Christians, virginity being a metaphor for fidelity to God.

Three angels appear to announce that the hour of judgement has come, that Babylon has been defeated and that any who worshipped the beast will be punished with fire and brimstone. A voice from heaven assures the world that Christians must be patient and long-suffering. Any who "die in the Lord" will be made happy.

The Jews had long previously been exiled in Babylon. Here that ancient name stands for any cities and empires hostile to the people of God.

The judgement itself is in two parts: an angel orders the earth to be harvested and the grapes to be picked and thrown into "the great winepress of the wrath of God". The grapes are pressed and blood flows in a river two hundred miles long ("1600 stadia").

Now begins the third of a series of parallel devastations. After the seven seals and the seven trumpets, seven angels, one at a time, spill the contents of seven bowls. These are the wrath of God, calamities that accompany the judgement and affect the entire world.

The first bowl brings a plague of foul and evil sores to all with the mark of the beast. The second makes the sea like the blood of a dead man, and everything in it dies. The third angel turns all the rivers and springs to blood. The fourth increases the heat of the sun, scorching men and the earth.

With the fifth bowl, the earth is plunged into darkness and men gnaw their tongues in agony, cursing God in their torment. The sixth bowl dries up the Euphrates River to "prepare a road for the kings from the east" Foul spirits that look like frogs emerge from the mouths of the dragon and the two beasts. They perform miracles and incite the world to battle. And the armies prepare for a great war at the plain called Armageddon.

The seventh angel empties the last bowl into the air and a loud voice within the Temple announces that this is the End.

There is lightning, thunder, earthquakes. Cities crumble. Mountains and islands vanish. But men continue to blaspheme God.

One of the angels takes John to show him Babylon, the woman with whom the kings of the earth had debauched themselves. She is drunk with the blood of saints and martyrs and is riding the red beast with the seven heads and ten horns. On her forehead is written "Mystery, Babylon the Great, Mother of Harlots and of the Earth's Abominations".

The angel explains that the beast which she is riding arises only to be destroyed. The seven heads stand for seven hills and for seven kings. A cryptic bit of mathematics follows: five of these kings have been dethroned, one is currently reigning and one is yet to come. There is an eighth king who will go to "utter destruction". The ten horns stand for ten kings who will reign in the future and will hand over their power and authority to the beast. They will go to war against the Lamb, who will defeat them.

The woman, the angel explains, is Babylon, the great city that has dominion over the kings, peoples, nations and languages of the earth. Another angel describes her as the city of drunkenness, wantonness and luxury. He announces that she has been destroyed and that she will be punished by death, sorrow, famine and fire. Her story is presented as a lament from the point of view of the kings who debauched themselves with her and the merchants and traders who grew rich from her. The city shall never again appear in its glory, says the angel, because all nations were seduced by her sorcery.

John hears the mighty roar as all heaven rejoices. The evil materialism on earth is contrasted with the spiritual joy and glory in

heaven. The passage is built around two hymns: in the first the angels sing of God's justice. In the second "the great multitude", the entire church, rejoices and introduces the idea of a wedding.

The bride (which is the church) is ready to be married to the Lamb. The elect are now cleansed and may be joined at once to Jesus. A wedding banquet is prepared; various voices cry "Hallelujah"—the only time that this traditional Jewish "praise Yahweh" appears in the New Testament.

Christ appears and is named as King of Kings and Lord of Lords. This is the climax of the Apocalypse. Jesus, his eyes like fire, his word like a sharp sword, his robe dipped in blood, rides a white horse. Following him are the elect—the 144,000—but their robes have been made white by Christ's sacrifice. They too are on white horses; they are the army of heaven.

The army of heaven faces the armies of the beast and the kings of the earth, but John describes no battle, only its aftereffects. In a grotesque parody of the wedding feast, birds pick at the flesh of mighty horses and men. The beast and the false prophet are captured and thrown into "the lake of fire". All their soldiers are killed.

There is one last force of evil left, and that is Satan, the serpent, the dragon. An angel shackles him with a chain for a thousand years and locks him into the great pit. Afterward he is set free "for a little while".

This is a remarkably confusing passage and the only place in Revelation—indeed in the New Testament—where there is a mention of a thousand year reign of Christ. But Christians have always taken this passage very seriously and have concluded that Christ and his

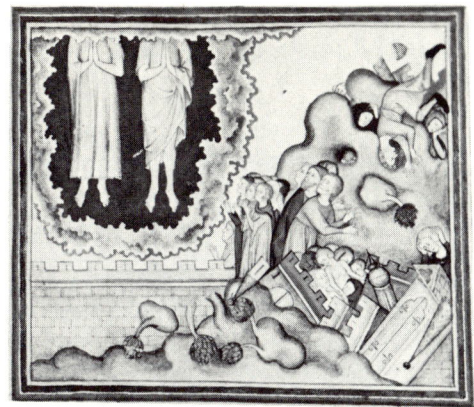

elect will first create a kingdom of God for a limited time only on earth.

Then Satan will be released from his prison and will fulfill the old prophecies of Ezekiel. He will lead the peoples of Gog and Magog into battle against Israel. His army will be enormous and will surround the Holy City only to be destroyed by fire coming "down from God out of heaven". Satan will then be thrown into the brimstone lake to spend "forever and ever" being tormented and tortured alongside the beast and the false prophet.

John's vision then focuses on the resurrection of the dead and the last judgement. All mankind rises from the dead to be judged according to what was written of their lives in two books. All those whose names are not found in the book of life are thrown into the lake of fire from which there is no hope of escape, death or resurrection.

In the presence of God on the day of judgement, "earth and sky fled away, and no place was found for them." They are replaced by a new heaven and a new earth. The new holy city, the new Jerusalem, descends from heaven, cleansed as a bride. The sea, symbol of primeval chaos and unconquerable forces, has vanished.

Henceforward God will live among men. There will be no more sorrow or crying, pain or death. All things will be new. God announces: "It is done. I am the Alpha and the Omega, the beginning and the end."

One of the angels, having some time ago taken John to see the judgement passed on the harlot Babylon, then shows him "the bride of the Lamb, which is the new holy city of Jerusalem, radiant with the glory of God".

The city sparkles like a jewel, surrounded by a great wall with twelve gates guarded by twelve angels. The gates, three facing each direction, are named for the twelve tribes of Israel. The wall has twelve foundation stones, and they are named for the twelve apostles.

The angel then measures the new Jerusalem and dictates the figures to John: the city is a perfect cube, its length, breadth and height all equal to 12,000 stadia, about 15,000 miles. The height of the wall, in comparison, is insignificant, only about 144 cubits (216 feet). John also lists the gold and precious stones that make up the wall and gates. The numbers and details, of course, are more important as symbols of the glorious completion of events than as dimensions and directions from which one could build oneself a new city.

There is no temple visible in the New Jerusalem and no need of sun or moon. Instead, the glory of God and Jesus permeates the city and there is always daylight. The gates are never closed and only believers may enter.

And through the middle of the city, directly from the thrones of God and the Lamb, flow the rivers of the water of life. On its banks grows the tree of life, which produces fruit year-round.

As a mark of the holiness that all the people have attained John is told that they will be able to see God's face—a privilege not given even to Moses in Exodus. "And they shall reign for ever and ever."

The last verses of the book simply close off the vision. The angel, John and Jesus testify to its truth, its imminence and that all the good that has been prophesied is promised to all who seek it.

John concludes with the stern admonition that God will strike anyone who alters his words with the disasters described in the book and take away his share of the tree of life.

He reminds us that Jesus said yes, he is coming soon, and ends his Revelation with a heartfelt "Amen, come, Lord Jesus!"

Irenaeus: The End Will Happen on Earth

Bishop Irenaeus of Lyons, the most influential writer of the late second century, made it clear that divine justice demanded a Kingdom of Heaven on earth. A ferocious defender of what one might call—even in these early years—the tradition of the church, he wrote five volumes whose collective title has been translated from the Greek as anything from *Against Heresies* to *The Destruction and Overthrow of Falsely So-Called Knowledge*. In this work he denounced the Gnostic gospels and others like them as heresy, "an abyss of madness and blasphemy against Christ".

Irenaeus attempted to answer the question "How does one recognize true belief?" by insisting on the written authority of Christ's teachings in the collection of gospels and epistles, and on the spiritual authority of the unbroken apostolic succession of bishops. He played down the role of so-called prophets (they had all but disappeared from day-to-day life by his time) but devoted a large part of one volume to a detailed description of the Antichrist and of the kingdom of God.

Christians had been, and would continue to be, vigorously persecuted in the Roman Empire. The Old Testament explained the redemption of Jews in terms of their eventual apocalyptic rewards and Irenaeus did the same for Christianity. He explained that "in that Creation wherein they labored, or were afflicted...in that same it is meet for them to receive the fruits of Suffering...and in what creation they endured slavery, in the same should they reign."

Irenaeus was one of the first to stress not only that the Christians would be rewarded for their persecution, but also, for God's reward to make sense after the end, the earth would have to once again become a paradise. The dead would be raised and would be the first to share in the glory of this kingdom. The enemies would be destroyed and their lands restored. The time was imminent.

Partial text of a Christian Trial at Carthage, 180 AD

It was their complete faith in the immediacy of the new age—and the rewards promised them by Irenaeus—that gave the early Christians the strength and courage to be martyred for their beliefs. Knowing they would rise again after the End of the World meant they could withstand all persecution.

Saturninus the proconsul: "You can win the indulgence of our lord the emperor, if you return to a sound mind."

Speratus: "The empire of this world I know not; but rather, I serve that God, whom no man hath seen nor, with these eyes, can see. I have committed no theft; but if I have bought anything I pay the tax; because I know my Lord, the King of Kings, and Emperor of all nations."

Cittinus: "We have none other to fear, save only our Lord God, who is in heaven."

Donata: "Honor to Caesar as Caesar; but fear to God."

Saturninus the proconsul: "Have a delay of thirty days, and bethink yourselves."

Speratus, a second time: "I am a Christian." And with him they all agreed.

Saturninus the proconsul read out the decree from the tablet: "Speratus, Nartzalus, Cittinus, Donata, Vestia, Secunda, and the rest having confessed that they live according to the Christian rite, since after opportunity offered them of returning to the custom of the Romans they have obstinately persisted, it is determined that they be put to the sword."

Speratus: "We give thanks to God."

Nartzalus: "Today we are martyrs in heaven; thanks be to God."

Montanus

One day, around the end of the second century, Montanus fell into a trance in the village of Ardabau in what today is western Turkey. Along with two women, Priscilla and Maximilla, he began to prophesy that the heavenly Jerusalem would soon descend upon the earth in Pepuza, a small neighbouring town in Phrygia, thus beginning the kingdom of God. Collections of their oracles were considered by their followers to have all the authority of revelations. Montanus himself was alleged to be a prophet foretold in a previously unnoticed passage in the gospel of John in which Jesus had said: "I have yet many things to say unto you, but ye cannot bear them now; but when he, the spirit of truth, is come, he shall guide you into all the truth."

That Christ may have admitted that his teachings were incomplete came as a shock to believers. Montanus had extraordinary initial success and the sect lasted until early in the fifth century.

Montanism had several very appealing features: it predicted the almost immediate return of Christ and called for urgent moral and disciplinary preparations; it accepted prophecy as a normal medium and authority; and, unlike Gnosticism, it made no attempt to replace the authority of the scriptures.

Its critics went further in describing the particular practices of the sect. Apollonius, writing in 196 AD, said: "If they deny that their prophets have accepted gifts, they will surely admit this, that if they are proved to have accepted them they are no prophets: I can provide endless proof of this. All the fruits of a prophet must be submitted to examination. Tell me, does a prophet dye his hair? Does a prophet paint his eyelids? Does a prophet do business as a moneylender? Let them say plainly whether these things are permissible or not, and I will prove that they have been going on in their circles."

Leaders of the more orthodox church correctly perceived Montanism as a threat. Montanus' argument was that his authority as the "spirit of truth" (called the Paraclete) was second only to that of Jesus. Bishops and the other Christian leaders were therefore left out entirely. They fiercely condemned both Montanus and the new movement.

Hippolytus, writing in 215 AD, explained that followers of the new movement "have been deceived by two females, Priscilla and Maximilla by name, whom they hold to be prophetesses, asserting that into them the Paraclete spirit entered....They magnify these females above the Apostles and every gift of grace, so that some of them go so far as to say that there is in them something more than Christ. These people agree with the Church in acknowledging the Father of the universe to be God and Creator of all things, and they also acknowledge all that the Gospel testifies of Christ. But they introduce novelties in the form of fasts and feasts, abstinences and diets of radishes...."

Maximilla, on one occasion had said: "After me there shall be no prophetess more." She was wrong about that; one meets many more prophetesses in this history. She went on to say: "Then will be the End." She was wrong about that, too.

Tertullian: A Very Reasonable Man with One Funny Idea

Born in Carthage in the 160s and converted to Christianity about 196 AD, Tertullian was a brilliant and prolific lawyer who greatly influenced generations of Christian thinkers. His most famous writing is one sentence: "The Son of God was born, I am not ashamed of it because it is shameful; the Son of God died, it is credible for the very reason that it is silly; and having been buried, he rose again, it is certain because it is impossible." For Tertullian this difficult paradox both describes and explains faith.

By 210 AD Tertullian had joined the Montanists. This should not have been a surprise. In the fourth book of his five-volume *Against Marcion* (his condemnation of the first major heretic to edit the New Testament), Tertullian had written that every morning for forty days a walled city had appeared in the sky in Judea, fading slowly during the day. It was a sure sign: the new Jerusalem was imminent and upon its descent to earth, following an order determined by their good deeds, believers would be resurrected and invited to move in.

(The vision of the heavenly city reappeared nine centuries later, exhorting the foot-soldiers of the Peoples' Crusades. The New Jerusalem was taking its time to descend but it was still on its way.)

Hippolytus and a Few Key Facts: 200 Years to Build a Shelter

After Irenaeus, another list of the succession of the bishops was compiled by Hippolytus, bishop of Porto, in about 235 AD. Hippolytus was involved in a dispute that eventually led to two bishops and two separate churches in Rome. The list he was compiling was to help legitimize the succession.

Hippolytus' apostolic list, along with charts of Roman emperors, Macedonian kings and Jewish high priests, was part of his chronicles of the world, tracing history from the Creation to the year 234. He calculated that 5,500 years separated Adam and Christ and that the life of the world was 6,000 years six full "days" of years until the seventh day, the day of rest. The empire foretold in Revelation that was to precede the era of the Antichrist must therefore be that of Rome.

His calculations that there were still at least two centuries left were a source of great encouragement and hope to a Christian community increasingly gloomy and racked by discord. Christians were not doing very well at their mission of converting and baptizing all the world. They could use a bit more time before the End.

The Chiliasmus Crassus of Cerinthus

"Chiliasm" is a specific term for the apocalyptic vision that holds that the millennium is a physical, material, future period after Christ's return to earth. The "heretic" Cerinthus was one of the wide variety of Gnostics living at the turn of the second century. He said he had learned from angels "that after the resurrection there would be an earthly kingdom of Christ, and that the flesh, that is, men, again inhabiting Jerusalem, would be subject to desires and pleasures.... There would be a space of 1000 years for celebrating nuptial festivals."

He went on: "The kingdom of Christ would... consist in the satisfaction of the stomach and of even lower organs, in eating and drinking and nuptial pleasures." There was great enthusiasm among his supporters for that End.

Origen and the Soul

Origen was the first important Christian to try to discredit the common notion that the Kingdom of Heaven would be a physical paradise. The Chiliasts were describing a New Jerusalem of gold and precious stones where believers would be rewarded by having their pagan persecutors as slaves. "Enough of this foolish literalness," Origen seemed to be saying, and he quoted Paul's first letter to the Corinthians: "Flesh and blood cannot inherit the kingdom of God."

(This enthusiastic reward-oriented materialism did not disappear with the Chiliasts. It returned often, and most vigorously with the Cargo cults and the Rastafarian movement of the twentieth century.)

Born in Egypt, a second-generation Christian (his father, Leonides, was martyred in 202), Origen spent a great deal of his youth studying the Greek philosophers, particularly Plato and the Stoics. He has been described as the most influential theologian of the early church; his influence is in a large measure the Hellenization of Christian doctrine, the spiritualizing of all its concepts, not just its apocalypse.

Origen explained that the heavenly eating and drinking that had been prophesied in Revelation and that so delighted the Chiliasts should be understood as nourishment of the spirit. The Christian's only hope is the hope of heaven, not on earth, but in the soul. Origen substituted a spiritual, individual kingdom for the literal and collective apocalypse that marked the church's first two centuries.

On the other hand, there was an abiding literalness in Origen's own life: in order to avoid suspicion or rumor while teaching the holy scriptures to women, he castrated himself.

Sibyl I

Santa Claus helps one understand Sibyls. The official Christmas is that of Christ and the Nativity. The popular one is that of Santa Claus and presents. Both survive together in today's church. The church has had this kind of split for a long time.

By the second and third centuries, power, prosperity and a degree of unanimity on major issues among church leaders meant they no longer had simply to respond to the arguments and heresies of outsiders; they could now decide with the weight of their ecclesiastical authority that Christians had spent too much time thinking about the End of the World. The heavyweights simply didn't want their flocks clinging to ideas of a new paradise—on earth.

But cling they did. Christianity had split into two separate religions: an official one, preached from the pulpits, concerned with canonical authority and liturgical detail, kept pure by bishops and priests; and a popular one, swept along by the fervent of the multitudes, making up its own mind on what it was prepared to believe—and willing to believe almost anything. This split would erupt in the later Middle Ages as the people insisted that the Pope was the Antichrist, leader of the false church, and would filter down to the twentieth century in minor skirmishes: the withdrawal of official approval of St Christopher, for instance, despite his continued popularity and success as a protector of travellers.

The popular medieval Christianity refused to be talked out of its fascination with apocalypse; consistently the End of the World appeared at times of great discontent, uncertainty or excitement. Sustaining the fascination was continuing reference to Revelation's vivid and horrifying images of good and evil. As a popular forum for their commentary, from about the third century on, Christians turned to an ancient literary genre whose thousand-year-old history was invariably tied to the End of the World: the Sibylline Oracles.

A prophetess called the Sibyl was known in the Greek colonies of Asia as early as the eighth century BC. Three centuries later the philosopher Heraclitus wrote of a seer who lived near Troy: "The Sibyl with frenzied mouth, uttering words mirthless, unembellished, unperfumed, with her voice penetrates through the centuries by the powers of the gods."

The Sibyl's most famous story is that of her encounter with King Tarquin the Proud. The Sibyl, in a dim cave filled with incense and the smoke of a large fire, offered the king, for an exorbitant amount of money, nine books that would contain all the answers he would ever need.

Tarquin declined her offer; she threw three of the books into the fire (all books were written by hand in those days) and told him she would sell the remaining six for the price she had originally demanded for the nine. He refused again; she threw three more books into the flames and offered him the last three for the same price. He bought them.

Tarquin need not have succumbed to her pressure tactics. Many people must have spent a lot of time concocting verses that they could then attribute to one of the ten historical sibyls: during an attempted purging of superstition by the Emperor Augustus, he collected and burned 2,000 books of Sibylline verse. Previous emperors had left the books in the hands of the quindecimviri, a special librarian priesthood, and consulted them in times of national emergency or unusual omens.

One could describe the Sibylline Oracles as religion's lowest common denominator. Each new era found itself rewriting the oracles in imitation of the ancient Greek and Roman verses. Of the fourteen books that have survived from the first Christian centuries, the earliest are Judaistic attempts to convert the pagans. Zealous Christians adapted existing verses to their missionary purposes and imitated the hexameter style to compose new ones. Sibylline cataclysmic histories of the world and verses cryptically prophesying impending annihilation continued to be immensely popular throughout the Middle Ages. Through the centuries they became more specific in their details and much more concerned with the End of the World.

The Eschatological Anti-Apocalypticism of St Augustine

If the Sibylline Oracles stand for popular religion, then Augustine, Bishop of Hippo in North Africa from 395 to 430 AD, represents official religion. Carefully argued, determinedly rational, his orthodox theology would attempt to stamp out "out-dated and inappropriate dreams of an earthly Paradise".

The scholar Tyconius expected the world to end in 380. He was one of a Christian North African nationalist sect called the Donatists. In his influential commentary on Revelation, he created many of the arguments that Augustine was to take over.

Most important of Tyconius' ideas was that the millennium was already in progress, brought about by Jesus' crucifixion; the figure of 1000 years given in the Book of Revelation explains only that the kingdom is not God's infinite rule in heaven, but a finite, earthly one that will last till the End of the World. In *The City of God*, his most famous work, Augustine explained: "The church now on earth is both the kingdom of Christ and the kingdom of heaven."

It was the popularization of a misconstrued version of this interpretation that later gave rise to the notion that the world would end in 1000 or 1035 AD. Augustine would have been horrified by such a literal reading of Revelation. His point of view was as firm as it was new: there is no reason to try to tie redemption and salvation to the earth-bound destinies of kings and empires. Although he gave the Sibyl a place in his City of God, he insisted that her prophecies were to be understood as allegories, the forces of good and evil struggling toward a final completion of history. He refused to predict a date for the End or to look for signs of its nearness in the political events then racking the Empire.

Rome, for instance, was sacked by the Goths under Alaric in 510. Although by this time the city was neither administratively nor strategically a vital piece of the Empire, it was still the spiritual center. The holy teacher Jerome, on hearing of Rome's fall, filled his letters with references to the previous collapses of Jerusalem and Troy. "What can be safe," he wrote, "if Rome in ruins fall?"

This was the question Augustine answered in *City of God*. He was meeting the pagan charge that Christianity destroyed the Empire, that Rome fell because it had stopped worshipping its original gods. Not so, Augustine said, writing "to correct the mistakes of some and refute the blasphemies of others". Rome's devastation was a just and inevitable result of its past sins and unrelated to the far more important issues of mankind's righteousness and redemption.

Augustine wrote of the tension between two ways of life: the godless and earthly life of people caught up with the temporal and the mundane, and the spiritual life of people united by divine love. The city of men shall pass away, he said, but the City of God has no end.

The City of God is attained through suffering, torment, fire and the destruction of all that is evil on earth. Augustine explained that "the figure of this world shall pass away in a conflagration of universal fire, as once before the world was flooded with a deluge of universal water. And by this universal conflagration, the qualities of the corruptible elements which suited our corruptible bodies shall utterly perish, and our substance shall receive such qualities as shall, by a wonderful transmutation, harmonize with our immortal bodies so that, as the world itself is renewed to some better thing, it is fitly accommodated to men, themselves renewed in their flesh to some better thing."

Certainly, in spite of Augustine's insistence on the spirituality of the End of the World, some earthly elements remained. The City of God, he said, promises "all that men honorably desire—life, health, nourishment, and plenty, and glory, and honor and peace, and all good things".

In 430 Augustine died during the siege of Hippo by a barbarian tribe of Vandals. A year later a council of bishops met at Ephesus in western Turkey. By decree they condemned as superstition the literal understanding of the millennium.

(Poor Bishop Irenaeus. Several embarrassing chapters of his *Against Heresies* now had to be expurgated. It was not until 1575 that they were rediscovered.)

Sibyl II: The Tiburtine

All the Sibyls were concerned with very little but the End. They were fanciful, but meticulous, explaining in great detail what the small steps would be in bringing about the Last Days. *The Tiburtine Sibyl*, for instance, foretold the names of all the emperors of Rome and the times of persecution. It said that the Christian Roman Emperor Constantine's two sons, Constans I and Constantius II, would succeed to his empire. Constans, a supporter of the church, would be murdered. It would be a "time of sorrows". These things came to pass. The Sibyl made almost no mistakes.

The *Tiburtine Sibyl* had an advantage over some other seers. It was written several centuries after the events it pretended to predict.

It lost some of its accuracy when it moved into predicting the future: Constans would return from the dead and vanquish the heathen, ushering in a golden Christian age of plenty. Reigning as the Emperor of the Last Days, he would plan to eventually hand his power over to God. Just before this could take place, the Antichrist would appear in Jerusalem and there would be a terrible final battle. Then and only then would the earth be ready for Christ's return.

When they grew tired of Constans, the Sibylline verses were updated: a new favorite king or emperor became the expected conqueror hero. With this kind of adaptability, it is not surprising that alleged translations of the oracles gained enormous circulation. After the invention of the printing press in the fourteenth century, they were among the first books printed. The bare bones hidden beneath their oft-revised prophecies were at least a thousand years old. But their face-lifts kept them young.

A Surprising Amount of Available Detail on the Antichrist

Sulpicus Severus, writing in the early 400s, tells us in his *Dialogues* that Nero will reappear and rule in the western empire "after subduing the ten kings". He goes on to explain that the Antichrist was born seven years previously (conceived with the assistance of an evil spirit in a grotesque parody of the birth of Jesus), and "will take over the empire when he comes of age".

About a century later, Quodvultdeus, in *Of the Promises and Predictions of God*, tells us that the Old Testament prophets Enoch and Elijah will be set against the Antichrist, and against them, in turn, three false prophets will rise. He explains that "the consummation and perfection of the times is to be completed in three years and six months" during which time Jerusalem is to be "trodden down by heretics, especially by the Arians". He identifies Gog and Magog as the Goths and the Moors.

The Revelation of the Holy Theologian John, an anonymous work, describes the Antichrist: "The appearance of his face is gloomy; his hair like the points of arrows; his brows rough; his right eye as the rising morning star and the left like a lion's. His mouth is a cubit wide, his teeth a span in length, his fingers are like sickles. His footprints are two cubits long, and on his forehead is the writing 'The Antichrist'." He will be hard to miss.

These descriptions are three of several hundreds that have survived from the Middle Ages. It's hard to imagine where their authors found so many dates and details, but it was all useful: it meant people were always alert and watchful, ready for the End.

Rome the Evil Becomes Rome the Good

It was perfectly obvious from the Book of Revelation that the Whore of Babylon sitting on the beast with seven heads stood for Rome and the Roman Empire. But as the Empire became Christian—and it was a great moment for the young religion when the Emperor Constantine was converted in the fourth century—it became difficult to continue to cast Rome as the personification of evil.

There was a period of transition. In the second chapter of the Book of Daniel the prophet interpreted Nebuchadnezzar's dream to suggest that there would be four successive empires. By the time of Tertullian, Rome had come to be identified with the last one, the one of iron and clay, a kingdom "partly strong and partly broken". Daniel goes on to say that in the days of the last empire, "the God of Heaven shall set up an empire which shall never be destroyed . . . and it shall stand for ever." Tertullian himself, fiercely anti-pagan, nonetheless prayed that the Roman Empire be preserved in order to allow time for the maximum number of conversions before the End of the World.

After Constantine's conversion, it was no longer heretical for Christians in the empire to be loyal to the emperor and his armies. Constantine took a forceful and visible role in reconciling the church and it feuding parts. It was inevitable that the people should come to see him as divinely appointed. With all the oracular predicting of the future, the next step was, of necessity to, find a role for him in the long-range scheme of things. He needed to have what the twentieth century might call "transhistorical significance".

Quickly, this role was created. It was immediately popularized in the Sibylline Oracles in a brand new apocalyptic myth, the legend of the Emperor of the Last Days.

And with a role for him, there had to be a role for the Empire. The Oracles offered a consistent line of optimism: in spite of all ups and downs, the Empire would last—with the loyal support of all Christians—until the End of the World. As goes the Empire, so goes the world.

Inventing Ends to Every Purpose

In the Middle Ages there were two ways in which visions of apocalypse related to the political, social and economic order: some interpreted already established Ends to stand for current events. They hoped in this way to influence the future, to move men to action. Other Ends attempted to give recent history the power of myth by rewriting the stories so that they would include recent political and social changes. This implied that the present made sense because it was all part of a plan tied in to the End.

In the twentieth century writers build Ends by exaggerating current situations, by taking them to their logical extremes. Just as in the Middle Ages, they have two choices: they try to account for what has already happened, insisting it's all part of God's plan—or they do their best to encourage us to change our ways.

Another Sibylline Oracle. Just When We Most Needed It

Pseudo-Methodius is the name now given to an oracle attributed to the fourth-century bishop Methodius. This oracle, astonishingly, was able to predict heathen forces overrunning Christians in the Middle East. Its secret was timing: the verses were in fact written in the seventh century, just after the forces of Islam overran the Holy Lands. Emboldened by its success in predicting the past, the oracle trained its sights on the future and offered hope in this dark hour.

The oracle announced, reassuringly, that a long-dead emperor would rise up against the heathen "and after those ten weeks of years they also will be overpowered and subjected to the Kingdom of Rome". After a peaceful golden age in which the formerly oppressed nations could return home, recover their properties and multiply, the Son of Perdition would appear, only to be defeated by Christ in all his power and glory.

Pseudo-Methodius brought two significant changes to the End of the World. The first was its suggestion of two separate redeemers for mankind: a mortal emperor and Christ himself. Over the centuries, the story merged into folklore, resurfacing as various legends of sleeping kings: Emperor Frederick Barbarossa, Camelot's King Arthur and Portugal's King Sebastian, all long-gone but awaiting the summons of their people to return.

At the time of its appearance, the Pseudo-Methodius oracle could not have been more inspired and appropriate. Its second contribution was a large step toward changing completely the role of Christians in the End. Until this moment, the End of the World was a passive event. Christians hasten it.

Suddenly—through the Emperor and the Empire—they had an active role. Once the forces of evil had been identified and the faithful had recognized the emperor as, indeed, the Emperor of the Last Days, they had a responsibility to serve him, and to overpower and subjugate the heathens.

62

The End in Feudal Times: Lull Before the Madness

The period between the middle of the fifth century and the middle of the tenth century was quiet. The papacy very slowly garnered the cooperation of kings and emperors and consolidated some political and spiritual authority over its own clergy. Heretics were rare and their heresies limited in their appeal and following. Life for most people was agricultural, near-subsistence, family-oriented and centered around the manor, a village-estate belonging to one lord.

The early medieval church encouraged both stability and tradition, supporting (and supported by) the structure of feudalism and insisting that the orthodox rituals and doctrines were more than adequate to deal with the fluctuations of nature and politics. There was virtually no world outside the manor—and no conception of common social injustices or grievances.

About 571 AD, in Mecca, Mohammed had been born. After spending some fifteen years meditating on the need for Arab religious reform, he gathered both disciples and enemies. In 622, he fled from Mecca to Medina. That event, the Hegira, is considered the beginning of the Islamic era. The new religion grew by leaps and bounds, and one of those leaps, in 637, was into Jerusalem.

Christianity was scandalized. It was as if the End of the World had been waiting only for the growth of public outrage against Islam as impetus for change. That feeling grew and grew and turned into the Crusades.

The Nature of the Beast

In 950 Gerberga, sister of Otto the Saxon and wife of Louis IV d'Outremer, king of France, sent a letter to Adso, a young scholar and teacher. She asked him to explain the Antichrist, of whom she had heard rumors.

Adso headed for the library.

The idea of an archenemy of the Messiah came from the old Jewish and Persian eschatologies, particularly from the notion that God and Satan would have a rematch in which God would be completely victorious. The name "Antichrist" first appeared in the New Testament Epistle of John: "As ye have heard that antichrist shall come, even now are there many antichrists, whereby ye know that it is the last time."

In about 200 AD Hippolytus had written a *Treatise on Christ and the Antichrist* and from that time forward the Antichrist had been interpreted allegorically to stand for the Roman emperors Nero, Domitian or Justinian, or for a variety of heretics and heresies.

Tyconius, in his *Commentary on Revelation*, identified the Antichrist as the church's own members engaged in evil works. This is a theme that would be popular for centuries, culminating in accusations that the Pope was the beast predicted in Revelation.

Beatus d'Asturias, a Spanish monk writing in the second half of the eighth century, calculated that 5,227 years had gone by between the time of Adam and the coming of Christ. Knowing that the world has a life span of six millennia, he was able to determine that the world should end in thirteen or fourteen years—in which case the Antichrist must already be born—but, ever the reasonable man, Beatus went on to explain that "whether these years are to be completed or to be shortened is known only to God".

Working from various sources and with a vivid imagination, Adso compiled the perfect bogeyman—and provided enough detail to give him flesh and a desire for blood.

The young monk began by explaining that the Antichrist will be the opposite to Christ in every respect: proud, wicked, exalting vices, reviving the worship of demons and calling himself Almighty God.

Adso went on: offspring of a man and woman (not a virgin alone, as others had predicted), the Antichrist will be born of the Jewish tribe of Dan in the city of Babylon, "conceived wholly in sin, generated in sin, born in sin". From his youth he will be instructed in the black arts by magicians and wizards and brought up in the company of demons.

In a political part of the letter, Adso recalled that these events would not come to pass until the Roman Empire passes away. He suggested coyly that "some of our learned men say that one of the Kings of the Franks will possess anew the Roman Empire". This king—presumably Gerberga's husband—would be the last. At the end of his reign he would surrender his crown and scepter on the Mount of Olives.

At that moment the Antichrist will appear in Jerusalem. Pretending to be the Son of God, he will boldly set up his throne in the Temple and will either convert or kill all Christians. He will perform great miracles such that "even those who are perfect and God's chosen ones will doubt whether or not he is the Christ who according to the scriptures will come at the end of the world". He will reign for three and a half years.

God will have sent his two prophets Enoch and Elijah to teach and defend the faithful and to convert all the remaining Jews to Christianity. The Antichrist will kill the prophets and martyr the rest of the Christians. At that time he will be killed by Jesus, either in person or through the archangel Michael. At this point, everyone who was led astray by the Antichrist will have forty days to do penance, and then, at whatever hour he chooses, God will come to judge the world.

Medieval Europe was looking for both scapegoats and explanations. Adso's *Letter on the Origin and Life of the Antichrist* caught the popular imagination and seemed to Christians—first of Adso's generation and then of later eras—mystically appropriate to their times. By the year 1100 it had been revised and redisseminated at least seven times and was considered so important that its authorship was attributed to many of Christianity's most famous writers and thinkers—among them St Augustine.

Note on the Rewriting of History

The *Oracle of Baalbek*, a fourth-century apocalyptic text, warned the city of Byzantium: "Do not boast!" According to the oracle, Byzantium would rule the Empire for only another sixty years, until the arrival of a Messiah who "will grant an exemption from paying a public tax and will restore all the people of the entire East and Palestine". Two centuries later a writer-editor noticed the prediction and noted that Byzantium was still the capital of the Empire. He took the liberty of amending the text to read "thrice sixty years". During the twelfth century, another creative editor, no doubt surprised that Constantinople (as it was now called) was still the imperial capital, amended the text to read "thrice six hundred years".

One cannot help but marvel at the transmutability of documents. Each time a text was to be copied, the copying was done by hand. Sometimes a copyist would notice that there were prophetic inaccuracies in the original, or details in predictions left out that now, with the advantage of hindsight, could be filled in. The temptation to make improvements was great. Prophecies had more impact if they could be shown to be part of a continuous line of successful predictions; surely there was no harm in adjusting mere numbers in order to accentuate the spiritual lessons of the old writings. Jesus' legal arguments in the Gospel of Matthew may have been created after his death and one knows better than to believe any contemporary oracles, be they in print or on television. Why treat the ancient ones with any less skepticism?

The Great Panic of the Year 1000 According to Raoul Glaber

The year 1000 marked the end of the first millennium since Jesus' birth, and, theoretically, the end of the sixth millennium since the creation of the world, and therefore, according to some, the time of the Second Coming. Most of the accounts of the turbulence and panic that accompanied the arrival of this ominous new year come indirectly from the *Histories* of Raoul Glaber, a Burgundian monk born in the late tenth century.

For medieval Christians from all walks of life, the story of Christ's time on earth was the most vivid piece of history imaginable. From about the eighth century onward, they became convinced that the greatest religious act they could undertake was a pilgrimage to the Holy Land, to pray where Christ had prayed, to be baptized in the stream where he had been baptized, to drink the clear blue waters of the Jordan River. The more difficult or dangerous the long trip to Jerusalem was, the more thorough it must be as a cleansing of their sins—and, over the centuries, the more popular as an act of piety.

Many thousands of pilgrims set off for Jerusalem. They endured weeks of slow travelling, and then, to their surprise and dismay, many were refused admission to the city. Although they were otherwise keen to have pilgrims visit, during the tenth century the Islamic Saracen governors of Palestine had imposed an entry tax of one golden bezant. The poorer Christians—who had begged or scrounged their way across Europe—were forced to camp at the gate awaiting the arrival of some richer pilgrim who would feel compelled as an act of charity to pay the tax for the whole crowd.

Once in Jerusalem, the pilgrims were an ecstatic, gullible mob. Filled with the blissful excitement of having accomplished their mission, they drank in every detail of the sites they knew so well from the Gospels. They were instantly thronged by charlatans and vendors of relics.

They were unable to resist. They bought little flagons of Jordan River water, little boxes of moss from the hill of Calvary, splinters of the true cross, tears of the Virgin Mary, even tiny scraps of cloth left over from the days when Paul the evangelist was still Saul the tentmaker.

Then someone noticed that the year 1000 was approaching and started talking about the End of the World. The idea electrified the mob and brought with it a holy terror. Everyone had seen the unmistakable signs: there were wars, invasions, epidemics and omens in the sky. Crucifixes and statues of the Blessed Virgin were seen to weep and groan. The devil was sighted in a variety of shapes and forms, grinning horribly. In 993 Mount Vesuvius had erupted causing great destruction. The church of St Peter in Rome had caught on fire. The next several years saw the deaths of many of Europe's most eminent churchmen and rulers, among them Pope Gregory V in 999. Two years earlier, in 997, according to Glaber, there appeared in the skies "an enormous dragon, coming out of the North and reaching the South, throwing off sparks of lightning". At about the same time Glaber described a five-year-long famine that covered the entire Christian world, so devastating that "it was feared the whole human race would be eliminated".

The pilgrims in Jerusalem realized that they had come to the right place. Where better— purged of sin and constantly in prayer—could they await the last judgement and the creation of the New Jerusalem? Word filtered back to Europe that there were wonderful apocalyptic omens in the Holy Land: earthquakes, meteors, hurricanes.

Glaber wrote: "When some of the more truthful of that time were asked by many what might be the meaning of such a great flocking together of people to Jerusalem, unheard of in previous centuries, they cautiously responded that it presaged nothing else but the coming of the Lost One, the Antichrist, who according to divine authority stands ready to come at the End of the age." And if the Antichrist was coming, could Christ be far behind?

Thousands more set off as pilgrims, leaving behind them homes, land, families and their work—for of what use would these be after the End? What they couldn't take with them, they donated as offerings to the church. All normal acitivities were suspended as the world prepared for the End.

It was a grim and glorious picture, and popular for many centuries. Unfortunately it has nothing in common with historic truth.

The Normal Passing of the Year 1000 According to Everybody Else

In 998 the Council of Bishops in Rome imposed a seven year penance on Robert II, saint, poet and king of France. In 999 Pope Sylvester II declared that henceforward the archbishop of Rheims would crown the kings of France. On March 27, 1000, he wrote to Stephen of Hungary conferring "upon you and your heirs and successors" the crown of king. Later the same year, the Emperor Otto III announced he would begin governing the empire from Rome.

Historians cite these and other examples as proof that life was going on normally, that there was no terrible millennial panic. They

offer the many wills and testaments that have come down to us from that era as evidence that people clearly anticipated a future. They go on to say that the opening clauses of the wills—"The End of the World being close, I hereby..." and "The World coming to its conclusion..."—cannot be linked to the year 1000 or even to a firm belief requiring action: these were the standard openings for legal documents from the sixth century through the end of the eleventh.

The major anti-Glaber argument is that if a great panic had actually taken place, there would be much more evidence than the twelve accounts that still exist. Of these, the most authoritative seems to be the chronicle of the monk Tritheim.

"In the thousandth year after the birth of Christ," Tritheim wrote, "violent earthquakes shook all of Europe and throughout the continent destroyed solid and magnificent buildings. The same year a horrible comet appeared in the sky. Seeing it, many who believed that this was announcing the last day were frozen with fear." He explained that for many years people had declared that the End of the World would arrive in the year 1000.

Five other texts discuss apocalyptic panics but they are all tied to events after 1000. The chronicle of William Godel, for example, written in 1124, tells us that in 1010, when news reached Europe that the Turks had captured Jerusalem from the Saracens, "fear and affliction overcame the hearts of many, and many feared that the end of the world was arriving". Fine, but nothing to do with the year 1000.

Even Glaber's enthusiastic accounts, upon close examination, actually suggest that the world would end in 1033 and there is some confusion as to whether all the omens he described happened around 1000 or 1033.

The abbot Abbo of Fleuri-sur-Loire in 998 wrote in his *Apologies* that when he was young he heard a sermon preached in the cathedral in Paris on the subject of the End of the World. "At the end of the year 1000", he recounted "the Antichrist would come and shortly afterwards the last judgement would follow."

Abbo opposed this assertion publicly "with

all my force" citing the Gospels, Revelation and the Book of Daniel. This event must have happened a long time previously. Surely if anyone were still excited about the year 1000, Abbo, writing only two years before that date, would have mentioned it. Instead the abbot went on to explain that "the rumor had filled the whole world that when the feast of the Annunciation coincided with Good Friday without any doubt this world will come to an end". People were convinced that the anniversary of the Lord's conception could not overlap with that of his death without dire consequences for the world. According to some sources this was to happen in 970, according to others, in 992.

But none of those serious historians who scoff at Glaber deny that the pilgrimages of the year 1033 were huge, unprecedented mass movements. That date, of course, was 1000 years after Christ's death.

Chapter Three

Theodicy and the Medieval Weather

A crucial word in the vocabulary of the origins of the End, "theodicy" has been described as the attempt by any church to answer the question, "Why does God allow suffering?" Churches have always had difficulty in devising understandable answers to this question.

Once a social milieu begins to change rapidly, any fixed set of doctrines or standards will generally be unable to keep up. When the social milieu appears to be changing for the worse, people are more likely to want to be able to count on the security of their beliefs. If those beliefs fail them in what they perceive to be critical situations, their disappointment or frustration will be greater than if those weaknesses had been revealed under happier circumstances. That disaffection will inevitably seek an outlet.

Traditionally that outlet has had three aspects: it made its presence felt in violence, in heresy and in a mass fascination with the End of the World. This was particularly true in the Middle Ages.

One should not imagine, as some millennialist historians do, that the inverse is true, that fascination with the End is necessarily proof of disaffection. The End of the World is not so easily explained. Its specter appears at moments of change for the good as well as the bad. In medieval Europe, the people's disaffection for the official Ends is only one of the causes of the popularity of the Sibylline Ends.

The continent had experienced profound changes. The Roman Empire—which had once surrounded the Mediterranean Sea—had given way to a Catholic Holy Roman Empire made up of the Kingdom of Italy (comprised of much of modern Italy) and the Kingdom of the Germans (which stretched from the Adriatic to the North Sea and included modern Germany, Austria, Czechoslovakia and Switzerland). England and France had come into existence when formerly barbarian tribes rapidly settled and became productive—the Franks to the point of outstanding political leadership—during what must be considered the birth of western European civilization. Severed from the Catholic church, the new Orthodox church with its capital in Constantinople was the backbone of the Byzantine Empire, which included Turkey, Greece and southern Italy. And the Moslem Empire stretched from the Middle East through northern Africa and the Iberian Peninsula nearly to France.

Population had grown during the several centuries of relative stability (interrupted by the occasional ravages of Norman, Saracen, Viking, Slav and Magyar invaders) and was shifting rapidly from the countryside to the new, booming towns. Villages of several hundred inhabitants grew to several thousand; when one hears of serfs escaping the manor to freedom by hiding in the towns, one is assured that the event was post-eleventh century: before then few towns were large enough to hide in. hide in.

In addition to the growing of food, milling, baking, brewing and the making of cloth and clothing, manors had fulfilled locally all requirements of religious observance and of protection in times of war or invasion; even marrying outside the community required the permission of the lord of the manor. But the development of new agricultural techniques and implements (particularly a new refined iron plow) freed many of the serfs from work on the manor.

Marketplaces had always been associated with the lord's castle. New towns grew up around the markets, at the base of the castle walls. The towns soon replaced the manor as the basic social, political and economic unit in early medieval life.

The settling in western Europe of the Vikings gave the continent access, through them, to a trading economy. The Vikings encouraged the establishment of wool mills and the making of cloth on a large scale through Belgium, Holland and northern France. These mills—and the other services that grew with them in the towns—were able to absorb large numbers of the new urban immigrants. Their lives, once supported by a strong tradition of family and community, were now dependent on the cooperation of strangers and the whims of international trade. At least one historian has commented that the medieval peasant's sense of the "source of fate" turned from God to the international wool market.

Not all newcomers to the towns found employment. While the family structure ensured that there was something for each individual to contribute—and to eat—at the manor, in town there was no comparable dynamic. While it would be very difficult for one person to go hungry surrounded by family and friends, one more beggar would not be noticed in town. The new urbanity created a new kind of poverty, a poverty of singular helplessness.

Even as the majority of the population was enjoying new-found mobility and independence, the new poor were appearing: beggars, the unemployed and unskilled workers. (The skilled joined guilds, which were an urban equivalent of the rural family support system.)

The new poor, as well as those peasants and farm hands who were not attached to manors, were fertile ground for the seeds of disappointment and frustration. This is where the concept of theodicy comes in. The poor sensed that the old stable religion was irrelevant to their new ordeals. They were desperately seeking explanations and outlets for their disaffection. They would pay attention to any new promises, theories, rumors, fantasies or even religions.

One of these fantasies suggested that the moral, social and political chaos, which the poor felt all around them, was inevitable. It had been foretold in the Book of Revelation. It was one of the signs of the End of the World. They had only to pray for their own forgiveness. But there was another side to the argument. It held that their way of life could be changed. They had seen the power of the guilds. They now sensed that if they, too, could form groups they could forcibly make new arrangements with their lords. Their new lives were proof that society wasn't static. They could begin to imagine it changing.

Don't Send *The Domesday Book* to the Printers Just Yet

In 1066 King William ("the Conqueror") of Normandy defeated the Anglo-Saxon King Edward and went on to subdue the rest of England. The country he took over was intensely agricultural and operating under a feudal organization of lords, villeins and serfs. It was blessed with large forests, with quarries, saltworks, ironworks and mines. Some 25 per cent of its land belonged to the church, 15 per cent to the king.

William found it a confusing piece of property to conquer: courts spent the first two decades of his rule trying to determine who really owned huge tracts of land. The courts themselves operated under three different legal systems, the Mercian, the Danish and the West Saxon, all of them unwritten, governed simply by custom and oral tradition. It was no easy matter for the king to get clear title to his new kingdom.

Preparations against a threat of Danish invasion demonstrated to William how little anyone knew about the human and economic resources of the country. Around 1085 he ordered work on a mammoth census and survey of the realm. This document, which came to be called the *Domesday Book*, was to record (according to the contemporary Anglo-Saxon Chronicle): "... what is the name of the manor, who held it in the time of King Edward, who holds it now, how many hides are there, how many ploughs in demesne and how many are held by the tenants, how many villeins, how many cottars, how many slaves, how many freemen, how many sokemen, how much wood, how much meadow, how much pasture, how many mills, how many fisheries, how much has been added or taken away, how much the whole was worth then and how much now, how much each freeman or sokeman had there or has."

There are two very similar explanations as to how the document acquired its gloomy name. The popular story tells us that the peasant class of England, God-fearing and superstitious, decided that the survey was being conducted in accordance with the twentieth chapter of Revelation, for "the book (wherein) the dead were judged out of those things which were written... and whosoever was not found written in the book of life was cast into the lake of fire." The folk wisdom

was that as soon as the compilation was complete, the world would end.

The stories aren't mutually exclusive. The other one comes from a book called *Dialogue de Scaccario* (Dialogue on the Exchequer) written by Richard fitz Nagel around 1179: "This book is metaphorically called by the native English, Domesday, i.e. The Day of Judgment, For as the sentence of that strict and terrible last account cannot be evaded by any skilful subterfuge, so when this book is appealed to on those matters which it contains, its sentence cannot be quashed or set aside with impunity. That is why we have called the book 'the Book of Domesday', not because it contains decisions on various difficult points, but because its decisions, like those of the Last Judgment, are unalterable."

Fortunately, the book was never completed (and the world didn't end). The document given to William before he left England in 1086 (never to return) was done carelessly and in great haste, full of errors, contradictions and missing sections. One of the largest blanks —having no statistics—was left open for the city of London.

71

Background to the Crusades

One learns a great deal about the mood of an era by learning what its collective longings are, longings one can discover and chart: they translate into fads and fashions, mass migration, hit records, bestsellers, large-scale public demonstrations.

To understand the Crusades, one must first understand roller skates or the hula hoop. Exhilaration can completely overwhelm a continent almost exclusively through word-of-mouth and example.

The first Arab conquerors of Jerusalem had been very cooperative with the Christians of Europe for several centuries, but the Seljuk Turks, who captured the city in 1071, barely tolerated Christian pilgrims.

Europe had been in a crusade mood for

about a hundred years before Pope Urban II's call to arms in 1095; various countries had had to defend themselves from sporadic Islamic incursions into their territories. The French epic poem, *Chanson de Roland*, which we usually associate with the Crusades, in fact, predates them. The idea of a holy war against Islam had been around for a while.

Several Centuries of Millennial Madness

The events that span the first centuries of the second Christian millennium and that history lumps together as the Crusades are in fact a series of wars, battles, campaigns, occupations, organized and unorganized group hikes, non-battles, non-wars, pilgrimages, pillages, pogroms, outright murders and frenzied, at times inexplicable, religious mania.

This is not the first era of mass communications; our era differs from previous ones only in that its communications are delivered simultaneously to entire countries.

Information has always been transmitted easily, over great distances, by travellers, traders, pilgrims, sailors, soldiers. As with rumors today, the information often travelled very quickly and changed over distance or time, becoming more exciting or provocative with each telling.

The Crusades got out of hand very quickly. Urban had had the idea of gathering some knights and noblemen to assist the Christians of Byzantium in recapturing Asia Minor from the Turks. This, he felt, would convince the eastern, Greek half of the church of his good intentions, and he would be able to heal the recent great schism, reuniting the two halves of Christianity.

It had not occurred to Urban that the idea of a holy war would inflame all of Europe. We have already seen how people in the eleventh century realized that there was no more logical place to await the New Jerusalem than in the old one. Christians for several centuries had been returning from pilgrimages to the holy land complaining about their poor treatment at the hands of the Moslems. They quickly determined that since the New Jerusalem would be the refuge of Christians after the day of judgement, surely it must be part of God's plan to have it reinstated as a Christian stronghold before that day could come. A war, with a successful conquest, was their chance to hasten the Second Coming.

Blessed Are the Poor, and the Rich, and the Bloodthirsty

The first crusade was in two parts: a crusade of the poor and a crusade of the princes. The first wave—the poor—was the most wretched of all the Crusades and also the one that felt most strongly that the End of the World was near.

Several hundred thousand of the poor people of France and Germany, called "pauperes" by themselves and by chroniclers, were prepared by the ever-popular Sibylline Oracles for all the excitement and adventure of the final battle.

They were still expecting an Emperor of the Last Days to appear. In the public fancy several of the nobles each took on the role for a short time, but then the poor were swept by the unshakeable conviction that Charlemagne had not died at all, but was sleeping in the hollow of a mountain. He would wake up to lead them to Jerusalem.

Charlemagne had been sent the keys of the city in 800 AD by the resident Christian patriarch. According to one source, the emperor was made a "protector of Jerusalem" and lord of the holy sepulcher by the Sultan Harun al-Rashid in 807.

The pauperes believed a completely different history. It was widely known that Charlemagne had once led a crusade to Jerusalem, had taken it back from the Moslems and ruled it as a Christian kingdom. They believed he would lead them again, three centuries later, to defeat the Islamic hordes and to raise the poor up to a new position of power and happiness in an age of bliss that would be climaxed by Christ's return.

In April and May of 1096, before the kings and nobles could oufit their knights and retainers, the poor were already following three charismatic and eloquent "prophetae" across Europe to Constantinople. Peter the Hermit, Gautier sans Avoir (also called Walter the Penniless) and the monk Gottschalk found themselves incapable of actually leading the hungry, unequipped, undisciplined fanatics that made up their army. This army hadn't yet left Europe before it started first massacring Jews and then razing Christian villages, plundering and murdering in search of supplies.

The mob, cut down by famine and the vengeance of the Hungarians and Bulgarians whose lands it had devastated, dwindled from roughly 300,000 to less than 25,000 to reach Palestine. Of these, 3,000 managed to escape death in battle or from starvation to retreat back to Constantinople. Not one of the first wave of Crusaders ever saw either Jerusalem, new or old.

The three largest divisions of the nobles' crusade arrived in Constantinople during the winter and spring of 1097. The Byzantine emperor, Alexius I Comnenus, had asked for help from the west to regain his territories in Asia Minor. What appeared instead were tens of thousands of troops with no interest whatsoever in becoming his army's reinforcements.

The nobles were eager to gain landholdings in the Middle East for themselves, but the poor who took part in the second wave wanted only to save Jerusalem. One of the chroniclers of the time recorded the popular sentiment: "The poorest shall take it: this is a sign to show clearly that the Lord God does not care for presumptuousness and faithless men."

The pauperes were led by King Tafur, a beggar-king who would expel from his troops anyone with money. They were convinced that their poverty gave them the humility and purity needed to find favor in God's eyes and to successfully capture the Holy City. The Tafurs, as they were called, began a tradition of self-righteous poverty that would resurface again and again in medieval history. The poor's distrust of the nobility would soon include all relatively well-off clergy and, later, the popes.

The Crusaders captured Jerusalem on July 15, 1099 and set up a western European style feudal state called the Kingdom of Jeruslem. French was the new language of the land; the official church was that of the pope in Rome. The previous rights of the Greek half of the church were ignored.

But the city could be held only by force. The Moslem power throughout the Middle East was growing and by 1145 Pope Eugenius III called for a second crusade. He asked the most famous monk of the day, St Bernard, founder of monasteries and unofficial secretary of state to the papacy, to travel and preach in favor of a crusade. Bernard, old and having retired to his monastery at Clairvaux, was hesitant.

His reluctance was overcome by reading the Sibylline Oracles. He became convinced, and he convinced many others to take part. But for the ambiguous enthusiasms of the cryptic verses, there would probably not have been a second crusade.

The oracle-reading public was sure that the French king Louis VII was the long-awaited Emperor of the East who would capture Babylon, the Antichrist's capital. The public was equally sure that before the events of the last days, heresies of any sort must be wiped out and God avenged. This meant that all Jews must be converted to Christianity, by being baptized, or be killed.

Saladin defeated the Crusaders at the Battle of the Horns of Hattin in 1187. Although the Christian kingdom continued to exist as a strip of land along the Mediterranean coast, that battle marked the end of continuing Christian rule in Jerusalem. The kingdom collapsed—following the eighth crusade—in 1291, after almost two hundred years of fighting.

The wars underlined a profound change in the nature of the End. People now knew that they had an active role to play in triggering the final days, and they were prepared for that role to be demanding even to the point of sacrifice of life and property. Crusaders were balancing two ideals simultaneously: they were actively preparing for God's kingdom and they were conducting down-to-earth battles and sieges.

Privileges Granted to Crusaders

Privilege Granted by Urban at the Council of Clermont, 1095:

"If anyone through devotion alone and not for the sake of honor or gain, goes to Jerusalem to free the church of God, the journey itself shall take the place of all penance."

Privileges Granted by Eugene III, 1145:

"Moreover by the authority vested by God in us, we who with paternal care provide for your safety and the needs of the church, have promised and granted to those who from a spirit of devotion have decided to enter upon and accomplish such a holy and necessary undertaking and task, that full remission of sins which our predecessor Pope Urban granted. We have also commanded that wives and children, their property and possessions, shall be under the protection of the holy church, of ourselves, of the archbishops, bishops and other prelates of the church of God. Moreover, we ordain by our apostolic authority that until their return or death is full proven, no lawsuit shall be instituted hereafter in regard to any property of which they were in peaceful possession when they took the cross.

"Those who with pure hearts enter upon such a sacred journey and who are in debt shall pay no interest and if they or others for them are bound by oath or promise to pay interest, we free them by our apostolic authority. And after they have sought aid of their relatives or lords of whom they hold their fiefs and the latter are unable or unwilling to advance them more money, we allow them freely to mortgage their lands and other possessions to church, ecclesiastics or other Christians, and their lords shall have no redress.

"Following the example of our predecessor, and through the authority of omnipotent God and of St Peter, Prince of the Apostles—which is vested in us by God—we grant absolution and remission of sins so that those who devoutly undertake and accomplish such a holy journey, or who may die by the way, shall obtain absolution for all their sins which they confess with humble and contrite hearts and shall receive from the Remunerator of all the reward of eternal life."

The Lateran Council of 1215 goes on to extend absolution to any kings, dukes, princes, marquises, counts, barons and other magnates who themselves cannot participate but send "a suitable number of warriors with the necessary expenses for three years".

The Invention of the Idea of Losing a Battle but Winning the War

The twentieth century has a relatively new and odd attitude to the goals of war: the point seems to be the systematic finding and demolishing of enemies' forces or, in some cases, enemies' civilian population—even when there is no territorial gain from doing so.

The tenth, eleventh and twelfth centuries, on the other hand, had a somewhat more sophisticated attitude.

The goal, by and large, was the straightforward acquisition of territory. For most of the Crusaders, the intention was the conquest of the Holy Land, particularly the walled city of Jerusalem. "Conquest" implies holding the city over time, that is, settling it permanently, and protecting it for Christendom. Certainly huge numbers of the Crusaders didn't plan on returning home; they intended to settle in Palestine and then send for their families to follow them.

Permanence requires security, and the leaders of the Crusades realized that they would have to conquer seaports and trade routes—as well as protective buffer areas—in order to hold Jerusalem.

A king engaged in fighting a war didn't come alone. He brought with him the same feudal structure that worked for him at home. He brought nobles, knights, retainers, servants, an entire system of vassals. In exchange for their services on his behalf, he would have to provide them with land and government. He would have to conquer land in order to assign small parcels of it to them; they in turn would continue to help protect all his lands.

Conquering land, at the time of the Crusades, was quite different from winning battles. Conquest required the capture of fortifications, of defensible castles or walled towns. If an army simply won a battle, then as soon as it moved on, its possession of the territory evaporated. (On occasion a defending army, for instance, in a village or on a plain, would attempt to engage the aggressors in battle and the latter would just walk away. If there was no tactical advantage, the Crusaders wouldn't risk the fight. They were only interested in attacking fortresses.)

Similarly, defending land meant holding onto the fortified places at all costs. Invaders would lay a siege and attempt to cut off the defenders from outside support. The best defence, therefore, included an army in the field, not to defeat the invaders in battle, but to dismantle their siege operations, to disrupt their supply routes, to force them to withdraw. Actual fighting was the least useful tactic for either side.

Why is all this important? Because it means that conquering Jerusalem was not a matter of besieging the city or attempting to slowly starve out the Moslem occupants. There was a whole network of linked components, a territory to be conquered. The first Crusaders realized, in the words of one military historian, "that Jerusalem could be won on the banks of the Nile".

Suddenly a complicated military strategy was the crucial first step toward readying the world for the End. It was the first time in history that there was such clear-cut action for Christians to pursue.

Tanchelm

When crusade furor died down in the later Middle Ages, the dislocated, the unemployed and the desperate found themselves all dressed up with nowhere to go. They were particularly susceptible to the eloquence of self-appointed prophets, saints and gods who would rechannel the mob's disenchantment with living conditions into, in many cases, open revolt.

In 1112 an eloquent wandering ex-monk named Tanchelm began preaching in fields across the Low Countries. A letter written at the time to the Archbishop of Cologne explained that Tanchelm—"like the Devil who must surely be his master"—had all the appearance of an angel of light. Claiming that he possessed the Holy Spirit, and was God to the same degree as Christ had been, Tanchelm announced a new Kingdom of the Saints and viciously attacked the church and the clergy. He quickly attracted great multitudes of blindly devoted followers.

He organized a bodyguard of armed disciples who routinely killed anyone who approached their leader except as a follower. Some reports state that they committed many massacres, which may be an exaggeration. (Often history's records of heretics were written by their enemies; in many cases there is no other corroborating evidence.) Nonetheless, there is no doubt that Tanchelm exerted a profound influence over a large area for decades after his death in 1115.

His main contribution to the mythology of the End was his insistence on holding magnificent banquets for his bodyguards and closest followers in imitation of the wedding banquet in Revelation. In a bizarre parody of the marriage of the Lamb of God to the church, Tanchelm announced himself betrothed to a statue of the Virgin Mary and, establishing a competition between the men and women present, demanded wedding gifts from all of them.

Through Ian, Jesus Christ Our Lord

One of the joys of medieval detective work is discovering that different details, in different accounts, refer to the same event or person. In histories of the End, one man's name appeared in many forms, revealing a great deal of imagination. It is possible, however, to make one story out of the conflicting dates and facts.

Ian de Stella, or Eon, Eys, Eons, Eudes l'Etoile, Eudo (or even Budo!), or most often, Eun, knew he was the son of God, come to prepare everyone for the End because all prayers ended with the same phrase: "per Eundem Dominum nostrum Jesum Christum". Priests thought this meant "through the same Jesus Christ our Lord"; the young, slightly mad Breton knew better: it meant "through Eun, Jesus Christ our Lord".

The winter of 1144 was a fierce one and was followed by two years of drought and famine.

Eon began preaching and prophesying in 1145 and within the year was travelling through Brittany with an armed band of believers, destroying churches, murdering monks and terrorizing anyone who did not accept him as the Christ of the millennium.

In 1148 the Archbishop of Rouen set a small army against Eys and easily captured him. The same day, a comet appeared, serving only to strengthen the belief of the followers.

At his trial before a synod in the Rheims Cathedral, Eudes declared to Pope Eugenius III that he was come "to judge the quick and the dead and the world by fire". He explained that he carried a forked staff to regulate the government of the universe: when pointed up, two-thirds of the universe was God's, one-third Eun's; when pointed down, the opposite.

The Quiet Calabrian Abbot

A person's influence on history is not simply the product of what he or she said or did. More important is what people think was said or wish had happened.

The monk Joachim has been called the most influential European until Karl Marx. Joachim would have been surprised. He did write three major works and a dozen smaller ones in his long life, but in the centuries afterward, a dozen major new works and many short prophecies appeared—under his name. Needless to say, the ideas attributed to him grew more and more unlike his own with the passage of time.

Born in about 1135 in Sicily, Joachim was the son of a court notary and became a minor official himself before he took part in a pilgrimage to the Holy Land and returned, converted to become first a hermit on Mount Etna, then a Benedictine monk. Later, about 1192, he founded a new order at San Giovanni da Fiore on Mount Nero, high on the Sila plateau.

In 1183, while at the influential monastery of Casamari, Joachim had the first of the visions that would drastically change the nature of the Christian End of the World. A year later, already with a bit of a reputation as an apocalyptic theologian, he was called before Pope Lucius III and encouraged to record his theories and visions.

For the next eighteen years, Joachim was a star. He was consulted by four popes, sought after (at his mountaintop retreat!) by kings, queens, emperors and princes. He became the most authoritative spokesman of the imminent last days.

He saw himself as someone to whom understanding had been given and who was obligated to spread the news of the impending apocalypse. In spite of seeing visions, Joachim did not think of himself as a prophet, merely a servant of God and the truth.

He had a complex sense of the world, of the End, of history and of the Trinity. He divided the past, present and future of mankind into three overlapping "states": the age or "status" of the Father and of the Law (a period of time beginning with Adam and lasting to Christ—Joachim described it as the order of the married); the status of the Son and of the

Gospel (the time of the order of clerics, it starts with Josiah, bears fruit with the life of Christ, and lasts until the defeat—in Joachim's day or shortly thereafter—of the Antichrist); and the status of the Holy Spirit, the time of the order of monastic contemplation, beginning with the life of St Benedict (the sixth century founder of the Benedictine order), culminating in the final days and lasting until the End of the World.

Joachim was convinced that the political events around him were signs that the second status was coming to a close. The continuing struggle between the church and the empire, the Islam resurgence, these for him were convincing. In an interview in 1191 with Richard the Lion-Hearted, Joachim announced that the Antichrist had already been born.

Joachim's scheme goes on to use a vivid set of images of trees, eagles, circles, psalteries, alphas and omegas to demonstrate a pattern of twos, threes and sevens throughout history and to explain the first and second stati as being completely parallel. There is some confusion as to how he imagined that the second status, the time of the New Testament, would end. Some passages suggest it would be the last historical age before the Kingdom of Heaven. If this is the case, then Joachim agrees completely with traditional theology.

But other writings seem to make it clear that the third age would be the next historical period, a time of renewal; a purified church—far less institutional and rational, far more spiritual—would reign over a peaceful, monastic world. For many in the thirteenth century these were revolutionary views, opposed by definition to the church as it then existed.

In the visions of Daniel and St John in Revelation, Joachim found clues as to the specific nature of the coming age: two new religious orders of "spiritual men" will arise, he said, to do battle with the forces of the Antichrist, one an order of preachers in the spirit of Elijah and the other an order of hermits in the spirit of Moses and imitating the life of the angels.

There is evidence in Joachim's writing that he expected the world to end within two generations. Later followers—particularly the Franciscan Spirituals—added details for him; before long it was assumed that the mathe-matics all came from Joachim himself: there were fourteen generations from Abraham to David, fourteen from Josiah to David and fourteen more to Christ. Fourteen is, of course, two (Joachim's mystic number of parallels) multiplied by seven (the most popular number in Revelation). Multiply that by three (for the Trinity and the three ages of history) and one has forty-two—the generations from Abraham to Christ and from Christ to the year 1260. (A generation is generally understood to be thirty years.) Forty-two is also the number of months foretold in Revelation as the length that the Holy City shall be trod underfoot.

After his death in 1202, Joachim's view of the Trinity was condemned by the bishops attending the Lateran Council of 1215. In 1255 his entire set of doctrines and writings was condemned. Since that time he has been treated both as a saint and a heretic and is the subject of great debate in academic circles even today.

An Example of Real Joachim Writing: From *The Book of Figures*

"After that wound [to the sixth head of the dragon] which has already in some part begun, there will be victory for the Christians and joy for those who fear the name of the Lord at the casting down of that head of the beast over which the sixth king reigns and at its being brought almost to destruction and annihilation. Then after a few years its wound will be healed, and the king who is over it (whether it be Saladin if he is still alive or another in his place) will gather together a much larger army than before and will wage general war against God's elect. Many will be crowned with martyrdom in those days.

"In that time the seventh head of the dragon will also arise, the king who is called Antichrist and a multitude of false prophets with him. We think that he will arise from the West and will come to the aid of the king who will be at the head of the pagans. He will perform great signs before him and his army .... The Lord will shorten those days for the sake of the elect so that they will not be longer than forty-two months.

"It is not to be thought, as the holy Doctors say, that the End of the world will come soon after he is judged, just because he is said to come at the End of the world. The End of the world and the last hour are not always to be taken for the very last moment, but for the time of the End, as John, who wrote a thousand years ago, openly teaches: 'Little children, this is the last hour, and as you have heard that Antichrist will come, there are now many Antichrists. And so we know this is the last hour.' (John 2:18)

"... After the destruction of this Antichrist there will be justice on earth and an abundance of peace. 'The Lord will rule from sea to sea, from the river to the ends of the earth.' (Psalms 71:8) 'Men will turn their swords into ploughshares, their spears into sickles. One nation will not lift up the sword against another; there will be no more war.' (Isaiah 2:4) The Jews and many unbelieving nations will be converted to the Lord, and the whole people will rejoice in the beauty of peace because the heads of the great dragon will be crushed."

Joachites

For the three centuries after Joachim's death almost all writing and thinking about the apocalypse was based on, or heavily influenced by, Joachimite ideas—notions that either were, or pretended to be, based on his writings. They found themselves in a fertile context:

•The world was still getting excited every several decades by Crusades that the clergy and nobility were encouraging, for reasons of their own.

•During the poor peoples' Crusades, intense anti-materialist feelings had been focused against the nobility and were still running high; they now started to turn against the wealthy, comfortable and often corrupt clergy. Joachim's call for a renewed church was powerful ammunition for his followers and indeed for all of European laity.

•Inspired, or somewhat mad, visionaries were capable of attracting loyal followings for any cause related to the End of the World.

•Most causes were related to the End; they had either been foretold as part of the Last Days or were evidence, or signs, of the coming of Christ or the Antichrist; Joachim's major works were all concerned with the End.

•People were—as indeed they still are—enamored by prophecy and particularly by specific and detailed predictions; Joachim's cosmology of symbols and myths was potent and very popular.

•The Sibylline and other oracles were, accordingly, as popular as ever; new ancient prophecies were appearing with regularity, explaining the future, drawing parallels between current events and the Last Days and labelling anyone—from the Emperor Frederick to various popes—as the Antichrist.

An Example of Pseudo-Joachim Commentary: From *On Jeremiah*

"The Temple is the Roman, or Universal Church, which is to be trodden down in general like the holy city for forty-two months from the time of Christ to the end of the second status. The forty-two months are forty-two generations in which the Christian people are to be afflicted. They will end in the year 1260....

"In sixty years the affliction of the Church will end. In the more particular sense, in three and a half years a more serious hardship will come. According to Ezekiel, it can come about that the new Chaldeans, that is, Germans, will come upon Tyre, that is, the kingdom of Sicily, laying it waste and bringing it into disorder because its king made his heart like the heart of God (Ezekiel 28:6)....

"Hear, Lord Emperor, (Frederick II) and attend to what is said: 'From the root of the serpent will arise a basilisk, and his seed will swallow the bird' (Isaiah 14:29). You are the serpent on the roadside, your successor is the horned basilisk in the road. Under him the empire will be stung, that is, will be divided, and any rider coming to it will fall. Like a winding snake you will be led forth from the kingdom; your successor, whose glance will scatter all, will spring out of his cave....

How far would writers go in reinterpreting the mystical Calabrian abbot? Very far. Later Joachim will be quoted as an indisputable source corroborating the doomsday prophecies of the Welsh wizard, Merlin—and this Merlin was, of course, a fiction himself. The real Joachim did once mention Merlin in his writings, in his Life of Saint Benedict. He considered him a prophet."

We're the Spiritual Men! No, You're Not, We Are!

After Joachim's death, new orders of monks consistently believed that they were the spiritual order he had predicted. One extremist and enthusiastic order was convinced that Joachim was wrong on only one count: the third status was inaugurated not by St Benedict, in the sixth century, but by St Francis, in the early thirteenth.

These were Franciscan Spirituals, who zealously called for a return to the absolute poverty rule established by St Francis. Most of them had been his companions and first disciples and disapproved of the order acquiring property and influence, participating in universities and cultivating theology; they wished really to go on living in hermitages and huts of twigs, working with the poor and the outcasts.

As far as they could see, they were obviously the new order of spiritual men predicted by Joachim. They adopted the Calabrian abbot as one of their own and adapted his work, producing explanations of it that would have astonished him.

They multiplied the forty-two generations from Adam to Jesus by thirty years per generation and in this way chose the year 1260 as the beginning of the End. In prophecies attributed to Joachim, they predicted that very soon all people—including Jews, Moslems and heathens—would be converted to a life of contemplation and poverty. The Spirituals themselves would be the leaders of the new age.

On Unspoken Conspiracy

Men and women were in the habit, through much of early history, of creating millennial or apocalyptic prophecies and attributing them to an earlier and more authoritative source. This was normal procedure. Thousands and thousands of people engaged in this petty fraud.

The only curious detail is that it kept happening. Surely, one imagines, there are only two possibilities: either the falsifications were public knowledge, or they weren't.

If they were, then it is difficult to imagine why anyone—particularly learned men like Joachim—took them so seriously. If they weren't, then there are two possibilities: either all these pseudonymous writers coincidentally wrote under the names of Joachim, the Sibyl, et cetera, or there was a great conspiracy of silence among the literate elect, similar to the alleged secrets of the Freemasons.

The only feasible explanation, and it is partial at best, is that a different notion of truth had currency. For some reason, if one felt oneself sufficiently inspired by Joachim, then it was alright to sign his name. Presumably one understood that all the other works signed with his name were also meant to be taken as inspired by him, and one could judge each on its own merits. But several questions remain:

Did monks admit to each other that they had signed famous names to their own writings? Did they consider that, because they were writing for the good of mankind, to warn of the signs or imminence of the End, forgery was no longer a sin? Who did they think they were, to change a date in a prophecy whenever it passed unfulfilled?

Were popes and bishops given secret initiation rites that allowed them to distinguish between prophecies that were most likely to be true and the others? Did they tell their closest friends to not believe anything they read? Did their friends tell their friends?

A Special Guest Appearance by Merlin, but Not Alone

Geoffrey of Monmouth's epic masterpiece *The History of the Kings of England* (written about 1136) made sense of a mass of mythic materials, and reconciled, for the first time, various legends about Merlin. He may or may not have written the slightly later 1500-line *Life of Merlin*, which tries to combine the Merlin of King Arthur's reign (known as Merlin Ambrosius) with the more traditional Celtic "wild man of the woods" called Merlin Sylvestris, a king gone mad who gains powers of prophecy.

In the early 1250s, a Franciscan writing under Joachim's name created *An Exposition on the Sibyls and Merlin*, which combined the three most potent apocalyptic sources of the day. The book joined a commentary on the Sibyl Erythea with a collection of *The Sayings of Merlin*.

As did so many authors, Geoffrey resisted taking credit for his powers of invention and fiction. The dedication to his *History* reads, in part: "Bishop Alexander of Lincoln, love of your nobility compels me to translate the prophecies of Merlin from the British into Latin...."

Merlin's best known prophecy is his explanation of a battle witnessed by Vortigern, king of the Britons, between two dragons, one red and one white. Under pressure from the king, Merlin called up his prophetic spirit and said:

"Woe to the red dragon for his destruction is nigh. The white dragon who signifies the Saxons you have called in will take his caves. The red dragon is the British people who will be oppressed by the white dragon—their mountains and valleys will be levelled and their river valleys will run with blood. Religious worship will be destroyed, the churches will be ruined. He who is oppressed will finally prevail and resist the savagery of the strangers ...."

Many other of Merlin's prophecies exist, composed at various times until about 1300 and in various places (but usually Italy). Merlin, once settled in Europe, took an interest in the traditional prophetic subject matter: in *The Prophecies of Merlin*, he expected a Last World Emperor—whom he called the Good Champion—to wrest the Holy Land away from the pagans, and to conquer "Rome and all Italy".

The Emperor would come from Merlin's homeland, Wales, and would be accompanied in his triumphs by the Doge and his armies from Venice. Curiously, the oldest manuscript of The *Prophecies* is in a half-French, half-Venetian dialect. Some key references suggest that it was composed about 1275, probably by a Franciscan monk for whom the use of Merlin's name brought a distinctive authority.

In Pseudo-Joachim works there are strong elements of religious commentary riddled with biblical quotations—following the precedents established by the real Joachim. Sibylline predictions are usually based on variations of great battles involving the Last World Emperor, the Antichrist and the European nations. Prophecies attributed to Merlin are more concerned with the fates of kings and kingdoms.

One begins to get a sense of the ready public accessibility to the authority of prophets. Anyone could (and did) write anything and attribute it to whomever seemed most appropriate. The prophecies of Merlin, the Sibyl and Joachim would be joined over time in anthologies and on library shelves with those —either real or attributed—of Amadeus, the monk Anselm, Fr Antonius de Hispania, Asdente, Fra Bonaventura, St Bridget of Sweden, Carion, Cassandra, St Cataldus, St Catherine of Siena, Cola di Rienzo, Cyril te Carmelite, Dandalus, Angelo Fondi, the Fraticelli, St Francis, Gamaleon, St Hildegarde, Isadore of Seville, John, hermit of Asturias, John of Bassigny, John of Bridlington, John of Rupescissa, the hermit of Lamposa, Johann Lichtenberger, St Malachy, Georges of Metes, St Methodius, the very famous Michel Nostradamus, Pierre Jean d'Olivi, Paracelsus, Paul of Middleburg, Rabanus, Raynier of Parza, Reinhard, Robert d'Uzes, Savonarola, Michael Scot, Telesphorus of Cosenza, the chronicler Tizio, Torquatus, St Vincent Ferrer and countless others.

These people had one quality in common: they described the future as if its details were facts—at the very least, ambiguous facts.

A Voice Crying in the Wilderness: David of Augsburg Speaks Out

"We are already fed up by what all sorts of soothsayers have to say regarding the arrival of the Antichrist. They alarm us with signs of the approaching judgment, the destruction of religions, the persecution of the church, the collapse of the kingdom and various other concomitant pressures creating havoc in the world.

"Even serious and devout men have made more out of these issues than is called for by extrapolating various interpretations from the writings of Joachim and other prophets, which though true and authentic, yet they have found many areas in which they could immerse themselves rather fancifully."

82

The Flagellants: Without Suffering There Can Be No End

Nearly one thousand years after St Augustine, the End of the World was still divided into official and popular camps. Bishops and popes were involved at a learned level, authoring critical and explanatory commentaries on Revelation. But the greatest interest in the End was somewhere between the literary, semi-official End, the concern of monks and scribes, the End built on the real or imagined prophecies of real or imagined prophets; and the so-called popular End, the colorful End of mass movements and mass madness. There was little direct intercourse among these three divisions although each contributed to the atmosphere that made the others possible.

Self-flagellation—the practice of flogging and scourging oneself in order to imitate the sufferings of Christ and thereby encourage God's forgiveness—in the mid-eleventh century was a form of penance among monks. By the mid-fourteenth, it was a full-fledged popular movement.

In about 1260—after the famine of 1258 and a plague in 1259—bands of men and boys carrying candles and banners began roaming through Italy from town to town. They would gather in the square in front of the local church and, with loud praying and wailing, flog themselves with iron-spiked leather whips into an ecstatic trance for hours at a time. These bloodied, half-naked penitants were both spectacular and disruptive as they visited towns and marched across the Italian country-side and into France, Germany, Hungary, Belgium and the Netherlands, gathering thousands of fresh adherents in their wake.

A mob is a pressure cooker for emotion. Chroniclers' accounts record the self-per-petuating internal forces that sustained the Flagellants: identifying strongly with Christ, they convinced themselves that their actions were assuring the redemption and salvation of all mankind.

The year 1260 was the date foretold in Joachimist prophecies as the beginning of the final earthly age, the age of the Holy Spirit. The Flagellants were simply the first instance of lay people taking on the religious attributes of Joachim's new order of spiritual men; soon, they were certain to be joined in religious devotion by all the rest of the population. The continent was tense and frenzied with the expectation of the Last Days. The Flagellants were both the product and the heralds of the frenzy. Their movement reappeared and sub-sided several times over the next few centuries.

The Road to Heresy Is Paved with the Best Intentions

Heresy, like truth, is in the eye of the beholder. Almost all existing records of religious sects that deviated from the teachings of the Roman church have come to us from their opponents. And it is always the opponents who give them the label "heretic".

Along with all the prophets and visionaries, Crusaders and mobs, the eleventh, twelfth and thirteenth centuries also saw the rise (and fall) of the Albigensians, an anti-clergy, anti-Rome subsect of the widespread Cathars; the Cathars, who believed that Satan ruled on earth, that earth indeed was hell and that people were reincarnated if they died unbelievers; of the Bogomils, who said that God had two sons, Michael and Satanail, and that Michael became Jesus but that his life was to be interpreted as allegory; the Lollards; the Paterines; the Petrobrusians; the Waldensians (or Vaudois), who believed that any layman could consecrate the sacrament and that, after the days of Constantine, the Roman church no longer represented the church as Jesus intended it. (Some went further, insisting that the church of Rome was the whore of Babylon described in Revelation.) The traditions of the Waldensians stayed alive in pockets of belief and later influenced the Brethren of the Free Spirit and the Hussites.

The Brethren, a heretical movement that by the fourteenth century had spread across Europe, was not content to criticize the church; its members had no interest in renewal or regeneration. Instead they virtually ignored it, feeling themselves completely above its authority. They believed they were incapable of sin.

Accordingly, they spent a great deal of time sinning. Their heresy was an anarchism based on personal salvation and ecstatic revelation; it was up to later theologians to construct a solid philosophical system around the cult.

Fourteen learned clergymen in Paris in the first decade of the 1200s believed that Joachim's third age had already begun, characterized by the Holy Spirit entering separately into each of them, a repetition of Christ's incarnation. Related philosophically to the Brethren, these men, called Amaurians, preached the immediacy of the last days, predicting a success so fast and sure that "Within five years, all men will be Spirituals, so that each will be able to say: 'I am the Holy Spirit.'"

They also prophesied that all the woes and catastrophes foretold in Revelation—wars, famines, earthquakes and heavenly fire—would take place during those five years, leaving only a small remnant of elect to enjoy the Kingdom of God.

Unfortunately, the Amaurians (they were named for one of their first members to be executed) became a small remnant first. Vigorously persecuted, they were tried and condemned as heretics. At one synod one of the sect insisted that "he could neither be consumed by fire nor tormented by torture, for he said that, in so far as he was, he was God."

Shortly afterward, he had a chance to test that theory.

From out of Nowhere, Prester John

While the Crusaders were fighting the Moslem Antichrist, and losing in their attempt to once again free Jerusalem, a sign appeared from the East that signalled the true End of the World. A great warrior arose in 1219 and with his host—much to the relief of the embattled Christians—smashed the infidel armies time after time.

The oracles seem to have come true: European Christians finally had their Emperor of the East. They believed him to be Prester John, leader of the lost Christian kingdom of the East, come to bring the tribes together in Israel. Stories and myths about the Prester, some associating his kingdom with Ethiopia, some with "the Indies" or the land "beyond Persia and Armenia", had intrigued Europe for at least a century.

The Christian masses predicted his final victory, marking the beginning of the End of the World, for the year 1265. But when the Mongol hordes appeared at the gates of Vienna in 1225, Europe realized that Prester John was not the new great Christian emperor. He was none other than Genghis Khan, whose name soon joined the lists of Antichrist.

The Peasants Are Revolting

Mankind's pursuit of paradise begat social implications in the aftermath of the Crusades of the Poor. Over time the belief took hold that some version of heaven was possible on earth—and either existed, just beyond the already explored realms, waiting to be found, or was a temporal state and would be brought about in the known lands in some near future.

The cult of poverty that had fuelled the crusading pauperes gave rise to a profound sense of injustice. That in turn led the poor to the certain understanding that part of the imminent Golden Age of God's rule would inevitably be the equalization of all lords and peasants.

A sermon attributed to the excommunicated English priest John Ball at Blackheath in the late 1570s explains the famous, and otherwise incomprehensible, proverb: "When Adam delved and Eve span, Who was then a gentleman?"

"If we are all descended from one father and one mother, Adam and Eve," the sermon asks, "how can the lords say or prove that they are more lords than we are—save that they make us dig and till the ground so that they can squander what we produce? They are clad in velvet and satin, set off with squirrel fur, while we are dressed in poor cloth. They have wines and spices and fine bread, and we have only rye and spoilt flour and straw, and only water to drink. They have beautiful residences and manors, while we have the trouble and the work, always in the fields under rain and snow. But it is from us and our labour that everything comes with which they maintain their pomp."

The traditional End of the World, God's day of judgement, with the incendiary preaching of numbers of impassioned priests, quickly metamorphosed into the Day of Revenge of the Poor upon the Rich. It was John Ball who insisted that that day was at hand.

The Peasants' Revolt of 1381 was a short-lived series of flare-ups quickly put down by bishops and lords. The English King Richard II acceded to some of the demands but the apocalyptic expectation that all the rich and clergy would be killed off and judged by the poor, who would be standing on the right hand of God, was not fulfilled.

Introducing the Plague

Life forms which may co-exist peacefully at a distance can cause trouble if they happen to converge. In the fourteenth century, large numbers of black rats infested the cities and towns of Europe and the Middle East. Rats often carry a plague bacillus that generally causes a mild infection. Occasionally the infection can kill the rat.

There is a particular type of flea that lives happily on rats and normally ignores human beings but whose sucking mechanism is blocked by the plague bacillus. The flea then spreads the disease as it repeatedly punctures any available creature in its delirious, desperate attempts to feed. This deadly coincidence caused the first near-End since Noah's flood.

The disease first appeared as swellings (called "buboes") in the groin and armpits. This was the bubonic plague. The swellings soon appeared all over the body. No medicines or doctors were capable of arresting their spread. Boccaccio, in the *Decameron*, explained that "the mere touching of the clothes or of whatsoever other thing had been touched or used by the sick appeared of itself to communicate the malady to the toucher."

Victims of the bubonic plague were highly susceptible to the far more deadly pneumonic plague, and they died within three or four days. Some small percentage of the victims contracted septicemic plague and died within a few hours.

Doctors who understood the nature of the contagion protected themselves by wearing elaborate leather costumes with metal beak-like masks and thick gloves. Priests, nuns and monks who attempted to care for the infected soon died themselves. Few could be found to bury the dead. Some of the very poor hired themselves out as "pickmen", bearing the corpses to the nearest church and the nearest grave. Soon Europe ran out of pickmen and bodies were tossed into huge overflowing trenches or left to rot in the streets where they would be torn apart by dogs.

It was inevitable that the healthy soon abandoned the sick and, if they could, fled the cities. This had the effect of spreading the epidemic to every small corner of Europe and of prolonging the first outbreak to nearly three years; some regions lost up to three-quarters of their population, some parts of England up to nine-tenths. As the disease spread, an overpowering feeling of complete helplessness grew with it. There was no reason for anyone to believe that the plague might lose its steam, that it might not eventually catch up to everyone.

There is a type of End of the World that is heralded by catastrophe or the fear of catastrophe. Jews often felt that an intensified persecution signalled the imminent appearance of the Messiah. Beginning in medieval times, Christians felt—as indeed they still feel today—that any widespread calamity could well be the precursor of the Second Coming and the last judgement.

We know from history that there are two normal responses to the panic that accompanies the public perception that the End has come: one can turn to God, or gods, with prayers and supplication, or one can grab at all available pleasures, living as if there were, literally, no tomorrow.

The second approach is the more popular. The most convincing widespread apocalyptic panic in written history was the one that accompanied the several waves of plague called the Black Death. As had happened in the mid-sixth century AD, during the bubonic outbreak known in some annals as Justinian's Plague, people at first reacted piously. But they soon learned that appeals to the Almighty had no visible effect and began to despair. Despair soon gave way to desperate debauchery, as millions died and all trappings of civilization were abandoned.

The Plague Foretold in Revelation

As many as thirty million men and women, roughly a third of what was then the population of Europe, died during the first—and worst—outbreak of plague, from 1342 to 1349. It was inevitable that people would remember the Book of Revelation's prophecy of plague and pestilence, and understand that this was the End.

A second epidemic broke out between 1357 and 1362 and killed nearly as many again. By the plagues of the early 1370s and 1380s, the people of Europe had built up some immunity and the disease seems to have lost its virulence: each later wave took about one-eighth of the population.

The early 1300s had been a time of optimism and plenty; the recurrence of plague after plague every ten to fifteen years for half a century gave birth to the idea that evil was gaining the upper hand in the world. Satan's forces were readying themselves for a major battle.

Demographically, the continuing reappearance of the plague meant that no sooner had one generation almost managed to recuperate from the staggering losses than it was struck again.

For scientific reasons still undiscovered, the plagues were somewhat selective: the first killed off a high proportion of older men—including a huge percentage of the clergy and many noblemen. Immediately afterward, records show a marked increase in the number of marriages and births. But the second outbreak seems to have killed mostly children. The situation could not have been more demoralizing.

John Clyn Fears He Is the Last Man on Earth

The narrator of H G Wells's *The War of the Worlds* stands alone amidst the devastated ruins of London, convinced that the Martian invaders are well on their way to uncontestable dominion over the earth. He thinks he must be the last person alive.

Centuries earlier, John Clyn, an Irish friar at the Convent of Kilkenny, surrounded by the blasted bodies of plague victims and with no reason to believe that the epidemic might cease and that human life might continue, movingly chronicled what he feared was the End:

"That pestilence deprived of human inhabitant villages and cities, and castles and towns, so that there was scarcely found a man to dwell therein; the pestilence was so contagious that whosoever touched the sick or dead was immediately infected and died; and the penitent and the confessor were carried together to the grave. . . . Many died of boils and abscesses, and pustules on their shins and under their armpits; others frantic with pain in their head, and others spitting blood; . . . I . . . am waiting for death till it come . . . so I have reduced these things to writing; and lest the writing should perish with the writer, and the work together with the workman, I leave parchment for continuing the work, if haply any man survive, and any of the race of Adam escape this pestilence and continue the work which I have commenced."

At this point in the manuscript someone else has written "Videtur quod Author hic obiit". ("Here it seems the author died.")

The Supernatural, the Natural and the Human Causes of the End

Giovanni Boccaccio said that there came in 1348 to his home town of Florence "the death-dealing pestilence . . . being sent down upon mankind for our correction by the just wrath of God".

For thousands of years God had sole responsibility for the timing and efficiency of the End of the World. By our wicked actions we could enrage Him and precipitate the End, but it was nonetheless God who sent Noah's flood, God who would convene the last judgement.

But the Black Plague changed all that.

Men and women have always had difficulty understanding personal suffering, but the magnitude and power of the epidemics that raged intermittently across Europe for two centuries baffled peasant and theologian alike.

The first plague came and went, either the wrath of God or the work of the devil. But when the second epidemic broke out, it was terrifyingly incomprehensible. The panic that ensued was far greater and far more volatile than that of the previous outbreak. Mankind had been punished and had suffered; was one plague not enough?

Clearly prayer didn't help. The clergy was at least as susceptible to the disease as the lay folk. But then came the revelation: one could avoid the contagion. (Everyone knew the disease was contagious; for much of history we have imagined that all forms of evil are contagious.) This implied that one could escape God's wrath.

Although they knew nothing of the actual causes of the plague, civic and medical authorities learned that one should isolate the sick and disinfect their clothes and possessions, that one could effectively quarantine a disease or even run away from it.

The Koran teaches that there is no cause of death other than the will of Allah. The Christian church taught that God's punishment fell upon the deserving. Any attempt to flee from the epidemic was evidence of a lack of faith.

But the plain fact was that men and women finally had some small influence on the progress and spread of the Black Death. This simple observation shook the religious foundations of medieval society. There were now two conflicting causes of plague and, by extension, of any End of the World: the natural and the supernatural. And they were becoming more and more difficult to reconcile.

During sixteenth and seventeenth century epidemics, clergymen in England were actively preaching that one should disobey the civil authorities who were trying to impose quarantines. Some doctors wanted to forbid church services because of the dangers of infection in large crowds—but churchmen explained that it was impossible to be infected while engaged in worship.

Having discovered that the plague was a natural phenomenon, mankind set the stage for the realization that we have a role to play in determining the exact nature of the End. From a humble beginning, we grew more and more powerful, more and more self-determining in our history, less and less dependent on the traditions of our religious Ends.

Boccaccio had explained that God's wrath could have been unleashed upon us "through the operation of the heavenly bodies or of our own iniquitous dealings".

We survived the Black Death. We were shaken up and completely baffled by God's relationship to the horror, but we survived.

Plagues continued to break out in Europe and around the world for many centuries. Accounts of particularly terrible epidemics in London in 1664, in Marseilles in 1720 and in India in the late 1800s, have become part of literature.

Not until 1905 did anyone understand how man caught the plague. No one had previously noticed the rat fleas. Without discovering them, and understanding only that the bacillus had to be made to enter the bloodstream, no one could make sense of the contagion.

A clergyman preaching in London in 1577 understood the Black Death better than most. He warned: "The cause of plagues is sinne, if you looke to it well: and the cause of sinne are playes: therefore the cause of plagues are playes."

The End as Successful Social Reformer: The Hussites

In the late fourteenth century, the church owned at least one-third of Bohemia (now the western part of modern Czechoslovakia). Enormously wealthy, the corrupt higher clergy was in a large measure German, a foreign minority amidst the restless Slavonic majority.

Jan Milicz began stirring up the people of Prague in the 1360s. The reign of the Antichrist had begun, he said, and announced that Emperor Charles IV was the embodiment of evil and that corruption in the church was proof that the End was imminent. He and others took up the cause of reform, insisting that change had to begin within the church.

Jan Huss, dean of philosophy at the University of Prague, was the most important preacher in the still loosely organized movement. Fiercely anti-papal, he announced "that if the pope sells benefices, if he is proud, avaricious, or otherwise morally opposed to Christ, then he is the Antichrist." Huss was burned as a heretic in 1415.

Almost immediately large numbers of townspeople and peasants joined together into a widespread movement named after Huss but far more extreme than ever he was. The Hussites—and later their even more radical and communistic wing, the Taborites—were attempting an economic and social revolution. They were the first such reformers to steep their insurrection completely in the language and tradition of the End of the World.

The Taborites took their name from the largest of the new mountaintop fortified towns that they founded. In the New Testament it was on Mount Tabor that Christ foretold his Second Coming and it was there he was expected to reappear.

In late 1419 a preacher announced that between the tenth and fourteenth of the following February the wrath of God would destroy by fire every city, town and village except the Taborite strongholds. In huge numbers, people moved to the mountains.

The Taborites believed that as soon as the world became free of sinners, Christ would appear on their Mount Tabor and then take his rightful place as the emperor of Bohemia.

The third of Joachim's ages would begin, there would be no need of a church, all men and women would be healthy, free and equal. As an added bonus, women would bear children without either intercourse or pain.

Although subject to vicious persecution, the reformers rapidly gained strength and numbers. When the world didn't end in 1420, they formed armies. The most radical were urged by their leaders to take upon themselves the responsibility of ridding the world of evildoers.

Soon Bohemia was in a state of bloody civil war with three sides: the Hussites, the Taborites and the Romanist-Royalist forces. Fighting continued until 1471, and the victorious Hussite religion became the established church of Bohemia until 1620.

Nostradamus: Several Centuries of Incomprehensible *Centuries*

Of all the prophets in this book, Nostradamus has best retained his popularity through to the present. Born in 1503 (note to astrologers: at midnight, December 14), in St Remy in the south of France, he was trained as a medical doctor and made a modest name for himself during outbreaks of plague.

In 1555 he published *Centuries*, a collection of 353 completely incomprehensible four-line poems.

One can describe the book in two ways. One could say that, using various foreign words, initials, anagrams and allegories, as well as a remarkable inexactness of time and space, the doctor-astrologer predicted an assortment of events most of which, despite their occasional odd detail, are so standard as to inevitably take place sooner or later. They include a fight between two brothers, the escape of a captive, an earthquake in May, a universal famine, Venice fearing barbarians, a great people tormented, honey becoming more expensive than wax.

Or one could take the opposite attitude: fearing for his life if very exact predictions suggested he was in league with the devil, Michel de Notredame purposefully set out to make obscure his verses. Luckily we are still able to make sense of them, and by looking closely we discover how very precise they are.

One twentieth century author insists he was a skeptic until he stumbled onto: "By night comes through the forest of Reines, two parts (a married couple perhaps), valley-tortuous, Herne the white stone, the black monk in grey into Varennes: Esleu (perhaps 'elected') Cap. ('Capet?') tempestuous cause, fire, blood, slice (as in sliced by a guillotine?)."

This, he suggests, can only refer to the aborted escape attempt under cover of darkness by Louis XVI—dressed in grey, with Marie Antoinette in white!—through the little town of Varennes. Indeed, he insists, Varennes has never had any other reason to be remembered. Nostradamus seems to have seen its importance some 200 years before the French Revolution.

By the end of his life, Nostradamus had published some one thousand quatrains. He was consulted by royalty and the famous throughout Europe. Every age since his has also managed to find relevance in his ambiguous details but, for our purposes, the good doctor is important because he created a brand new genre of End of the World: he predicted an End unencumbered by the religious trappings of centuries of prophesying. He treated apocalypse as just another political event among the many he covered. He never spoke of the last judgement or of a paradise under God.

Nostradamus took for granted the common belief of the time that life began four thousand years before Christ and, as predicted in the *Book of Enoch*, that the world would last for "a week of years", that is, seven thousand years. Describing the beginning of the End, he wrote: "In the year 1999 and seven months, from heaven will come the great King of terror."

He gave some details: "The third Antichrist soon annihilated, twenty-seven years blood will last his war, heretics dead, captive, exiled, blood, human bodies, reddened water, hail upon the earth." Mars will reign happily, there will be great and calamitous wars, until finally—and a 1926 commentary on the *Centuries* suggests a date of June 21, 2002— "there will be a new king anointed who shall long keep the earth in peace".

Finally, says the seer, "the wolf, the lion, the ox and the donkey, the timid deer, will lie down beside the mastiffs". This is the most specific Nostradamus ever is in describing the eventual Kingdom of Heaven on earth.

Rediscovering the End in the Age of Discovery

Christopher Columbus just happened to be the first to sail to America. For fifteen centuries—since the great sailing days of Greece, Phoenicia, Carthage and the Roman Empire—sailors and geographers had been pushing themselves closer and closer to openly admitting that one could probably reach the Far East by heading west. But no one seriously considered such a trip until the mid-1200s, and when it happened, curiously, much of the impetus came from the Roman church. It was hoping to precipitate the End of the World.

By the end of its first thousand years, Christianity was confined geographically to a small part of southern Europe and northern Africa. Slowly its missionaries gained converts among the Danes, Norwegians, Swedes, Poles and Hungarians. During the twelfth century Finns, Lieflanders, Estonians, Pomeranians and other Slavs were converted. The Greek half of the church had christianized the Russians and Nestorian Christians in China had made a powerful convert in a Khan who had been ordained a priest. His son had been defeated by Genghis Khan.

In the Gospel of Mark, the resurrected

Jesus instructs the apostles "Go ye into all the world and preach the gospel to all creation." Accordingly, the Roman church entusiastically sent missionaries to the East. Their reports made it clear that they fully expected that their conversion of the Tartars was a major step in the conversion of the entire world to Christianity.

For these missionaries, the ninth verse of the seventh chapter of Revelation provided the critical urgency. In his vision, John had seen that there will be 144,000 chosen to be saved from among the tribes of Israel after the breaking of the sixth seal. He then saw a "great multitude", more people than could be counted, clothed in white robes after the tribulation. This number was "of all nations, and kindreds, and people, and tongues".

The logic is very straightforward: surely if this wide variety of people is to be saved, each must first become Christian. For this to happen, clergy and missionaries can and must take an active role in preparing the world for the last days.

John of Rupescissa, a Franciscan monk living in the Catalan and a disciple of Joachim's writings, predicted that the conversion of the Tartars would be followed by the conversion of the Jews and the extermination of the Moslems. At that moment, mankind would have accomplished all it could reasonably be expected to do; the only other event left in history would be the Second Coming of Christ.

Genghis Khan and the Tartars were not interested. China was never again Christian. But Rupescissa was the first person to suggest that part of God's scenario for the End of the World must be the conversion of all of Asia—that is, all of the rest of the world as he knew it—to Christianity.

The breathtaking possibilities of the Age of Discovery, the four centuries from about 1100 to 1500, meant that missionaries could preach the gospel to Gentiles and heathen around the world, a vision, in the words of one historian, "so blinding and radiant that its fulfillment must inevitably foreshadow the rapidly approaching end of the world".

Rupescissa made possible the voyage of Christopher Columbus.

The Divine Mission of Christopher Columbus, Franciscan

The Franciscan Spiritualist monk Father Juan Perez had been chosen by Queen Isabella to be her confessor, but court life didn't agree with him. He received permission to retire to the Andalusian convent of La Rabida where in about 1484 he met Christopher Columbus.

In the same convent lived Father Antonio de Marchena, a noted cosmographer keenly interested in the discovery of the New World. In one of his letters, Columbus later wrote that in the beginning everyone ridiculed him except for two friars. Indeed, after the Spanish court turned down his plan to sail west, it was Perez who talked him into submitting the proposal directly to Isabella. (Columbus was on his way to see the king of France when he stopped in La Rabida.) Perez travelled to see Isabella on the navigator's behalf.

When the Nina, the Pinta and the Santa Maria set off in August of 1492, it was Perez who blessed the fleet.

The Atlantic was so wide that previous explorers had been intimidated: they zigzagged up and down the ocean looking for islands they had been hearing of for centuries, islands that would be a halfway post en route to the Orient. Columbus' contribution to history was the result of his deciding that there were no new territories between Europe and the east coast of Asia. He simply sailed with determination due west.

In 1493, Father Perez sailed on Columbus' second voyage and celebrated the first mass in the New World. Upon their return to Spain, Columbus appeared in the streets of Seville wearing the sackcloth garment of a repentant Franciscan, grateful for the order's support and beginning to get a reputation as a mystic in the tradition of Joachim.

Now an admiral in their majesties' fleet, Columbus undertook a third voyage from 1498 to 1500. The will he wrote just before sailing left a portion of the annual income from his estate to a fund that would help finance the liberation of the Holy Sepulcher in Jerusalem. In the course of the voyage he travelled as far south as Brazil and conclusively identified the Orinoco River as one of the four rivers of the garden of Eden.

On his return to Spain, Columbus composed a mystical-apocalyptical commentary on the Psalms and other scripture which he entitled *The Book of Prophecies*. In the winter of 1501 he drafted a partly biographical letter to Ferdinand and Isabella intended to be the book's introduction.

He explained that all of his learning—religious, mathematical, geometrical, astrological—had not been the cause of his decision to sail west. That decision came directly from the Holy Spirit.

At this time the Moslems were in complete control of the Holy Land. Columbus was convinced that another of the conditions for the End of the World was the Christian conquest of Jerusalem. He now thought of himself in a holy partnership with Ferdinand and Isabella: "Not unworthily nor without reason, Most Splendid Rulers", he wrote, "do I assert that even greater things are reserved for you, when we read that Joachim the Calabrian Abbot predicted that the future ruler who would recover Mt Sion would come from Spain."

Joachim, of course, had never made such a claim. Columbus was gathering ammunition from any origin for his grandest scheme: he announced that David and Solomon had built the first Temple at Jerusalem with precious stones from Panama. Now that he had discovered Solomon's legendary mines, he could rebuild the Temple himself with materials from the original sources.

His plan was to liberate Jerusalem. He first proposed the idea to Ferdinand and Isabella in August, 1492, on the day before he sailed on his first voyage, telling them he would bring gold from the Indies for that.

In 1501, Christopher Columbus, navigator and admiral, announced that he was the Messiah prophesied by Joachim. His geographical discovery of a direct route for missionaries to the Orient—he died without ever learning that he hadn't reached the East Indies—was the climax of the fifteen centuries since Christ. The next climax in history would be a successful last crusade. His calling was to lead the Christian armies.

Columbus went further: he allowed 155 years for all mankind to be converted to Christianity. Then the world would end.

A False Messiah Is Better Than No Messiah: Shabbetai Tsvi

From the time of the Babylonian exile and the rebuilt Temple at Jerusalem, hardly a generation went by without the appearance in one of the scattered Jewish communities of a messiah or, at the very least, a messenger fulfilling Elijah's role in announcing the Messiah.

These false messiahs almost always gained some local following, but rarely a more widespread one. The celebrated exception was Shabbetai Tsvi, a young rabbinical student born in Smyrna to a merchant family in the mid-seventeenth century. His studies focused on the kabbala.

Today the kabbala is considered the occult, esoteric, mystical part of Jewish doctrine. In the 1600s it was not yet the province of circles of initiates but rather a dominant influence in normal Jewish life. At about this time, a new form of messianic kabbala appeared across Europe, Asia Minor and north Africa, arguing quite convincingly that the end of time had come.

Into this ripe ideological environment stepped Tsvi. Always given to moodiness he seems to have swung from a melancholic depressive to a euphoric, charismatic, natural leader. On one of his up days he met the Rabbi Nathan of Gaza, who instantly succumbed to an ecstatic trance and awoke to announce that God had told him "This is my son. This is the redeemer of Israel." Jewish tradition demanded that the Messiah must be legitimized by a prophet and, accordingly, Nathan proceeded to play Elijah or John the Baptist.

The surprised but willing Shabbetai Tsvi led a triumphal march from Gaza to Jerusalem and slowly toward Constantinople, the seat of the Ottoman Empire, which then dominated the eastern and southern Mediterranean.

The time was right. Within eight months Tsvi's movement sent the entire Jewish world into a messianic frenzy from Poland to Morocco, from Kurdestan to Amsterdam. The English diarist Samuel Pepys recorded that bets were being made at the London Stock Exchange as to when the Messiah would lead the Jews to Israel.

Tsvi lapped up the attention and the authority. He announced—as St Paul had done 1,600 years earlier—that the advent of the messianic age heralded a break from the old Laws. He actively encouraged sins—from eating forbidden foods to sexual profligacy. He went so far as to reword the ritual blessing to "Blessed are thou God who permittest those things which are forbidden."

It has been suggested that, because Tsvi performed no miracles or other physical messianic actions, he felt compelled to depend on startling symbolic gestures to assure his followers that this was indeed the new age.

It couldn't last, of course. Tsvi was taken prisoner by the Ottoman sultan and given a choice between a slow, exquisite execution or conversion to Islam. Without hesitation, he chose the turban.

One can imagine the surprise of his thousands and thousands of followers. Naturally most were horrified, embarrassed and quick to forget their heady zeal. But remarkably, some of his followers, after their "disconfirmation" of his role as messiah, became even more adamant in their support of him.

They had committed so much of themselves to Tsvi's cause that to admit being wrong was impossible. Instead, their rational, rationalizing minds reformulated a set of beliefs after the fact. Just as the early Christians accounted for Christ's death (and therefore their disappointment in his not leading them in successful insurrection against the Romans) by saying that he redeemed them through his death, so too the Shabbetaians—knowing that the gravest sin for a Jew is to renounce his religion—claimed that Tsvi took upon himself the ultimate sin, on their behalf.

The sultan eventually banished Tsvi to Albania, where he died. The movement petered out slowly; the last clump of Shabbetaians (still living in Salonika) finally vanished during the First World War.

The Fifth Monarchy Men

In 1534 King Henry VIII announced that he was "the only supreme head in earth of the Church of England", thereby eliminating the pope's authority and encouraging the most militant of reformers to think that he would proceed upon a wholesale cleansing and renovation of the church. Henry, however, still regarded himself as an orthodox Catholic and would go no further.

The most ardent reformers continued to urge a purification of the English church. By the 1560s they were called Puritans; by the 1640s, they controlled Parliament.

One of their most extreme sects culled the biblical prophecies of Revelations, Ezekiel, Zechariah and Daniel, and announced that it was not safe "to coin metaphors of Scripture," that the Bible must be taken literally. The four kingdoms described by Daniel, they explained, were the Assyrian, Persian, Greek and Roman empires. The fifth kingdom, which would be the government of Christ on earth, was about to begin, in England, under the leadership of Oliver Cromwell.

One wrote that "all the teetering and tumbling affairs on Earth now (which is universally shaking into a new Creation) are an History of Christ's coming to reign...." Another described the state of the world as "these overturning, overturning, overturning days".

When the so-called Barebone's Parliament was convened in 1653, it was composed of religious men nominated by the Independent churches. The sect—which called itself the Fifth Monarchy Men—rejoiced.

The country, they proclaimed, was about to be governed by saints. God had called Parliament specifically "to destroy Antichrist in his Dragonical and Priestly power, with their appendancies, and to advance the Kingdom of Jesus Christ," not just in England, but throughout the world.

God, they insisted, would lead Cromwell and his armies across the Jordan River (which today we call the English channel) into the biblical land of the Canaanites—Europe, and particularly Rome, the bastion of the Antichrist. While the Pope was being defeated by the English, the Jews of the world would be returning to the Holy Land where they would defeat the Turks (the now traditional Gog).

Naturally, the Fifth Monarchist theoreticians could not resist the temptation to predict when all these events would come to pass. Their logic, which is only a little more ingenious than that of most who make predictions based in part on reason, is worthy of note:

"Some that have heard that the end of Paganism is placed in the year 395 ... will easily be induced to believe that the famous number, 1260, ought to be added to it, and then ... 1655 must be pointed out for an apocalyptical epocha. Others pitch upon the year 1656, because, having summed up the lives of the patriarchs in the fifth chapter of Genesis, they find 1656 years from the creation to the flood, and thence infer, that the coming of Christ will be the next year, because it must be as in the days of Noah. To 325 (the Council of Nicea was in) add 1332, that is, twice 666, the sum will be 1657. Others will wait three or four years more, hoping that the 1260 years must be reckoned from the death of Theodosius.... Nor need we wonder, if we find some confident that eleven years hence we shall see the fatal change, because of the number 666."

If they had been content simply to discuss the impending End, the Fifth Monarchy Men would have been just another of the many vigorous and slightly mad English sects. But their strong pushing for social reform and their continual harassment of the government for its shortcomings—all of these within a fiercely apocalyptic context and timetable—set them apart.

They had a divine mission. And when even Cromwell failed to live up to their expectations, they turned against him. He dissolved Parliament; they grew belligerent, and then violent, and attempted to trigger the End of the World by armed insurrection in 1657 and 1661. They were defeated and their leaders executed. After that, they simply faded away.

A Tudor Inventory

The Antichrist—indeed, the whole End—was very big in England. After Wycliffe, John Huss and then the Lutheran Reformation, Protestantism burst quickly into Europe and with it came the certain knowledge that the pope was the enemy. The best label for any enemy was still that of Antichrist.

The Reformation was a time of re-examination of the biblical writings and traditions. Inevitably, as scholars were moved to comment on the New Testament and on prophecy, they landed on the Book of Revelation and saw in it what they felt (as everyone had before them, and has since) were remarkably appropriate descriptions of the temper of their times.

Even a partial list of some of the hundreds of pamphlets and commentaries serves to eloquently demonstrate the mood of Tudor England:

•Babilon is fallen. Wherein briefly is unfolded All the matters of greatest moment, which hath hapned from the rising of Julius Cesar Emperor of Rome, to the present affaires (now) in Germany: And which shall ensue to the Worldes end. Published according to the first Copie, Printed, Anno Dom. 1595.

•Bullinger, Heinrich: A commentary upon the seconde Epistle of S. Paul to the Thessalonians. In the which bedydes the summe of oure faythe, ther is syncerelye handled and set forth at large, not onely the fyrst commyng up and rysyng with the full prosperyte and dominion, but also the fall and utter confusion of the kyngdome of Antichriste: that is to saye of Mahomet and the Byshop of Rome. 1538.

•Bullinger, Heinrich: A hundred Sermons upon the Apocalips of Jesu Christe, reveiled in dede by Thangell of the Lorde: but seen or receyved and written by thapostle and Evangelist. S. John. 1561.

•Daneau, Lambert: A treatise touching Antichrist. Wherein, the Place, the Time, the Forme, the workmen, the Uphoulders, the Proceeding; and lastly the ruine and overthrow of the Kingdome of Antichrist, is plainly laid open out of the word of God: where also manie darke, and hard places both of Daniell and the Revelation are made manifest. Meete in these dayes to be considered, where-in the kingdome of the Beast is by force and trecherie sought to be revived: And published for the encouragement of those which joyne in the intended actions against the Spaniard and otherwise, for the further overthrow of Antichrist, and enlarging of Christ his kingdome, with the pure preaching and sincere government of the same. 1589.

•Dent, Arthur: The ruine of Rome: or an exposition upon the whole Revelation. Wherein is plainly shewed and proved, that the Popish Religion, together with all the power and authorite of Rome, shall ebbe and decay still more and more throughout al the Churches of Europe, and come to an utter overthrow even in this life before the end of the world. Written especially for the comfort of Protestants, and the daunting of Papists, Seminary Priests, Jesuites, and all that cursed rabble. 1603.

•Draxe, Thomas: An Alarum to the Last Judgement or An exact discourse of the second comming of Christ, and of the generall and remarkable Signes and Fore-runners of it, past, present, and to come; soundly and soberly handled and wholesomely applied. 1615.

•Fleming, Abraham: A bright Burning Beacon, forewarning all wise Virgins to trim their lampes against the comming of the Bridegroome. Conteining A generall doctrine of sundrie signes and wonders, specially Earthquakes both particular and generall: A discourse of the end of this world: A commemoration of our late Earthquake, the 6. of April, about 6. of the closcke in the evening 1580. And a praier for the appeasing of Gods wrath and indignation. 1580.

•Geveren, Sheltco: Of the ende of this world, and second comming of Christ, a comfortable and necessary Discourse, for these miserable and dangerous dayes. 1578.

•Gualter, Rudolph: Antichrist, That is to saye: A true reporte, that Antichrist is come, wher he was borne, of his Persone, miracles, what tooles he worketh withall, and what shalbe his ende. 1556.

•Harvey, Richard: An Astrological Discourse upon the great and notable Conjunction of the two superiour Planets, Saturne and Jupiter, which shall happen the 28, day of April. 1583.

•Huss, John: ed. by Otto Brunfils, entitled: De Anatomia Antichristi (etc) Locorum aliquot ex Osee (etc) Sermonum Ad Populum, Tomu Terius. (1525?)

•Joachim of Fiore: Expositio in apocalipsim. Ed. S. Meuccio. Venice. 1527.

•Joye, George: The exposicion of Daniel the Prophete gathered oute of Philip Melanchton, Johan Ecolampadius, Chonrade Pellicane and out of Johan Draconite etc. A Prophecye diligently to be noted of al Emprowrs and kinges in these laste dayes. 1545.

•Kirchmeyer, Thomas: The Popish kingdome, or reigne of Antichrist. 1570.

•Knox, John: The First Blast of the Trumpet against the monstrous regiment of women. 1558.

•Morton, Thomas: Ezekiel's Wheels: A Treatise concerning Divine Providence: very seasonable for all Ages. 1618.

•Osiander, Andreas: The conjectures of the ende of the worlde. 1548.

•Pont, Robert: A newe treatise of the right reckoning of the yeares, and ages of the world, and mens lives and of the estate of the last

decaying age thereof this 1600 year of Christ, etc. 1599.

•Sheldon, Richard: Man's last end, The glorious vision and fruition of God. 1634.

An Embarrassment of Ends

The astute reader will have noticed that many of the events touched upon or recounted in this history are indeed the same events that he or she remembers—but remembers without such a strong apocalyptic thrust. All these stories, the life of Jesus, the Crusades, Merlin, the discovery of America and others, are often told without mentioning their connection to the End of the World.

Curious. All of them have an undeniable concern with the End; indeed, not just concern, but motivation, impetus, force. It seems an odd whitewash to have not learned in Sunday School that all Jesus' parables were about the Kingdom of Heaven, to have not learned in school that Columbus thought he was the next messiah.

Why not admit these facts? Are we now so cocksure in our religious disbelief that we are embarrassed to remember that our past is the history of people who thought that God might, at any time, cancel his enthusiasm for our little world?

The whitewash is complete: Merlin is considered a wizard although for ten centuries he was better known as a prophet. The Peasants' Revolt and the Hussite uprisings are always described as "reform movements" and examples of social discontent, despite their profoundly millennialist expectations.

Perhaps our current embarrassment stems from our realization that mankind has been crying wolf for nearly 2,000 years. We would have been happy, around the 1700s, if the End had become more rational, more industrial, more technological in line with everything else in the sphere of our knowledge.

Chapter Four

We Are Perfectly Capable of Ending the World, Thank You.

Columbus was almost right. But he was forgotten quickly, and it was Hernando Cortes who ensured that the world would end for nearly all the natives of the sixteenth century Americas. He was fulfilling a prophecy: the lore of many native tribes and races anticipated the disastrous effects of the white man on their lifestyles.

We have difficulty in knowing with any certainty how many of their predictions were written after the fact—or perhaps by tribes that had heard of the arrival of the Europeans but had not yet had dealings with them. Mythologists have difficulty knowing, for example, whether alleged old folktales are simply the reworking and retelling of an early missionary's teaching of a similar story. Also there is no reason to assume that the first North and Central Americans were any less likely than Europeans to construct or embroider their tales of impending apocalypse after the white man arrived, bringing with him the literal End of their World.

The New World:
One Large Step for the End

Late in the evening on October 11, 1492, Christopher Columbus emerged from his cabin and climbed to the forecastle deck on the bow of the Santa Maria. His eyes picked up what appeared to be a faint light, low on the horizon. Unsure of his discovery, and fearful of raising an unnecessary alarm with his crew, he descended to turn in for the night. Later in the evening, Rodrigo de Triand—the lookout on one of the Santa Maria's sister ships, the Pinta, spotted land.

It is doubtful that Columbus knew what Rodrigo de Triand's sighting meant. His purpose was to find a direct route to the East and thereby provide Spain with a new trade route to the Orient's rich spice and textile markets. He had no way of knowing that he had discovered a continent so strange and different that it would assume the title "the New World".

Columbus began to explore. He was struck by the strange flora and fauna of the islands. After the first few days, he wrote in his journal: "All the trees were as different from ours as day from night, and so the fruits, the herbage, the rocks, and all things." Then he ran into the natives: he was as baffled by the Arawak Indians living in the islands as they were by the men who floated across the water in the bellies of wooden boats. They gathered around the Spaniards and kissed their hands and feet, "marvelling and believing that they came from the sky...feeling them to ascertain if they were flesh and bones like themselves".

The ancient Greek and Judeo-Christian explanations for the order of the world—the building blocks of Western civilization—no longer provided enough answers. The Book of Genesis with its promise of one God, one creation, and the survival of the species in Noah's ark, held no explanation for the strange new animals and plants that were part of this New World.

Moreover, how, looking so different, could the natives of these new lands be descendants of Adam and Eve?

In 1493 the pope decreed that Ferdinand and Isabella, on behalf of Spain, had sovereignty over "all islands, mainlands found and to be found, discovered, and to dis-covered". But other nations argued that the church of Rome had jurisdiction only over descendants of Adam and Eve. If the natives of the New World had no connection to Adam and Eve, then Rome's decrees had no authority in the New World. Many Europeans were not ready to accept that they were linked by common descent to the strange natives Columbus found in the Indies. Phillipus Paracelsus wrote in 1520 that, "those who have been found in the out-of-the way islands" were probably "descended from another Adam".

In the theater of conquest there is little time for lengthy intermissions while questions of creation and cosmogony are debated. Spain, and indeed all of Europe, wanted to get on with the business of laying claim to the New World and its inhabitants. The court of Ferdinand and Isabella soon came up with a remedy they hoped would set the issue straight. The document, *The Requirement of 1512*, was to be read by the conquistadores to the Indians of the New World as part of the conquest package. A formality incomprehensible to the natives, the *Requirement* began with the statement: "The Lord our God, living and Eternal, created Heaven and Earth, and one man and one woman, of whom you and I, and all the men of the world, were and are descendants...."

Having made a comfortable place for the New World in the dogma of the Old, the Europeans were now prepared, with the authoritative approval of Rome, to claim, conquer and settle.

According to the traditions that had grown out of Revelation and the Sibylline Oracles, to bring about Christ's new kingdom earth, the entire world had to be Christian. This belief justified and gave a zeal to exploration and missionary activity that a desire for real estate alone could not explain.

The conquistadores now knew that their enslavement and slaughter of the Indians in Mexico, Peru, and throughout America were nothing less than essential to the millennial mission of the church.

The Aztecs Predict the End of Their World

Munoz Camargo was of Spanish origin but married into the Tlaxcala nobility upon his arrival in the New World. During the conquest the Tlaxcaltecs allied themselves with Cortes and his troops. Munoz Camargo presents the conquest from the Tlaxcala point of view. It coincides with other contemporary accounts.

"Ten years before the Spaniards came to this land, the people saw a strange wonder and took it to be an evil sign and portent. This wonder was a great column of flame which burned in the night, shooting out such brilliant sparks and flashes that it seemed to rain fire on the earth and to blaze like daybreak. It seemed to be fastened against the sky in the shape of a pyramid, its base set against the ground, where it was of vast width, and its bulk narrowing to a peak that reached up and touched the heavens. It appeared at midnight and could still be seen at dawn, but in the daytime it was quelled by the force and brilliance of the sun. This portent burned for a year, beginning in the year which the natives called 12-House—that is, 1517 in our Spanish reckoning.

"When this sign and portent was first seen, the natives were overcome with terror, weeping and shouting and crying out, and beating their palms of their hands against their mouths, as is their custom. These shouts and cries were accompanied by sacrifices of blood and of human beings, for this was their practice whenever they thought they were endangered by some calamity.

"This great marvel caused so much dread and wonder that they spoke of it constantly, trying to imagine what such a strange novelty could signify. They begged the seers and magicians to interpret its meaning, because no such thing had ever been seen or reported anywhere in the world. It should be noted that these signs began to appear ten years before the coming of the Spaniards. . . .

"The second wonder, sign or omen which the natives beheld was this: the temple of the demon Huitzilopchtli, in the sector named Tlacateco, caught fire and burned, though no one had set it afire. The blaze was so great and sudden that wings of flame rushed out of the doors and seemed to touch the sky. When

this occurred, there was great confusion and much loud wailing and shouting. The people cried: 'Mesicanos! Come as quickly as you can! Bring water jars to put it out!' Everyone within hearing ran to help, but when they arrived and threw water on the fire, it leaped up with even greater violence, and thus the whole temple burned down.

"The fourth wonder was this: comets flashed through the sky in the daytime while the sun was shining. They raced by threes from the west to the east with great haste and violence, shooting off like bright coals and sparks of fire, and trailing such long tails that their splendor filled the sky. When these portents were seen, the people were terrified, wailing and crying aloud.

"The fifth wonder was this: the Lake of Mexico rose when there was no wind. It boiled, and boiled again, and foamed until it reached a great height until it washed against half the houses in the city. House after house collapsed and was destroyed by the waters.

"The sixth wonder was this: the people heard in the night the voice of a weeping woman, who sobbed and sighed and drowned herself in her tears. This woman cried: 'O my sons, we are lost. . . . My children, we must flee far away from this city. . . . O my sons, where can I hide you?'

"The seventh wonder was this: the men whose work is in the Lake of Mexico—the fishermen and other boatmen, or fowlers in their canoes—trapped a dark-feathered bird resembling a crane and took it to Motechuhzoma so that he might see it. He was in the palace of the Black Hall; the sun was already in the west. This bird was so unique and marvelous that no one could exaggerate its strangeness or describe it well. A round diadem was set in its head in the form of a clear and transparent mirror in which could be seen the heavens, the three stars in Taurus and the stars in the sign of the Gemini. When Motechuhzoma saw this he was filled with dread and wonder, for he believed it was a bad omen to see the stars of heaven in the diadem of that bird.

"When Motechuhzoma looked into the mirror a second time, he saw a host of people, all armed like warriors, coming forward in well-ordered ranks. They skirmished and fought with each other, and were accompanied by strange deer and other creatures.

"Therefore, he called for his magicians and fortune tellers whose wisdom he trusted, and asked them what these unnatural visions meant....

"But when they wished to advise their lord on what seemed to them so wondrous a thing, and to give him their judgments, divinations and predictions, the bird suddenly disappeared; and thus they could not offer him any sure opinion.

"The eighth wonder and sign that appeared in Mexico: the natives saw two men merged into one body—these they called Tlacantzolli ('men squeezed together')—and others who had two heads but only one body. They were brought to the palace of the Black Hall to be shown to the great Motechuhzoma, but they vanished as soon as he had seen them, and all these signs and others became invisible. To the natives, these marvels augured their death and ruin, signifying that the end of the world was coming and that other peoples would be created to inhabit the earth. They were so frightened and grief-stricken that they could form no judgment about these things, so new and strange and never before seen or reported."

The Aztecs Were Right

A message arrived for the Aztec emperor, Motechuhzoma, delivered by a macehual, a common man: "Our Lord and King, forgive my boldness. I am from Mictlancuauhtla. When I went to the shores of the great sea, there was a small mountain floating in the midst of the water, and moving here and there without touching the shore. My Lord, we have never seen the like of this, although we guard the coast and are always on the watch."

These small mountains were the ships of the Spanish forces under Hernando Cortes.

The news of strangers landing on the coast was first interpreted as the fulfillment of an ancient prophecy promising the return of Quetzalcoatl, a great hero who led the Aztecs during their settlement of the valley of Mexico in the mid-thirteenth century. Quetzalcoatl unexpectedly left the city of Tenochitlan promising to return over the waters now known as the Gulf of Mexico.

Believing Cortes and his ships to be the returning Quetzalcoatl, Motechuhzoma assembled five messengers to greet the Aztec messiah. "Come forward my Jaguar Knights," he said, "come forward. It is said that our Lord has returned to this land. Go to meet him. Listen well to what he tells you; listen and remember."

Hernando Cortes landed on the coast of Veracruz on Good Friday, April 22, 1519. Accompanying him were roughly six hundred Spaniards, who seemed, indeed, to be supernatural, wearing rock-hard detachable shins that radiated like the sun and that defended them against arrows. They carried thundersticks—powder muskets—that spat fire and could tear apart a human being. And they sat astride great spirit-dogs; the Aztecs had never before seen horses. But Cortes' greatest weapons in his conquest of a native population nearing several million were smallpox and influenza, European diseases to which the natives had no natural immunity.

"Sores erupted on our faces, our breasts, our bellies.... The illness was so dreadful that no one could walk or move. The sick were so utterly helpless that they could only lie on their beds like corpses, unable to move their limbs, or even their heads. They could not lie face down or roll from one side to another. If they did move their bodies, they screamed with pain....A great many died from this plague, and many others died of hunger. They could not get up to search for food, and everyone else was too sick to care for them, so they starved to death in their beds."

Two years after landing, Cortes, who for one brief moment had seemed to be a messiah, captured the Aztec capital.

The Ten Lost Tribes Appear, in the Nick of Time

Not everyone was puzzled by the origin of the Indians of the New World. The Book of Revelation makes it clear that there will be twelve tribes at the last judgement, but common knowledge from the Middle Ages onward was that ten of the Jewish tribes never returned to the Holy Land after the exile in Babylon. For them to be part of the upcoming last days, they had to be found.

Luckily, they were. One of the most popular myths associated with the New World was that its inhabitants were the lost tribes, whose remarkable primitiveness was part of God's punishment for their various sins.

A Dominican historian named Duran went one step further: God had promised the people of Israel that he would send them much hardship; the conquest of the New World by the Spaniards was part of the suffering that the Jews must endure as atonement to prepare them for the day of judgement. The God-fearing Spanish soldiers, along with their missionaries, were the instruments of God's divine plan.

(A Jewish origin for the aboriginal population of North America remained a popular notion until early in the eighteenth century, particularly among the Puritans of New England. Like their strict counterparts in England, the Puritans were in the mood for apocalypse.)

The Tupi-Guarani and Brazil-Fried Chicken

Brazil has been a great melting pot for the End of the World, mixing the native with the new, one race with another, and intermingling legends and myths from any source. It is no easy matter sorting out who influenced whom, or even deciding which movements were truly concerned with the End.

When the Portuguese missionaries began to appear, in the mid-1500s, they found some tribes, notably the Tupi-Guarani, curiously excited. A few of the tribes were obviously newcomers to the coast—they didn't know how to sail or fish—and were in a state of religious expectation and disappointment. At first the missionaries assumed these Indians were typical nomads, moving to the rhythms of climate and food cycles, who were now in the coastal part of a cycle. But on closer observation, they realized the Indians were driven by odder urges: they were making pilgrimages to their god.

The Tupi-Guarani believed the world had been created twice. It had already been destroyed, long ago, when all mankind drowned in a great flood. It had, fortunately, been rebuilt, but the second time the construction had an eccentric twist. The rebuilt world was suspended like a chicken on a spit. Someday the spit was going to give way, plunging the earth into the fire, which would end all life for the second time. There was, however, a salvation, for those so inclined. If they repented their wrongdoing, and practised ritual praying and dancing, they could purge themselves of evil. Then they could join their god in his kingdom, a place they called the Land Without Evil. And of one thing they were certain: this paradise lay to the east.

The Indians, believing the world was coming to its second end, migrated east in great numbers until they were stopped by the Atlantic Ocean. Just then, on the same coast, the first Jesuit missionaries arrived by boat. The Tupi-Guarani were split into two groups. One group believed that it must simply keep travelling east, that god lay on the other side of the ocean, wherever these white people had come from. The other group was more pragmatic. The directions had simply been wrong. The Land Without Evil was to the north,

further up the coast. These believers soon migrated again.

The Jesuits, meanwhile, were appalled by these peripatetic savages and their heathen beliefs. They immediately began to follow the Indians, moving when they moved, settling where they settled, preaching the Catholic gospels. The missionaries and the colonial governors banned the old religion with all its rituals, insisting that the Indians learn the one true faith. The Portuguese hoped this would settle the natives down, but the new laws had the opposite effect. The Tupi-Guarani rebelled and began a new round of mass migrations back into the interior, where they could pray and dance as they pleased, without interference from the newcomers.

But resist as they might, the Indians could never return to their simple vision of the End. Their myths and the Christian stories had begun to mingle.

End by Alcohol: The Deerskin Trade among the Cherokee and Choctaw

Since ancient times, when the world seemed Endless, the white-tailed deer was the basis for a hunting and gathering economy that sustained the Cherokee, Choctaw and Creek tribes in the southern United States. Sought primarily for their skins and meat, the deer also offered entrails and sinew to make cord and threading for baskets, nets and bowstrings. Antlers were used to make needles and even the brains were used to help tan the skins.

Toward the end of the sixteenth century, drawn by expanding European markets for leather, the English began exchanging European goods—guns, beads, cloth and tools—for deerskins obtained by tribes during their winter hunts. Unfamiliar with the workings of mercantile economy, the Indians saw the exchange as a form of reciprocity between brothers.

But the trade was much more than a reciprocal exchange. As it grew, so did the link between the mercantile system of the Old World and the hunter-gatherers of the New. As the link became stronger, more entwined, so did its stranglehold on a way of life the Cherokee, Choctaw and Creek tribes had known for centuries.

The prosperity of the trade for the Europeans depended upon the volume of skins shipped to England each year. The traders soon found that once the Cherokee and Choctaw's needs for durable goods such as clothing, guns and metal tools were met, they had little desire to continue on with the trade. To guarantee that the volume of skins grew each year, the Europeans had to fix the natives' dependency upon the trade. The first step was to advance the natives credit at outrageous rates, thereby locking them into a commitment to deliver more deerskins to relieve their debts. The second step involved finding a trading product for which the natives had an almost insatiable desire. Rum, shipped in from the slave plantations of Jamaica, seemed to serve this purpose perfectly.

The Indians began to buy more rum, began extending their hunting season, putting even greater pressure on the white-tailed deer population. As the trade slowly destroyed the woodlands ecology, the presence of alcohol among the Indians slowly destroyed the tribes. One observer wrote in 1777: "I came thro' their town and I saw nothing but rum drinking and women crying over the dead bodies of their relations who had died from rum...."

The alcoholism and alcohol-related diseases shattered an already faltering sense of harmony between the natives and the world around them. As these diseases wiped out whole tribes, it became increasingly difficult for the natives to find any explanation for the event within their culture—just as it had been impossible for western Europeans to understand how God could sanction the Black Plague.

Feeling betrayed by nature, the natives grew more dependent on their lucrative deerskin trade. They waited eagerly for the traders who came to the villages bringing rum, trade goods and the End of a way of life.

Messiahs Emerge Among the Native Tribes

We've seen these symptoms before. And one of the ways we know that native North and South Americans are indeed descended from the same Adam and Eve is that they reacted just as the Europeans did to disillusionment, calamity and the inexplicable abandonment by their gods.

They looked for explanations and for saviors.

So-called primitive tribes throughout the world reached the same conclusions about the next age as had so-called civilized nations: they looked for a return to the old, happier ways, or they looked for a new and better future.

While some of the Choctaw said that the spirits of the animals and forest had turned against them because of their involvement in the fur trade, that they must stop trading with the whites, the Ojibway threw away the sacred bundles that gave them protection, prepared to rely on the vagaries of whatever the new world would bring with it.

But explanations are never quite enough; to achieve a better world, either new or old, one also needs a course of action. That action, almost always in history, is inspired or directed by one individual. We call him or her a messiah.

The shaman had traditionally been the supernatural mediator in native culture: now messiahs and prophets appeared, promising deliverance from the destructive forces, spokesmen for the apocalyptic vision that surfaced among the native tribes.

Popé Yemo Comes to the Tewa Pueblo

Since 1598, the Spaniards had been settling the land of the Pueblo in the upper Rio Grande Valley. They brought with them protection from the marauding Apache, as well as a fairly consistent dose of Franciscan Catholicism. As the Franciscans increased their efforts to convert the Pueblo, they also began to threaten the deeply codified Pueblo religion which was the basis of all organized tribal life. This assault quickly escalated into a cultural conflict.

In 1680, a medicine man appeared among the Tewa and San Juan Pueblo. He claimed to have returned from Shipapu, the great body of water where the Tewa originated. This shaman, Popé Yemo, called forth the Kachina spirits, who informed the tribal leaders that, to save their world from destruction, the Pueblo nation must rise up in revolt and drive the invaders and their strange religion from the land.

In response to the messiah's vision, knotted pieces of cord were sent to all the Pueblo villages. Accompanying the cords was a message instructing each chief to untie one knot with every sunrise. When the final knot was untied, all the Pueblo would rise up in revolt against the Spanish.

As a response to the almost certain destruction of their culture and end of their religious world, the natives succeeded in organizing the largest revolt to date on the North American continent. Popé's message was carried to Pueblo and Navaho groups from El Paso to Santa Fe. In August, 1680, the battles began. By October, inspired by Popé's vision, the Pueblo, Hopi and Navaho successfully drove every Spaniard out of the large territory known as Nueva Mexico.

The Master of Life Speaks to the Delaware

Since 1754 the British and French had fought for control of the Ohio Valley and the promise of gaining the heartlands of America in the French and Indian War. When its governor-general, the Marquis de Vaudreuil, gave up Montreal, the last French outpost, on September 8, 1760, all that kept the British from complete control of the continent were the native tribes along the Ohio River and throughout the Mississippi Valley.

The English traders and settlers began taking possession of their newly won territory with a cavalier disregard for the natives living in the region. The end of the lucrative fur trade with the French, coupled with the encroaching British settlers and the disease that followed in their wake, brought the tribes to the rude realization that not only were their lands being taken away, but their very existence was in jeopardy.

A series of dreams inspired a Delaware Indian, later known as the Delaware Prophet, to undertake a ten-day journey into the wilderness in hopes of meeting the Master of Life, creator of all things.

During his journey he met a beautiful woman dressed in white garments. Aware of his search, she told him to remove his clothes, bathe in a nearby river and climb to the top of a smooth-faced mountain using only his left foot and left hand. The prophet obeyed. At the summit he met a man who gave him a hat bordered in gold to use as a seat. He sat down, identified himself as the Master of Life and began to preach.

"This land, where you live, I have made for you and not for others. That is why I give you warning, that if you suffer the English among you, you are dead.... You might live wholly as you did before you knew them.... Did you not live by bow and arrow? You had no need for their guns or foul smelling powder, nor the rest of their things....

"Unite, drive them out. Make war on them. I love them not, they know me not, they are my enemies and enemies of your brothers. Send them back to the country which I made for them. There let them remain."

The Delaware Prophet returned home to his village and described what he had seen. Soon his teachings spread throughout the Ohio River Valley and to the tribes living along the Great Lakes. In the spring of 1763, Pontiac, chief of the Ottawa tribe, was inspired by the Delaware Prophet to call together more than 400 Huron, Ottawa and Potawatomi into a council near Fort Detroit. The bands synchronized an attack on all the British outposts from Niagara Falls to the Straits of Mackinac. By the end of June, 1763, all the British posts in the Ohio Valley and Great Lakes region, except Forts Detroit and Pitt, were in the hands of Pontiac's warriors.

But they could not last. By November, the Indians were running low of food and clothing. Their dependence on the European trade and the requirements of fighting a sustained campaign against the British left them helpless, unable to gather enough food to last through the winter. Discouraged and defeated, on October 31, 1763, Pontiac finally surrendered, not only the war, but also the hope of building a new world free of the whites.

Lauliwasikaw and Tecumseh: Resisting the End

By 1770 the Cherokee and Iroquois had relinquished much of their lands through a series of colonial treaties. The Delaware, Wyandot and Shawnee were shattered by the revolution and the loss of their lands in the Treaty of Greenville in 1765.

One day in 1802 the Shawnee shaman, Lauliwasikaw, was found unconscious in his cabin. He claimed he had fallen out of his chair while lighting his pipe, although there is some evidence to suggest he had been drinking rum. Presuming he was dead, his friends gathered for a funeral. During the ceremony, he woke and began to shout that the Master of Life had revealed the path the Shawnee must follow to avoid the destruction of their world by the whites.

First of all, the Master of Life said, the Indians must give up drinking. Rum was a poison, and drunkards would spend the rest of their lives in the afterworld with an eternal flame burning from their mouths. He then said that the Indians should throw off the white man's clothing and wear the traditional buckskins of the tribe. They must not intermarry with the whites.

By 1806, now known as the Shawnee Prophet, Lauliwasikaw learned of an imminent eclipse. Preaching that the Master of Life had given him power over heaven and earth, the Shawnee Prophet told his followers that he would soon darken the sky. When the eclipse did occur, news of his powers spread all the way from the Creek in Florida to the Blackfoot in Saskatchewan.

The Shawnee Prophet had a brother possessed of a strong hatred for the whites and known as Tecumseh, the "Panther Crouching in Wait". Together they began to consolidate a confederacy of tribes to rise in revolt against the whites.

Tecumseh's powers as a shaman equalled his skill as a diplomat. Once in the Creek town of Tukhabatchee, Tecumseh was put off by the tribe's cool response to his call for an uprising. In a fit of rage he announced that he would travel to Detroit and upon his arrival stamp both feet on the ground with such force that the homes of Tukhabatchee would come tumbling down to the ground. On the morning of his visit to Detroit the earth began to tremble and shake. By the end of the day, Tukhabatchee was in ruins, the Mississippi River had begun overflowing its banks, and numerous other towns and villages were completey destroyed.

During the culmination of their campaign, Tecumseh and Lauliwasikaw encouraged a number of Indians to move into the Appalachian foothills to await the Battle of Tippecanoe. While Tecumseh was away, the Shawnee Prophet became over anxious to begin the attack. The Indian alliance suffered enormous losses, in part the result of the Shawnee Prophet's promise that the bullets from the whites' guns would bounce off the warriors' chests and fall to the ground. Finally, Tippecanoe was abandoned.

Tecumseh sided with the British in the War of 1812. During the Battle of the Thames, he cast off his British sword and put on his native buckskins to face the overwhelming attack of American calvary units. The Panther Crouching in Wait was brought down in battle a thousand miles from his tribal lands. During the heat of the battle, after he fell, Tecumseh's body was whisked away from the field and never seen again.

The Ghost Dances

The Ghost Dance movement of 1890 was the climax of the cultural apocalypse that was destroying the native American world. A Paiute named Wovoka, "The Cutter", worked as a ranch hand for a family in Mason Valley, Nevada, but was known among the tribes as a messenger from the Great Spirit.

Wovoka foretold the coming of a new world, a world that would come like a whirlwind crushing all in the present world that was bad and old. He had met God in 1889 and was told that the Indians should stop their wars, do no harm to anyone and practise the sacred Ghost Dance that God taught Wovoka. Equipped with sacred red paint and two eagle feathers, a Ghost Dance follower would enter into the new promised world after going through the dance ritual.

Wovoka's message spread throughout the West. The Arapaho believed that the dance would cause a wall of fire to descend, engulfing the white man and driving him back to his old lands. The Arapaho would be lifted up above the flames and rain would fall for twelve days. The Kiowa trusted in their dance feathers to preserve them while the new world came over the old, like a wind from the west. The Cheyenne expected a new world for both the dead and living. The old world was worn out and filled with evil people; in the new world there would be large herds of buffalo and elk to feed all who were hungry. The Sioux were the largest surviving tribe in the United States. The Ghost Dance was the most visible element of their struggle to preserve their culture.

In 1889, approximately 26,000 Sioux were moved onto eleven million acres of land along the Grand River in South Dakota—the last piece of the Sioux territory which had once stretched all the way from the banks of the Missouri River. The buffalo herds had been killed off by the transcontinental railroad crews, and the white settlers were moving into the Black Hills looking for gold. In 1888 a disease called "the black leg" almost wiped out the Sioux cattle. A year later epidemics of smallpox and influenza spread through the tribe. And in 1890 a drought dried up all the reservation crops. At the same time the United States Congress enacted drastic legislation cutting the Sioux food rations in half.

Diseased and starving, the tribe faced almost certain extinction as the winter of 1890 approached. A council was called during which plans were made to hold a large gathering for a Ghost Dance. The time had come to bring the new world down from the skies to earth.

Alarmed at the sudden gathering of the Sioux, the United States Cavalry was sent in to keep an eye out for any outbursts of rebellion. Frightened by the presence of the troops, a band of Sioux, under the leadership of Short Bull and Kicking Bear, fled to the Badlands. Determined to stand his ground, Sitting Bull, shaman, chief of the Hunkapapa Band and leader of the Little Bighorn Massacre, continued to perform the ceremony with the other members of his tribe.

The cavalry units descended on Sitting Bull's camp and the Battle of Wounded Knee began. One Ghost Dance leader, Yellow Bird, asked his followers to put on the "ghost shirts" that held the magic capable of repelling the Cavalry bullets. Within minutes the Hotchkiss guns had decimated an entire band of two hundred men, women and children.

The long-awaited new world of the Great Spirit never came. Sitting Bull and his tribe were gunned down in the midst of a South Dakota blizzard, their bodies left to freeze in the blowing snow. No messiah, no ritual, no prayers were capable of holding back the End.

Chapter Five

Life as We Know It: the End Today

The boundary between madness and charisma is a fuzzy one—just as is the line between heresy and genuine, inspired belief.

In the past mankind has created arbitrary rules: if an individual attracted followers, he or she was more likely to be taken seriously. If he or she ranted or raved alone, insanity seemed a more likely label than sainthood.

Was Columbus crazy to think he was the new messiah after discovering a new world? Was Tecumseh crazy to think he could lead his people against the conquering whites? Was St John crazy to imagine complicated visions of the End?

What about Tanchelm and Eudes? They had the popular support of their peers but certainly subscribed to some odd convictions.

The problem becomes even more overwhelming when one looks at the body of literature written by the Gnostics, or the long-term influence of the Hussites on life in Czechoslovakia.

The eighteenth and nineteenth centuries, recent enough to have left a legacy of written accounts, provide a wealth of confusing detail. Some prophets went too far, but others, equally steeped in the love of the End, gave us beliefs and religions with millions of adherents.

One can only follow one's intuition to decide which of the spirited groups are cults and which are sects; which are aberrations and which genuine religions; what are prophecies and what are ravings.

Bell to Bedlam

On February 8, 1761, London was shaken by an earthquake, not an unusual event in itself. But on March 8, a second seismic tremor hit the city and woke up a soldier named William Bell. Bell, a man with a calendar, went on a speaking spree and told anyone who would listen that there would be another great upheaval exactly four weeks after the second one. This one would be the End of the World.

By the appointed day, April 5, there was mass hysteria, affecting even those who had originally been skeptical of Bell's warning. Thousands of Londoners fled the city and went to the comparative safety of outlying villages, where the local inhabitants were charging exorbitant rates for food and shelter. Many of those who remained in the city took to boats on the Thames, thinking that the End would be ushered in by another flood.

The day passed uneventfully. The next morning, Bell was arrested and locked up in Bedlam, London's famous insane asylum.

There Are No Baby Shakers

In the 1750s in Manchester, England, a small group of millennialists, for the most part ex-Quakers, met regularly to pray in an enthusiastic manner. They were hot-gospellers, given to shouting, physical gyrations, trances and doomsaying. Their neighbours took to calling them Shakers, short for Shaking Quakers.

Among them was a young woman named Ann Lee. She lost her faith for awhile, but in 1770 it returned with a vengeance. While sitting in jail—she had profaned the Sabbath—she had a revelation: it told her that she was to be the leader of the sect. Calling herself Mother Ann, in 1774 she led eight followers in an emigration to America, the new land.

(The outside world was changing rapidly around the sect. A machine for spinning cotton had just been perfected, and the initial roar of the Industrial Revolution could be heard throughout Great Britain.)

The Shakers contained within themselves the seeds of their own disappearance. Mother Ann was vehemently anti-sex. (Some writers have suggested this was an emotional backlash against the deaths in infancy of her own four children.) Her husband followed her to America but she would no longer defile herself with a carnal relationship and he eventually left her for another woman. Her followers, as well as the new converts, gave up cohabitation, the men lived with the men and the women with the women. Married converts were de-married in a curious ritual; women and men could not eat together at a table unless chaperoned; and it was forbidden to watch the copulation of animals. Three young women, who had watched two flies mating, were once ordered by an elder to strip off their clothing and whip each other, in order to purge their sexual inclinations. When the Shakers said "to take up the cross", they meant to pursue celibacy. No marriage, no children, no sexual intercourse.

Does this seem extreme? Procreation was unnecessary. The world was ending. Mother Ann's revelation in jail had been the Second Coming, and the millennium would officially begin in 1792. The very creation of the sect meant the sanctuary had been cleansed and that the believers had overcome sin. The Shakers would soon be living in the Kingdom of God.

Ann Lee died before 1792. She never made it to the kingdom, but the church continued to thrive until the time of the Civil War, after which its following dwindled away. There are still a few Shaking Quakers around today, but they are getting lonely.

Jesus' Little Sister

Elspeth Buchan, the Scottish seer, led a normal country life until her forties, when she separated from her husband. There were reasonable causes: she was being less than faithful and he was out of work. But there was one additional strain: she had become a religious zealot, a seeker. In 1781 she left him and went up to the city of Glasgow.

Mrs Buchan fell under the spell of the Reverend Hugh White, a heavy-handed preacher of the Relief sect, a secessionist group that had split from the Church of Scotland. White, for his part, was equally entranced by Buchan, recognizing her as the Woman Clothed with the Sun, anticipated in the Book of Revelation. He insisted, moreover, that she was the saint who had been sent to rid the world of the Antichrist. His churchgoers would have none of it. They demanded of White that he dismiss both Mrs Buchan and his heretical beliefs and, when he refused, had him suspended from the ministry.

The pair left Glasgow, followed by some of the old congregation, and settled in Irvine, where they held regular meetings. The townspeople didn't like the new sect, began to discriminate against its members and, in a final fury, attacked the new saint one night and drove her out of town. To them she was immoral (in her relationship to the married Reverend White) and heretical (in her growing belief that she was the Holy Ghost of the blessed trinity).

The Buchanites moved on. They lived communally wherever they went, farming and spinning yarn for a living, often helping neighbours for no fee. (Why take money? They believed, after all, that the End of the World was near.) Buchan often excited the group with the expectation that the midnight cry, signalling the return of Jesus, was to be heard that night. Jesus, who she claimed was her elder brother, never appeared

Buchan died in 1891 and White, after waiting in vain for her resurrection, emigrated to America with thirty followers a year later.

Notes on the Transferability of Prophecy

Around the end of the eighteenth century the British Parliament, with very little opposition or public interest, passed a law allowing Jews, for the first time, to become naturalized British subjects. Bishops and archbishops had already given their support to the bill and no one expected the extraordinary commotion that suddenly inflamed England.

The lower clergy and country parsons, with sermon after sermon, managed to incite their congregations against the new law. The period was one of tension between France and England as well, and new, bold grafitti covered blank walls in city and country: "No Jews. No wooden shoes." There was no logical connection between the Jews and Napoleon's France.

The higher clergy retracted, resolving that some concessions to the outcry were necessary. They admitted they had made no attempt to examine the truth or falseness of the public's accusations. They put forward a representation to the Duke of Newcastle, the current prime minister, urging him to repeal the law because the populace found it offensive.

And of what was the citizenry so afraid? They were convinced that if Jews were allowed to become naturalized, all of the historic prophetical curses that were in store for Jerusalem and the Holy Land would instead fall upon Britain.

The law was repealed.

God's Nephew Neither Preaches nor Pays His Rent

Richard Brothers was born in Placentia, Newfoundland, on December 25, 1757. It was perhaps his birthday that first led him to think he was of divine lineage.

His father was a soldier in the local garrison, stationed there to fight the French, and wanted his son to follow in his military footsteps. So when Brothers came of age, he was sent off to England to join the navy. In 1786, ashore for a brief spell, he married an Englishwoman and went immediately back to sea for three years. Upon his return home he discovered that his wife was living with another man and had children by him. Crushed, Brothers moved to London.

Brothers began to write. In 1794 and 1795 he published the two volumes of *A Revealed Knowledge of the Prophecies and Times*, which predicted the millennium would begin on November 19, 1795. Brothers himself—"Prince of the Hebrews and Nephew of the Almighty" —would lead the ten lost tribes back to Jerusalem. The books sold rapidly and were reprinted, stimulating strong discussion and debates throughout England. Even *The Times* took to calling Brothers "the great prophet of Paddington Street". He was gaining followers rapidly although he never preached or appeared at public meetings.

Brothers made one mistake. He included political exhortations among his prophecies. In one he informed King George III that God wanted Brothers to wear the crown. He went on to tell the people of England that the war with France was contrary to God's will. In March, 1795 he was arrested on suspicion of treason and subsequently committed to a lunatic asylum.

The Second Virgin Birth

The Industrial Revolution was in full swing, now, with the introduction of the new high pressure steam machine. Mechanized ships and trains were being designed, and there were many who believed that the millennium, if not already at hand, was certainly approaching. What else could this progress mean?

Joanna Southcott was a daunting woman from her early years. She had a strict religious childhood but was also attractive to men. She rejected marriage proposals well into middle age, preferring to maintain her virtue. And then, at the age of 42, in 1792, she became a prophetess.

She made many predictions and was right often enough to win a reputation as a seer. Her information, she said, came from divine visitations. She gained a large following.

In 1814 her spiritual visitor made a startling announcement. She, Joanna Southcott, sixty-four years old, was to give birth, by immaculate conception, to the second Jesus Christ. The Second Coming would lead almost immediately to the final judgement. Joanna saw twenty-one doctors, seventeen of whom verified that she was pregnant. Suddenly, all of London was expectant.

The child was due in the fall, but by November there was no birth. She began to doubt herself and her mission, and the symptoms of pregnancy began to disappear. She became sick and weak and, on December 27, she died. The body was wrapped with towels and hot-water bottles in the hope that she would come back to life on the fourth day.

Joanna Southcott began to decay and, as the doctors performed an autopsy, spectators watched from the corners of the room, smoking to disguise the smell. There were no signs of disease nor any of pregnancy.

Back to Brazil: the Return of Sebastian

While most millennialists—particularly the students of Christian missionaries or prophets —wait for the return of Jesus Christ, not all do. As we've seen, some expect other figures, equally mystical, to reappear.

By the early 1800s the population of north-eastern Brazil was a thorough mixture of Indian, black and Portuguese elements. Each brought its own legends, religions and histories, so the local mythology was somewhat confused.

One unusual belief resurfaced among these people from time to time. King Sebastian, a medieval Portuguese king who was killed while fighting the Moors, was expected to come back to punish the wicked and lead the faithful into the Kingdom of God. It was a hybrid belief—central Europeans had been expecting the return of the Emperor Frederick, Welshmen the return of King Arthur and so on—and a little out of place in the 1800s, but it wasn't without a related precedent. Some Portuguese had believed the same thing back in the 1400s.

The early 1800s was a time of many uprisings in Brazil—the country was going through the trauma of independence—but not all of them were warfaring.

The Pedra Bonita incident in Pernambuco province, for example, was bloody in another way. One group of believers, borrowing from unChristian religion, thought that human

sacrifices would entice Sebastian to return. (To come for the first time actually, since he had never been to Brazil.) They sacrificed children in his name, but to no avail.

Another group, known as the Rodeador movement, took another tack to encourage Sebastian to come. They were a pacifist people, organized along army lines but unwilling to fight. They proposed a military crusade to Palestine to liberate Jerusalem and the Holy Land. They believed there would be no blood-shed, their enemies bowing down to Sebastian at the appointed hour.

These peaceful crusaders still believed in a supernatural victory when they were attacked by Brazilian troops. They did not retaliate. They thought, right to the last, that the attackers would suddenly convert to the Sebastianic faith.

The Golden Egg

In 1806 in a hamlet near Leeds, England, a hen laid an unusual egg. Precursor to our modern billboards and bumper stickers, it was normal in size, weight and color, but on the side were the words "Christ is Coming". Word spread quickly, and hundreds gathered from miles around to witness this sign of the Kingdom of God. Local priests, believing the End was near, quickly organized the curious into impromptu prayer meetings.

A local doctor, skeptical of miracles, came to inspect the blessed hen and deduced that the egg had been inscribed with corrosive ink and forced back into the fowl's body, where-upon the crowd dispersed, simultaneously disappointed and relieved, but not without first offering thanks to the Lord.

The Mormons Get the Last Laugh

It has always been easy to ridicule the Mormons, but constant mockery and persecution has unified and strengthened the sect. The newness of the religion, the isolation of its central miracle and the partiality of its witnesses, all make it seem less than credible. Yet the Mormons have withstood a century and a half of disbelief and now have a following of about two million Americans.

The story began when the Smith family of Sharon, Vermont, moved to Palmyra, New York, in the early 1800s. All the family members except for Joseph, a teenaged son, became members of the Presbyterian church. Joseph was undecided, confused by so much contradiction and quarrelling between denominations. Joseph knew he was a Christian, so he looked to his Bible for advice and sought his God through prayer. As he knelt praying in the woods, in the spring of 1820, he saw his first vision. The Father and the Son appeared to him, instructing him to join none of the existing churches with their abominable creeds.

He complied. Later, a messenger of God (named Moroni) came to Smith, telling him that God had work for him to do and showing him where to find the *Book of Mormon*, written on golden plates. The book was written in what Smith called "Reformed Egyptian" but, fortunately, it was accompanied by devices that helped him translate the work. When he had finished the task, he allowed his three closest followers to accompany him back to the woods where they all saw a vision, an angel turning the golden pages leaf by leaf. To further substantiate his claim of divine guidance, Smith later called eight more witnesses to view the plates, and to give their testimony. The problem—from the disbeliever's point of view—was that the eight new witnesses were all immediate relatives of Smith or the original three. Furthermore, they didn't get to touch the original book. Moroni appeared and turned the pages for them. When he left, he took the book.

Nonetheless, the church had begun. In 1830 it was officially incorporated as the Church of Jesus Christ of Latter-Day Saints. It had, to begin with, six members. A month later it had forty, and it went looking for new converts with a missionary zeal. Not everybody welcomed these evangelists and trouble awaited the Mormons wherever they tried to settle. They tried to stay in two separate towns in Missouri, but each time they were run out of the area. The second time, the state militia intervened during a battle and threw the believers into a jail from which they escaped. They fled, but Illinois was no friendlier than Missouri. Smith ordered his followers to burn the offices of an anti-Mormon newspaper and was imprisoned. This was a turning point for the young church. Some angry citizens stormed the jail, killing Smith. The Mormons had a martyr.

Brigham Young became the president of the organization and moved it to Utah where, in 1847, he founded Salt Lake City. By the time Young died, thirty years later, the church had 140,000 members and was flourishing.

The Mormons believe the End of the World will come after three great gatherings. First, the tribe of Ephraim, the Mormons themselves, will gather in Zion, which they believe to be Independence, Missouri. (Unfortunately, they were chased out of this Zion in the 1800s.) Then the tribe of Judah—the Jews—will gather in Palestine. (After Jesus returns to earth he will reign simultaneously from two capitals, Jerusalem and Independence.) And finally, the ten lost tribes of Israel will be found and will gather in Zion. At this point Christ will return to begin the peaceful millennium.

His first act, as the millennium begins, will be to burn the wicked and unfaithful. Satan will be bound. And, at last, the mockery will stop.

William Miller, Adventists and Strength through Disappointment

William Miller, a New York farmer and atheist, saw the light some time around 1830, repented, and turned to his Bible. After a careful reading of Daniel and Revelation he concluded that the world would end on April 3, 1843. He began to preach this wisdom in 1831 but no one paid much attention until meteor showers in 1833, and frequent comet sightings later that same decade, turned their thoughts to apocalypse.

By 1843, the predicted year, the *New York Herald* had begun to take Miller seriously. It published his prophecy that the world would be consumed by fire. There was an outbreak of murders and suicides among his followers, who believed they stood a better chance of going to heaven one at a time instead of with the mob at Armageddon. On the final day, nothing happened. Unruffled, Miller predicted a new final day, July 7. His following grew rapidly.

On that date, and again on March 21, 1844, and again on October 22, 1844, the cult believers gathered to greet the impending cataclysm. The followers wore white ascension robes, which they bought from Miller, and waited next to carefully dug graves. The End refused to come. Eventually the Millerites, who numbered 100,000 at their peak, split into factions, most of them having lost confidence in their leader. The strongest of these factions, the Seventh-Day Adventists, still exists as an organized religion today.

Their history begins with the Millerite movements of the 1840s and they refer to October 22, 1844, the last of Miller's appointed days, as the Day of the Great Disappointment. As with the followers of Shabbetai Tsvi or the twentieth century Mrs Keech, the disenchantment (or, to use the sociological term, disconfirmation) by no means spelled the end of the set of beliefs. When Christ failed to present himself, the Millerites broke into smaller groups, their enthusiasm intact; some later reassembled to form the Seventh-Day Adventist church. Miller lost his personal hold on the believers but several local spiritual leaders rose to take his place.

Hiram Edson of New York explained away the Great Disappointment. The predicted Second Coming was a misinterpretation of the Bible, he said. Christ had been in action on that day, it is true, but he had moved from the heavenly sanctuary to the heavenly holy of holies, the upper house of the spiritual kingdom. A simple mistake. Anybody could make one. Some of the doubters, after a period of skepticism, regained their faith.

A theologian, Joseph Bates of Massachusetts, and a preacher, Frederick Wheeler of New Hampshire, worked together to give the young cult the foundation of its belief in the holiness of the seventh day, Saturday. The two borrowed from the Jewish and Seventh-Day Baptist faiths and came to the conclusion that the papacy had been incorrect in declaring Sunday, the first day of the week, holy.

The other local leader to spring from William Miller's followers was Ellen White, a Maine visionary, who began to see the way into the City of God. Her visions began immediately after the Great Disappointment. She believed she was uniquely guided by Jesus and that she could lead the Adventists into the Promised Land. She is reported to have had as many as two hundred visions.

In 1860 the name "Seventh-Day Adventist" was taken as the denomination's official name. Within three years the separate groups had convened in a great conference and organized themselves back into a unified religion. Almost immediately the church began energetic missionary work and today three-quarters of its believers live outside North America.

What do they believe? They believe, as a central doctrine of their faith, in the literal, physical and personal return of Christ. They no longer try to predict the date, appreciating the lessons learned by Miller, but they believe the Lord's return is imminent, at a time that is near but not disclosed. They believe that Armageddon, which has come to stand for the great holy war in the Middle East, will be ended by the sudden appearance of Christ who will crush his enemies. And they believe that, during the millennium, believers will live with God in heaven and the unbelievers will live with Satan on a desolate earth, scorched by a sea of fire, the "fathomless pit" of the Bible.

The Taiping Rebellion and Imaginative Misunderstanding

As has been seen repeatedly throughout this book, practical Christianity at any given time often resembles the beliefs of its current leaders and is adapted to suit the contemporary situation. It has been flexible throughout the ages, always open to one more interpretation. In China, in the mid-1800s, Catholicism was banned but there remained a Protestant influence through books and with the presence of one American missionary, Issachan J Roberts. This influence cleared the way for a millennialist cult and the Taiping Rebellion.

(Millennialism was going through a slow period in the west at this time. Charles Darwin had just published *On the Origin of Species*, and many people were beginning to reject the literal interpretations of the Bible.)

The Taiping story begins with the failures and frustrations—some say the insanity—of one man, Hung Hsiu-ch'uan. Hung wrote the entrance exams for the civil service four times and failed each time. He began to have visions that he interpreted freely, based on his recollections of the teachings of the American missionary, Roberts. Hung became convinced that God had chosen him as the new messiah, and that he would restore China to the true faith, leading the nation into the final millennial peace.

Preaching a rich mixture of militarism and Christianity, Hung quickly gathered a large following in a mountainous part of Kwangsi, a province known for its rebelliousness. His was an eccentric Christianity. Because of rough translations and a sketchy understanding of the Bible, Hung and his disciples chose only those parts that supported his millennialist visions. They believed in the Creation, they believed in Noah, and they believed in the exodus from Egypt. They saw themselves as the lost tribe, who would remove the Manchu dynasty from China and set up the "Taiping t'ien Kuo", the Heavenly Kingdom of Great Peace. They also added some peculiar features of their own. Christ, for instance, was believed to be the Heavenly Elder Brother of Jesus.

The rebels seized Nanking and held power in one area or another from 1851 through 1864, when the rebellion was finally crushed. Hung, isolated from his military generals and withdrawn into his religion, committed suicide a few months before the Taiping headquarters fell. The cult faded quickly.

116

James Jershom Jezreel and the Jezreelites

To our eyes, the present seems cluttered with sects, subsects, cults and a great variety of truths. It was ever thus. And, somehow, most prophets, no matter how obscure, have seemed able to find support and followers.

James White was a private in the British Army. In October, 1875, he joined the followers of Joanna Southcott who at the time were called The New House of Israel. (They were an offshoot of the Christian Israelite Church, founded in 1822.) Within ten weeks he was asked to leave and with seventeen others formed The New and Latter House of Israel. Two months later he was posted to India.

On his return he announced that he was the messenger of God and he received revelations that he wrote down (at God's request) in "The Flying Scroll". He changed his name to James Jershom Jezreel and married Clarissa Rogers, who changed her name to Esther, Queen of Israel. They toured America and began attracting converts.

Incredibly successful, they bought twenty acres of land and, using donations equal to $500,000, built an entire community with houses, shops and a college. They began construction on a temple large enough to hold 20,000 people. Despite the lack of biblical instruction on such questions, they grew their hair long and wore purple velvet caps.

They were, of course, part of the ten lost tribes of Israel, the first batch of the 144,000 elect of God foretold in Revelation, awaiting the very imminent End. After Jershom's death they split into various camps, one under Queen Esther. Little else is known about the Jezreelites except how important the End of the World was to them. Their name is the clue: Jezreel is the plain at the present site of ancient Armageddon.

Millennialism for Atheists: Marxism

For those unable to believe in religion and unwilling to see popular millenialism movements as madness, there remains the class-struggle argument. There is, to the Marxist, no divine intervention, since there is no God. It follows, then, that there are no prophets, either, and those who claim to be prophets are irrelevant, if their teachings are embarrassing, or else they are simply good leaders. Millennialism is a sign of the masses unified in pursuit of the paradise that has always been expected to accompany the End of the World.

It is often difficult to separate the revolutionary from the millennial. Every time a nation has a revolution or a civil war (Russia, France, China and the United States are all good examples), the End raises its head in some form or another. There are always those who will believe that political upheavals are signs of the millennium. And colonial situations, which gave rise to many of the End cults in this book, are equally fruitful grounds for Marxist analysis.

The Marxists' dream, after all, is that there will be a last judgement. They call it the revolution. The millennial kingdom—which they call the dictatorship of the proletariat—will be established, here on earth, by man's own will. The Marxists are millennialists, without being spiritualists.

The strength of Marxism, however, is also its failing. It believes in the perfectibility of man and the perfectibility of social and political life. But what Marxism delivers is what any centrally controlled totalitarian government delivers: the promise, but not the perfection.

What communism offered under Stalin, finally, was the same as Nazism did under Hitler—a new world, but not the promised one.

Charles Russell and the Invisible Advent

The precocious Charles Russell was pushed into adulthood at a young age. His character was shaped partly by his mother, who hoped and prayed he would become a minister, and partly by his father, who made him, at the age of eleven, a partner in his furniture store.

Young Charles thought at the time he would grow up to be a foreign missionary. During adolescence, however, he was bothered by the notion of a God who could mete out eternal torture to the damned. Russell became a doubter and remained so until he encountered his first Adventist preacher, a man under the sway of William Miller. Part of the Adventist's sermon was an explanation that the soul was not necessarily immortal—the souls of the chosen were immortal, he said, but the souls of the wicked died with their bodies. No more eternal torture. Charles Russell regained his faith.

Shortly afterward he began to improve upon that faith. He believed, like the Adventists, that Christ would return to establish the Kingdom of God on earth, but he did not believe in a visible and tangible Second Coming. Christ would come back, and soon, but he would do so invisibly, like a thief in the night, with only the faithful knowing he had returned. In 1875 Russell wrote a book called *The Object and Manner of Our Lord's Return*, which sold 50,000 copies.

And then, in 1876, he became convinced that the Adventists had been right in teaching that the Second Coming would take place in 1874. Christ, Russell decided, had already descended for the second time. Invisibly. He sold his furniture business and set out to tell the world. The kingdom was at hand.

First he tried to convince the local clergymen (of Allegheny and Pittsburgh) that he was on the true path. They didn't subscribe. So he began to lobby the Adventists, travelling with them and winning some of their followers. In 1879 he began to edit and publish a new magazine, *Watchtower*, the journal that still bears his imprint.

His movement took no name although critics called his followers "Russellites". It was held together in large measure by Russell's fantastic publishing ability. During his career he wrote 50,000 pages of religious material, some of it published as books, most as *Watchtower* articles. The sect can be seen as a gigantic publishing house, with the followers serving as distributors. The motivation was simple. Only those who preached—the distribution of religious literature was considered preaching—were part of the church; and only those who belonged to the church would be saved. Very straightforward: you push our pamplets, we'll see you aren't overlooked on the day of judgement.

According to Russell, the prophesied 1,000 years of Christ's rule on earth did not begin with the Second Coming. The millennium would commence in 1914. Its inauguration would be seen by all in the overthrow of the earthly kingdoms. Russell died in 1916, convinced that the first world war was the first sign of the millennium. He didn't live long enough to see the British force the Turks out of Palestine. It was at that moment of prophetic fulfillment that millennialists around the world began to take heed of Russell's predictions, many believing that the way was prepared for the Jews to return to the Holy Land.

Russell's movement grew and grew, eventually becoming the Jehovah's Witnesses.

Jehovah's Witnesses

After the death of Charles Russell, his organization became less and less democratic. Under Russell, each congregation had governed itself, the *Watchtower* had an editorial committee of five and the corporation served the religion. (The corporation was the Watchtower Bible and Tract Society, established in 1884 under the presidency of Russell to publish the thoughts of the church.) In 1917 all that changed. The new president was a very political man.

Joseph Rutherford, the corporation's legal counsellor, became the top man in a controversial election. There are those who claim it was rigged. These facts are certain: nominations were closed immediately after Rutherford's name was put forward; the convention did not vote, since only one candidacy had been announced; and many delegates, clearly supporting other leaders, were given no chance to lobby for their favorites. The furor died down a year later and Rutherford was re-elected, under careful scrutiny from all quarters, by a substantial majority.

Rutherford moved quickly to establish the corporation as the central governing body of the church and to gain control of the editorship of the *Watchtower*. By 1925 he was publishing articles against the wishes of the majority of the editorial board. And in 1931, the same year the church officially became the Jehovah's Witnesses, he removed the names of the other editors from the magazine. Rutherford was in control. It seems one no longer had to be a prophet to lead a sect—a good lawyer could do it too.

There were, of course, rebellions and schisms resulting from this political maneuvering, but the tenets of the faith remain much as Russell had envisaged them: Christ is among us and his kingdom began in 1914. Satan himself began the First World War, enraged at the interruption, by the Second Coming, of his rule on earth. That war, however, pales beside the great battle of Armageddon which, according to tracts published in the 1950s, will take place within a generation. On the one side will be the Jehovah's Witnesses (144,000 of them) with followers, known as the sheep. On the other side will be all the nations of the world, the United Nations and all other organized religions. The faithful will not have to fight. Christ will intervene on their behalf, striking with earthquakes, floods, plagues and fires, killing over two billion disbelievers.

Then comes the kingdom, after which Satan is freed. He tries one last time to win over the faithful, then he is destroyed. Finally there is total peace on a perfect sin-free earth, made all the more perfect by the absence of politics. And nobody around, except the handful of Jehovah's chosen.

Brazil, Land of Millennial Zest: Of Armies and the End

By the turn of the twentieth century, civilization was radically different from that which had existed when the Jesuits first showed up in Brazil. Technology was pervasive, the Church had softened its dogma, Darwinian thought was acceptable and H G Wells had given fiction an apocalyptic school. But in Brazil the End of the World was one of the unchanging presences of life, undergoing only minor mutations and reincarnations.

The mass migrations were over, and even the most faithful had given up on Sebastian, but one critical element was constant. The millennialist movements continued to be an affront to the government, a rebellion against the authorities. The government, in turn, continued to purge the cultists, using the force of the military. The Brazilian End of the World was in a fatal rut.

The Canudos movement, which ended in 1897, was remarkable by any standards. An insane man, known first as Antonio Conselheiro and later as Bom Jesus, wandered from town to town near Bahia, living on alms and doing a little freelance preaching. His was a mixed doctrine that included an imminent End accompanied by the return of the real Jesus. He gathered thousands of followers and finally settled at a large ranch called Canudos, where his disciples led a promiscuous and lawless life.

Government officials, embarrassed by this anarchy, decided to intervene. Clergymen were sent in first to show the cultists some reason, to let them see the error of their ways. When this didn't work, provincial police arrived to explain the laws of the land. They were sent packing. In 1896, two separate expeditions of federal troops were dispatched to capture the ranch. The first was defeated handily by the millennialists. The second army, a much stronger body of fighters, seized Conselheiro's stronghold after savage fighting, but just at the end of the battle, a stray bullet killed the colonel who had led the expedition. His soldiers fled in panic and disarray, believing they were in the presence of supernatural forces.

Conselheiro became a hero, and a hero with a large arsenal of guns and ammunition, left behind by the government troops. His throng

of followers grew, impressed by his religious and military reputation. In 1897 the military returned in force, taking the community hut by hut, crushing and devastating everything in sight. The fighting was long and fierce—the army alone lost 5,000 men—and it was also decisive. The movement was over, most of the followers dead.

Another millennialist disturbance occurred in 1912. In an area called Contestado (a piece of land in the interior claimed by two provinces), a mystic called Joao Maria began to predict the Second Coming and the End of the World. His followers, uneducated peasants, gathered frequently to pray. Joao Maria believed himself to be the prophet and saint who would prepare the world for the return of Jesus, and went on to insist he was above all other civil and religious authorities. The government, ever contrary, believed he was just another in a long line of apocalyptic troublemakers. Alarmed by his popularity, and by now well trained in handling these zealots, the federal government made a preemptive strike. In 1915 a full division of 6,000 men marched into the Contestado and wiped out the believers.

For Brazilians the pattern became clear. Joining the army offered a better future than believing that the End was nigh.

Cargo Cults and the Gods of Paperwork

Perhaps the most peculiar of the modern visions of the End belongs to the cargo cults of Melanesia, the group of islands that includes New Guinea, Fiji, the Solomons and the New Hebrides. Although they have a complexity of social organization and religious ritual, the native inhabitants remain primitive today, their technologies based on stone and wood. They were not prepared for their first encounters with the white men who arrived as explorers and missionaries in the late 1800s and the early 1900s.

As late as 1946 an Australian government patrol found the people of New Guinea's central highlands in a state of religious fervor. The arrival of the whites, with their incomprehensible technology, was the signal that the End of the World was at hand. They killed off all their livestock in the belief that more would appear magically from the sky. The End was nigh and many thought they would now be able to change their black skins for white ones.

Their entire vision was based on a simple misunderstanding. These stone-age thinkers had no comprehension of jet-age technology, nor did they grasp the ideas of manufacturing, factory production, freight shipping or international trade. What they saw was white-skinned Europeans—and later Australians and Americans—writing on pieces of paper and later receiving shiploads of crated cargo. Manufactured goods, clothing and preserved foods. Machines. To the Melanesians it was all cargo, and its arrival was magic, the result of a religious faith and ritual of which they were ignorant. The question they tried to answer was how they, the black Melanesians, could attain the proper state of grace so they, too, could receive cargo.

Traditional Melanesian belief is based on magic. Nothing can be done without the help of magic, no gardening, no canoeing, no childbearing. They believed the cargo must have come from the Land of the Dead. Somebody had to be helping the Europeans, since all they did was sit in offices all day, scribbling on sheets of paper, while the blacks worked. The cultists observed the whites who ran the missions and began to imitate them in ritualistic ways. They formed cabals, dedicated to the magic properties of paper and collective writing, for the most part illiterate doodling. Other cults had secret gatherings at which they sat around tables, containers of flowers before them, dressed in European clothes, waiting for the materialization of cargo. To us it seems a satire of bureaucratic life; for them it was a search for the path into the Kingdom of God.

European missionaries had not been able to shake the natives' faith in magic. They had simply added new features. The Melanesians loved the concept of the millennialist End of the World and were enchanted by the idea that all Christians, black or white, are equal in the eyes of God. They believed that the whites were already part of the Kingdom of God and that they themselves would soon join them, when the cargo secret was revealed.

One group of natives in the Madang district of New Guinea, at the turn of the century, went in a group to the mission, presenting a petition demanding that the secret now be revealed. They had been Christians for forty years, the petitioners said, and forty years was patience enough.

The Modern Miracle at Fatima

There have been many fanciful versions of the three letters of Fatima and it's difficult to separate the fact from the fancy. It took 25 years before the story became widely known in North America and, as is so often the case, the doubts had thickened with the years and the details had changed somewhat.

There are two certainties about the events at Fatima. First, there were no letters. Instead the Blessed Mother revealed three secrets to a shepherd child, one of which has not been made public to this day. (The letters were actually reports, based on the child's descriptions, written by church authorities.) And second, there was a miracle. At Fatima in Portugal, in 1917, with 70,000 witnesses. A modern-day miracle.

This is the story. On May 13, ten year old Lucia dos Santos and her two cousins saw a figure of a lady brighter than the sun standing on a cloud perched on an evergreen tree. The lady asked that the children return to the spot on the thirteenth of each month until October, when she would reveal who she was, show them a miracle and tell them what she wanted. They returned the following month, attended by fifty curious locals who had listened to their story. The lady appeared again but was only visible to the three children, although others saw the arrival and departure of the cloud and saw movement in the tree. Nonetheless, the first doubts were planted. The townspeople began to believe that Lucia and her playmates were having hallucinations or, worse, were being possessed by demons. Lucia's mother insisted that these were tricks of the devil, and Lucia became fearful herself. She became confused and frightened and decided against keeping her appointment on July 13. But at the last moment her fears vanished and she ran happily to the site, where more than a thousand persons were waiting. The lady appeared and showed, to Lucia and her cousins, a vision.

The earth disappeared, replaced by a sea of fire through which lost souls, like transparent black animals, tumbled in pain, on fire within and without, shrieking uncontrollably in their agony. The children were terrified but the lady reassured them, explaining that they had seen hell, where the souls of sinners go. She spoke of the war (this was 1917) and said it would soon end but that God was offended. She also predicted the Second World War, saying it would begin during the term of Pope Pius XI. (Pius died in February, 1939). And she said further that if Russia were not to be converted and consecrated then the Russian errors would spread throughout the world, initiating wars, annihilating nations and persecuting the Church.

It was ten years before the Church allowed Lucia to reveal the first two secrets: the vision of hell and the necessity of religious devotion to peace. There was a third secret, written and sealed in the archives of the local bishop that was not to be made public until 1960.

The three children were kidnapped on August 13 by a Portuguese civic official, who interrogated them for two days, making them miss their monthly appointment. Some 18,000 spectators showed up, but the Blessed Virgin did not. Instead, she appeared six days later to the three children in a nearby field. When Lucia returned home that evening she brought her mother a piece of the branch on which the lady had rested her foot. Her mother, while examining the branch, was conscious of a fragrant perfume, never before smelled in those parts, which came from the leaves. For the first time, she believed her child.

On September 13, Lucia was one of a crowd of 30,000 who saw the cloudless sky change color as a luminous globe moved across it, changing into a cloud that stopped on the usual tree. The scene was repeated on a rainy October 13, when 70,000 persons, including newspaper reporters, witnessed it. And on this day the Blessed Mother produced her miracle.

This is what the children saw: a series of heavenly visions, of the Lord as a grown man dressed in red, of Jesus as an infant with Joseph and Mary and, lastly, of Mary herself in brown robes. This is what the crowd saw: the rainclouds parted and the sun shone through, turning pale and then becoming a silver disc. Multicolored light then surrounded the sun, every color of the spectrum, and the skies seemed to revolve as the sun spun madly

on an axis, painting the crowds with fantastic patches of color. Three times it spun like this, and three times it stopped. As the crowd fell to its knees the sun was suddenly wrenched from the sky and came hurtling, in a zigzag fashion, down to the earth, coming closer and closer, getting hotter and hotter, terrifying the masses. It stopped, very close to earth, hovered for a moment (drying the rain-drenched clothes of the assembled throng), and then ascended, once more in a zigzag manner, to its natural place. The people looked up in astonishment, 70,000 of them, happy and dry, and the miracle was over.

Lucia's cousins died as young children. She herself became a nun. And the third secret?

The letter was reportedly opened on schedule in 1960 by Pope John XXIII who read it, fainted and had it resealed. What did it say? Few people know. The most common story is that it predicted a fiery End of the World during the term of the fifth pope after the letter was opened. Since that time we have had Paul VI, John Paul I and John Paul II, the present pontiff.

The story tells us that the letter, whose contents are read by each new pope, is kept secret because the Church fears that the masses would become suicidal and immoral if they were to know that the world was ending. In cases like this, the truly wise are often silent.

Prophecies of Russia and Israel: Two Down, One to Go

When our Lady of Fatima chastised Russia for its errors and predicted that an unconsecrated and atheistic Russia would provoke a major war followed by a great peace, it was old news to the millennialists. They knew it from biblical prophecies. Nonetheless, when the Blessed Virgin produced the miracle of the sun in October, 1917, they were reassured by the sign. But the miracle was, for them, only one sign of three. Within the next month the Balfour Declaration announced British support for an independent Jewish nation in Palestine, and the Bolsheviks revolted in Russia. Events were unfolding as the Bible said they would, and the End of the World was near.

According to biblical prophets (in Ezekiel 37, Deuteronomy 30 and Isaiah 11) the Jewish people would return to Palestine, gathering from around the world, to recreate (for the third time) the nation of Israel, as they did in 1948; they would return to Jerusalem, which they did during the Six Day War in 1967; and they would rebuild Solomon's Temple. This they have not yet done; on the site now stands the Dome of the Rock, one of the holiest of Moslem temples.

And paralleling the re-creation of Israel is the rise of Russia as her enemy. Russia (identified as "the uttermost parts of the north" in Ezekiel 38, and as one of "the nations which are at the four corners of the earth" in Revelations 20) will be led by the prince of darkness, and will attack Israel and desecrate the temple, provoking the final war of wars, Armageddon. With the 1917 revolution came a swing to official atheism and a policy of exterminating religion. The purge has not been successful. Christianity thrives in the western USSR, Islam flourishes in the south, and there are, scattered through the republics, some three million Jews living in conditions that amount to house arrest. And it isn't only at home that Russia has shown her anti-Semitism. Abroad, she has armed any country in the Arab world that will be an enemy to Israel: Egypt in the 1960s, Libya and Syria in the 1970s and 1980s.

Today there are over eight million millennialists in the United States alone. They are watching every sign. Russia will invade Israel, damaging the temple and provoking Armageddon. God will be offended, Russia will be crushed, there will be a global holocaust, and Jesus will descend for the second time, to establish the Kingdom of God on earth.

Commentaries that have appeared sporadically since the 1700s have made it clear that Israel must re-emerge as a nation in order to bring about the End of the World. But it was up to Hal Lindsay, writing in the United States in the late 1960s, to explain the detail of the events that would accompany the apocalypse, and to fit Israel into the scenario.

Let's Talk for Just a Moment Longer about the Dome of the Rock

The hill called Mount Moriah sits surrounded by the city of Jerusalem, the ancient site of Judaism's most holy temple, the present site of Islam's second holiest shrine and, according to many prophecies, the future site of the temple that will be built just before the world ends.

Long ago Abraham prayed at its summit, and Elijah, and later King David. The Ark of the Covenant rested on it, and Solomon built his temple using the rock atop the hill as the foundation of its altar.

This was the temple from which Jesus

chased the moneylenders, the temple destroyed in 70 AD by the Romans who left only one part of one wall standing, the Wailing Wall. When Israeli forces captured Jerusalem during the Six Day War, soldiers flocked to the wall, to kiss it and to pray. They brought with them a wooden ark of the scrolls, and a crude hand-painted sign announcing "Beyt Knesseth" —this is a temple. Moshe Dayan, then defense minister, announced "We have returned to the holiest of our holy places, never to depart from it again."

The blue-and-white flag of Israel was flying from all the buildings of old Jerusalem except one, a large beautiful mosque that stands just slightly above the Wailing Wall on the hill, the Qubbet es Sakhra, Islam's Dome of the Rock.

Out of respect for a religion that, until recently, has always treated Jews considerably better than Christianity has, the Israeli forces after the war left the golden crescent flag still fluttering above the mosque at the summit of Mount Moriah, the mosque built on the ancient site of their Temple.

For it was at this same spot that Mohammed prayed, and with such earnestness that, as he started to ascend into heaven, the rock followed him. It had to be restrained by the angel Gabriel, whose fingerprints are its only decoration. The bare rough rock, fifty-six feet long and forty feet wide, is the centerpiece of the mosque. Beneath it, enormous cisterns are carved deep into the summit. Moslems believe, in fact, that the rock is suspended in the air, still trying to reach after Mohammed.

They also believe that Mohammed drove four nails into the rock. They are slowly working their way downward, one having already disappeared. The Moslem guide taking tourists through the building tells them that when all the nails have shaken through the rock, and fallen into the small cave below, Mohammed will return to earth to announce the End of the World.

The Haile Unlikely Ras Tafari Movement

One of the world's most bizarre millennialist cults was born in Jamaica in the 1930s. The Ras Tafari movement was a religious offshoot of the Universal Negro Improvement Association, founded in the 1920s by Marcus Garvey, a Jamaican.

The Rastafarians believed that they were reincarnations of members of one of the ten lost tribes of Israel, and that they had been sent to the West Indies because of their sins. They believed that Africa was the promised land and that the emperor of Abyssinia would make arrangements for all the black exiles to come home to the millennial kingdom. They believed, in fact, that Ethiopia (formerly Abyssinia) was heaven, and Haile Selassie, its emperor, was the living God.

Who was this Haile Selassie? He was born Prince Tafari Makonnen. (Ras simply means prince.) He became His Imperial Majesty, The Conquering Lion of the Tribe of Judah, Elect of God, King of Kings, Emperor of Ethiopia. The Ethiopian constitution (based on Abyssinian legend) claims he is descended, without interruption, from the dynasty of Menelik I, son of King Solomon of Jerusalem and of the Queen of Ethiopia, known as the Queen of Sheba. (Jesus Christ was also descended from the line of Solomon, so it can be argued that Selassie was related to two of the men who personified God's will on earth.) He became famous throughout the world in 1936—he was called the conscience of humanity—when he appeared in a black cape before the League of Nations to decry Italy's invasion of his homeland. Ethiopia had become the first battleground of fascism, Mussolini's first grab at expansion.

The League of Nations heard this riveting speaker correctly prophesy that the League would collapse if it did not move to protect Ethiopia from Italian aggression. His fame would last for decades. Throughout the 1950s, for example, he was the premier spokesman for an independent and united Africa. When the Shah of Iran celebrated the 2000th anniversary of Persia's Peacock Throne, Selassie sat at the head of the table, the highest ranked leader in the world.

He went to Jamaica in the 1960s to see for himself this cult that carried his name. It is said he refused to leave his plane for a long time, bewildered by the sight of thousands of dancing, chanting Rastafarians with braided hair. After that one visit, he never returned. He was deposed as emperor in 1974 and died in 1975 after a prostate gland operation, thus depriving the cult of its Living God.

Luckily, many Rastafarians don't believe he really died.

It Can Happen Here, and Now

In the early 1950s, three social psychologists from the University of Minnesota, Leon Festinger, Henry Riecken and Stanley Schachter, were interested in the effect of the lack of fulfillment of prophecies on the lives of people who had made a serious commitment to those prophecies. They were somewhat frustrated by the lack of complete data on the followers of such End-of-the-Worlders as William Miller and Shabbetai Tsvi. But one can imagine their delight when they read the following story in a daily newspaper: (They have changed all names of geographical locations and of earthlings.)

"PROPHECY FROM PLANET. CLARION CALL TO CITY: FLEE THAT FLOOD. IT'LL SWAMP US ON DEC. 21, OUTER SPACE TELLS SUBURBANITE.

"Lake City will be destroyed by a flood from Great Lake just before dawn, Dec. 21, according to a suburban housewife. Mrs. Marian Keech, of 847 West School Street, says the prophecy is not her own. It is the purport of many messages she has received by automatic writing, she says.... The messages, according to Mrs. Keech, are sent to her by superior beings from a planet called 'Clarion'. These beings have been visiting the earth, she says, in what we call flying saucers. During their visits, she says, they have observed fault lines in the earth's crust that foretoken the deluge."

The three Minnesotans, as well as several hired observers with backgrounds in sociology, infiltrated the small band from October (presumably of 1954) through the period of the expectation of the flood, following up into January of the next year. *When Prophecy Fails*, a straightforward account of those times, details the course of their observations. (Their admirable and objective detachment must have frequently been put to the test by some of the more outlandish beliefs of Mrs Keech's followers. The only hint of this in the book is the date of their introduction: it celebrates the first anniversary of the non-flood.)

Mrs Keech had had some minor dealings with the occult and was keenly interested in theosophy, scientology and UFOs (which were still called flying saucers at that time). She was surprised when Higher Forces chose her to receive their messages. One of them introduced himself as Sananda, the contemporary identity of Jesus Christ.

Mrs Keech called the communications "lessons". There were several hundred of them, always received through automatic writing. Together they created a complicated cosmogony that included the destruction of a previous world (called Car) by one of the two groups of its inhabitants, "the scientists" led by Lucifer, who eventually settled on earth—only, Mrs Keech learned, to begin the cycle anew, leading again to destruction.

Details of the impending destruction came in bits and pieces. One lesson read: "the Earthling will awaken to the great casting of the lake seething and the great destruction of the tall buildings of the local city... You shall tell the world that this is to be, for such it is given."

Another communication was more detailed: "And the scenes of the day will be as mad...a great wave rushes into the rocky mountains—the ones of the covered area will be as the com [group] of the newly dead. The slopes of the side to the east will be the beginning of a new civilization upon which will be the new order, in the light.... Yet the land will be as yet not submerged, but as a washing of the top to the sea, for the purpose of purifying it of the earthling, and the creating the new order." France, England, Russia and much of the United States would be submerged; the lost continents of Mu and Atlantis would rise again; the Egyptian desert would become a fertile valley.

That part of the population, however, which is receptive to the "Light" will escape from the Earth, before the End, in flying saucers. It was to this group that Mrs Keech eventually turned her attention. She was not active in seeking converts, preferring for the most part to keep the information to herself and immediate acquaintances. Primarily through connections to flying saucer enthusiasts, their families, girlfriends, boyfriends and college roommates, a small circle of followers did grow up around Mrs Keech in Lake City and her most influential disciple, Dr Thomas Armstrong, who lived some 200 miles away.

It was Dr Armstrong who first attempted to alert the world to the imminent disaster. A seven-page press release gave geographical and philosophical details, but no date. It was ignored until a second, shorter release named date, time, and listed places of safe refuge from the floodwaters. In spite of the attendant publicity, the group made no effort to attract attention to itself or to gain membership.

About fifteen individuals could be considered part of the group at that time, eight of them very seriously committed to it. Such commitment was very important to the infiltrators, who were trying to determine if there would be a correlation between level of conviction (as evidenced by quitting jobs, facing familial discord, using up personal savings) and ability to withstand what they called "disconfirmation" of the prophecy.

Buoyed up by meetings with much of the flavor of seances, the group became more and more excited as December 21 approached. Mrs Keech and Dr Armstrong were terse but polite to reporters and the public but still made no effort to win support. Telephone inquiries would often receive a simple "No comment".

The believers survived several disappointments. A telephone message informed them they would be picked up by a flying saucer in the Keech backyard at 4 pm Friday, December 17. They removed all metal—including zippers and buttons—from their clothes in preparation for boarding, but the saucer never appeared. The household convinced itself that the false alarm had been a test drill.

The same night Mrs Keech received a communication that the pick-up would take place half an hour later, at midnight. There was a flurry of activity and the group—again metal-less—stood outside in the cold and snow for several hours. By the next day no one was talking about the second disappointing rehearsal. Curiously, the group became more serious and more vocal in the attention it lavished on the dozens of interested visitors who appeared at the house. (Previous callers had had to be quite forthright and ask lots of questions to learn anything about the predictions. Now—for the first time—that information was volunteered readily.)

Later the group managed to convince itself that five clever, skeptical college students who arrived and asked a number of detailed and pointed questions were in fact spacemen testing the will and readiness of the believers.

On December 20, at midnight, they waited again. The flood was scheduled to take place at dawn, but they hoped by then to be in the flying saucers, far from earth. By 4 am, their disappointment was acute but they could find no satisfactory explanation. Mrs Keech at one point said, "We don't have to understand everything. . . . We don't know what the plan is but it has never gone astray." A short while later, she burst into tears.

At 4:45 am, Mrs Keech received another communication through her automatic writing. It was entitled "The Christmas Message to the People of Earth" and it explained that God had saved the world from otherwise certain destruction because of the goodness of the little group of believers.

"From the mouth of death have ye been delivered," the message said, ". . . Not since the beginning of time upon this Earth has there been such a force of Good and light as now floods this room and that which has been loosed within this room now floods the entire Earth."

Mrs Keech and Dr Armstrong started telephoning the newspapers and wire services. This was the most active they had ever been in seeking publicity—and this, we note with some curiosity, was after their prediction had failed.

They dealt with reporters and broadcasters all that day, patiently, enthusiastically. Group members that previously had refused to talk to the press were now willing, and all questions were answered freely and at length. Members that had been somewhat skeptical before the disconfirmation now seemed convinced of the correctness of the cause and of the celestial origin of the messages.

The group now began to suspect that various visitors to the house were in fact from outer space, and they plagued these callers for instruction and orders. They began to make short-term, desperate predictions that inevitably did not come to fruition.

Finally threats of police action broke the group up, and they returned to their homes. The leaders felt compelled to keep moving, the Armstrongs to tour the United States, lecturing (mostly on UFOs), and Marian Keech, under an assumed name, to Arizona.

Sananda's Last Lesson

"A man with a conviction", say the authors in *When Prophecy Fails*, "is a hard man to change.... Suppose an individual believes something with his whole heart; suppose further that he has a commitment to this belief, that he has taken irrevocable actions because of it; finally, suppose that he is presented with evidence, unequivocal and undeniable evidence, that his belief is wrong: what will happen? The individual will frequently emerge, not only unshaken, but even more convinced of the truth of his beliefs than ever before. Indeed, he may even show a new fervor about convincing and converting other people to his view."

The Montanists remained strong for several centuries after the New Jerusalem declined to descend at Pepuza. Some of Shabbetai Tsvi's disciples were faithful long after their leader was imprisoned, even after he converted to Islam. Thousands of Millerites sustained huge disappointments month after month before fizzling out. There are countless other examples.

But why does this happen? It seems to boil down to the very basic: no one likes to be seen a fool. And the more he or she has risked, the more difficult it is to admit to having been wrong.

After the prophecy is seen to have not happened, the believer works overtime to convince as many other people as possible of the correctness of the belief-system that gave rise to the prophecy—and thereby justify and vindicate his or her involvement.

Festinger and company give an additional, arresting example. They point out that if one thinks of the crucifixion as unequivocal disconfirmation, then early Christianity fulfills the five conditions. The Jews expected a warrior messiah who would avenge them and certainly never let himself be crucified. For some people, that event was clearly shattering.

Perhaps, therefore, part of the psychological impetus for the early Church's evangelism was the unwillingness of so many followers to admit that they had been duped.

An interesting idea, but there is an easy counter-argument: Jesus explained more than once that he would be made to suffer and be crucified. Subsequent events confirmed that prediction rather than disproving that he was the Messiah.

Bad Odds in Eschatological Roulette

Mrs Keech and her friends draw attention to another lesson, too: prophecies about the End have failed far more frequently than they have been realized, and yet, over history, there has always been no lack of men and women willing, not just to predict the End, but to commit themselves completely to the idea. They have given up jobs and homes, risked scorn and ridicule and have preached and proselytized. They have built arks in public, believing they have been promised a rainbow, and they have been wrong.

Most of the prophets of the late twentieth century, risking less, have been careful to couch their predictions in perhapses, probablies and distant times. If there is something to be gained by being right, then by risking less, they have had less to gain; the more accurate their prophecies, the more gifted prophets appear to be.

Nonetheless, there does seem to be a powerful motivation at work in the world, a motivation one could call the Noah Urge: the desire to predict the End, to be right, and in so doing, to escape that End. It is a gift given to few.

Hal Lindsey Is Our Adso

We saw earlier how, in 950 AD, the young theologian Adso compiled and augmented existing concepts of the Antichrist in terms so completely appropriate to the mood of his times that his *Letter on the Origins and Life of the Antichrist* could easily be termed a major medieval bestseller. Other authors, before and after, were much more specific in their interpretations—and they would select key quotations from the Bible to make a convincing argument in each case. The Antichrist, they told us, was certainly Nero, or Mohammed, the pope, Napoleon or Hitler. The King of the North, prophesied in Ezekiel, was variously the Goths, the Vikings and, as we have seen, centuries later, the Russians. Babylon was variously interpreted as Rome, everywhere but Rome, Persia, Babylon, and, in recent times, the United States. And virtually every era has managed to find proof that it was deserving of the title "last days", the final stage in the development of the world.

Hal Lindsey is in good company. He is as eloquent as the most eloquent of early doom-sayers and more popular than most. His major book, *The Late Great Planet Earth* had over two million copies in print by 1980. The back cover of its paperback edition asked, "Is this the era of the Antichrist as foretold by Moses and Jesus?"

Lindsey begins by pointing out that the first appearance of Jesus on earth fulfilled *"300 specific predictions"* (his emphasis) in the Bible. The Second Coming, he tells us, will fulfill an additional 500 prophecies in the Gospels, the Book of Revelation, as well as in Daniel, Ezekiel and Zechariah.

The Late Great Planet Earth translates for us the events of recent history into the biblical signs that announce or pave the way for the imminent End of the World. Several stand out:

• The return of the Jewish nation to the Holy Land and particularly to Jerusalem.

• The ecumenical movement in combination with the liberalising of the Church, as well as the popularity of astrology, drugs, demon and idol worship. These together, Lindsey says, comprise the one-world religion that Revelation calls Babylon.

• The existence of various kingdoms that could and will rise up against Israel: the North, which is Russia; the South, the combined forces of Africa and the Arab states; and the East, Red China.

• The coming into power of the European Economic Community—the ten-horned beast prophesied in Revelation and the heir to the Roman Empire.

All of these events are locked into their order and place, as part of the last days, by one event still to transpire: the reconstruction of the temple at Jerusalem.

Apparently the present conflict in the Middle East will escalate until it brings the rest of the world to the brink of World War III. The leader of the European Economic Community —a man who will have gained instant prominence in a mock-Resurrection by recovering from what should have been a fatal wound— resolves the crisis. According to Daniel (according to Lindsey) the Roman leader, who is none other than the Antichrist, will begin construction of the temple.

At this time Jesus will return and millions of Christians will rise up to meet him "in the air", to join him for eternity. This event is called the Rapture or Translation. The last trumpet will blow and believers will be metamorphosed into new, immortal but recognizable bodies. "If you're not too satisfied with the face or body you now have," says Lindsey generously, "you will have a glorious new body."

The rest of the world will be flabbergasted. In the twinkling of an eye millions of people will have vanished.

Those who are left behind will endure the

seven years of tribulation predicted in Revelation. They will be under the rule of the Antichrist who will bring peace and security to the chaotic, war-torn world. In gratitude the world will let him crown himself as the new Great Roman Dictator. He will work miracles and be worshipped as a god. He will be strong, powerful, attractive, self-assured, proud and a charismatic public speaker.

The Antichrist will be assisted in his endeavors by a Jew from the tribe of Dan who will be called the "second beast", the False Prophet. Lindsey explains that this devilish lackey "will be given control over the economics of the world system and cause everyone who will not swear allegiance to the Dictator to be put to death or to be in a situation where they cannot buy or sell or hold a job. Everyone will be given a tattoo or mark on either his forehead or forehand, only if he swears allegiance to the Dictator as being God." That mark will be the number 666.

The next few years will be rife with complex patterns of war. Lindsey tells us that Magog, first mentioned in Ezekiel, stands for Russia, and Gog for its leader. Its army conquers Israel and the rest of the Middle East but then is attacked in turn and defeated by the Western Europeans under the leadership of the Antichrist. This army goes on to do battle with forces from the east, presumably the Red Chinese, at Armageddon.

Just as the battle, in Lindsey's words, "reaches its awful climax and it appears that all life will be destroyed on earth—in this very moment Jesus Christ will return and save man from self-extinction." This is the Day of Judgement. It will be followed by 1000 years of Christ's kingdom on earth and then he will create a new heaven and earth.

Lindsey's great success is attributable to several factors. In spite of the incredibly complex scenario he outlines, he speaks as if with authority; he claims to be able to understand the truth behind certain ambiguities that no one else can satisfactorily sort out; he, like all the most popular apocalyptic theoreticians in this book, does come up with an answer to the basic question, "How do our lives fit into history?"; and, also like so many others, he conveniently ignores any statement in the Bible that doesn't fit into his scheme.

Perhaps two of the most important such statements are in the writings of Luke. After the Resurrection, Jesus was with the apostles and they asked him whether he would now restore the kingdom to Israel. Acts I records his reply: "It is not for you to know times or seasons which the Father has fixed by his own authority." Hal Lindsey and many others have gone beyond the decent bounds of interpreting the lessons of the Bible and seem to be trying to read God's mind.

Luke, in chapter 17 of his Gospel, also wrote: "Being asked by the Pharisees when the kingdom of God was coming, he (Jesus) answered them, 'The kingdom of God is not coming with signs to be observed... for behold, the kingdom of God is within you.'"

We Pause for a Brief Moment of Heresy

If one goes along with those people whom Hal Lindsey dismisses as "liberal theologians" and decides not to take every word of the Bible as true fact, or description of potentially true fact, then all his arguments crumble.

As with any oracle, the Bible demands a willingness on the part of its readers to accept its authority, and within the restrictions of that authority it builds a complete, albeit self-referential, closed case. Most people are willing to accept a certain historical authority of the testaments—some call that "faith"—but Mr Lindsey cannot do justice to those powers he so boldly attempts to explain.

This, perhaps, is to pick, unfairly, on Hal Lindsey. His appearance in this History of the End is symbolical: he stands for the many well-intentioned Christians who get carried away with theorizing—but all of whom couldn't be fit into these pages.

Chapter Six

Until Recently, the End of the World Has Been Something to Hope for

From the days of Daniel, the times immediately preceding the End had usually been imagined as terrifying—the presence of terror in the world had always been a sign of impending apocalypse. For sinners, both the End and damnation promised to be torture, but the deserving could certainly look forward to paradise. As long as mankind believes in a future paradise, the End is a positive—even optimistic—step in the earth's continuing eternal history.

But even as cults, sects and latter-day prophets were unravelling the End's mysterious workings, humanity was convincing itself that the world could be understood through science. Simultaneously these notions were being explored in science fiction, and soon the End came to be seen as simply a horrible event devoid of religious meaning, severed from the notion of the Kingdom of God.

As the technical details of the End became all-important, afterlife became irrelevant. Fewer people talked about it. People with strong religious convictions ignored the Ends postulated by science and science fiction, knowing that the End of the World must include Christ's Second Coming.

Everyone else, however, ignored the redeeming features of Armageddon, looking forward with horror to any End that incorporated both scientific plausibility and collective finality.

The scientists were latecomers, admittedly, but they made up for that by creating a brand new apocalyptic myth. They were the first to imagine a depersonalized End, a scenario with no survivors, no redemption, no paradise. While this History demonstrates that much more of our past was tied into the End than one might imagine, science today warns that many of our futures—perhaps even most of our futures—tend towards the End.

The Industrial Revolution Spawns Dr Strangelove

For many people in the 1600s, utopias were an obsession. While a deluge of explorers and adventurers were charting new coasts and continents, writers were equally busy turning the facts of geography into myths and stories. These stories underlined the proximity of earthly paradises. Writers of utopian fiction—Sir Thomas More, Roger Bacon—created the new Atlantis, Christianopolis, the City of the Sun, all of them places that pretended to exist but had not yet been found.

The utopias were the same old paradises brought to earth in new guises, millennial kingdoms built out of new philosophies, new geographies, even new science.

But by the late seventeenth century, excitement over the notion of progress pushed the End of the World out of people's minds. It was a time to look to the future, to envisage what could be created through ingenuity and hard work. Life was getting better, understanding greater, and it seemed this progress would continue forever. When the End of the World returned to popular consciousness a little while later, it had undergone a radical change.

By the late 1700s the Western world had lived through the Industrial Revolution, although no real revolution had taken place and the changes were as specific to economics, farming, demographics or philosophy as they were to industry. The methods of food production were enormously improved, factories had emerged as the most efficient way to manufacture goods, coal was being widely used as a fuel and the steam engine had been invented. The time was ripe for entrepreneurs and capitalism.

The world had changed, and man's faith had changed. When man first tried to fly, he had resorted to magic. When this didn't work, he lost his faith in magic and learned to believe instead in machines. We see the results all around us.

(Not everybody believed in the machines, of course. Even in Great Britain, in the very heartland of the Industrial Revolution, the great apocalyptists—Mother Ann, Elspeth Buchan and Richard Brothers—were promising their followers the millennium.)

Science stopped being the concern of only a few intellectuals as it pursued technologies that affected everyone. Experiments and inventions were no longer isolated. They became part of a greater plan to conquer and exploit nature, to have it serve humanity.

The churches, particularly those which were Protestant, supported this new emerging order. They saw the possibility of more and more economic improvement. They advocated strict obedience to the word of God, and ceaseless, selfless work on earth. Successful work was seen as a sign of inner grace. "To redeem time is to see that we cast none of it away in vain" was the recurring cry of the preachers. With the clergy on the side of the Industrial Revolution, the Protestant work ethic was being invented. The clergy, however, had no idea where it would all lead.

What lay ahead seems now, with the advantage of hindsight, perhaps to have been inevitable. Science and religion could not stay cozy; science would contradict dogma. More to the point, science would stop apologizing for itself. When Copernicus pointed out that the earth swung in orbit around the sun, he had apologized. He dedicated his book to the pope, fearing censure, and his publisher included a preface saying this new theory was merely a hypothesis. Defiant scientists like Galileo had been rare. Deference to the church had been the rule.

But now men were learning to think in a different way. Religion was static, claiming external and absolute truths, while science, always tentative, was designed to understand and prove the laws of constant change. And this notion of change, of development and gradual growth, springing from Newton's theory on the origin of the universe and Darwin's theory on the evolution of species, would be a serious blow to the doctrines of the church.

Darwin shook everyone's beliefs. No one's old perceptions could hold any longer. Man changed. God changed. And the relationship between the two changed. Essentially Darwin had two points: he said, first, that no species stands alone; each lives in a symbiotic relationship with the rest of nature. And second, he showed that Homo sapiens is a child of the past and a parent to the future, a moment in a continuing evolution—like any other species.

Any way you looked at it, Darwin diminished the power of God and desecrated the relationship between the deity and his most intelligent creatures. It was uplifting to believe that reptiles had evolved into birds and it was reassuring to understand that wolves had been tamed into dogs. But it was unsettling to think that one's ancestors had once swung from branches in the jungle, and that their ancestors had dropped their gills and crawled out of the swamps onto dry land. What about Adam and Eve? What about our creation "in God's image"? And what about man's God-given dominion over all other creatures? In classical theology man had been the center of the world. Now, in the light of new findings by biologists and astronomers, he was growing less and less important. A grain of sand. A seed on the land.

It was equally unsettling to imagine that humanity was not fully developed, that it could continue to evolve. Did this imply that if Jesus' Second Coming didn't take place soon we might already have become something new, some strange futuristic beasts? Our egocentric vanity would not tolerate the notion: we collectively resolved that the End of the World would come some time during this glorious present stage of our development.

For a while, before Darwin's time, some philosophers had tried to straddle the gap between the old and the new. Kant, in the excitement of the Enlightenment, was the last of these. He saw the Kingdom of God as a new global ethic arising out of progress, "the highest good possible on Earth". Kant believed in God and progress. "Two things fill the mind with admiration and awe," he said, "the starry heavens above and the moral law within." With a leg on each side of the schism that separated the new astronomy and the old religion, Kant was balancing cautiously.

Others were boldly making the leap. The rise of scientific empiricism—"Show me! Prove it!"—brought a renewed age of reason. All of nature was seen as being deterministic: one could predict the path of every particle by studying the forces acting upon it. God became, for the first time, a hypothesis, and therefore debatable. What was his role? Was he an active, interventionist God, or did he merely start the ball and leave it to roll where it

would? And what of man? The rationalists believed that he (and society) could be made perfect by logic, by discovering and maintaining the natural balance.

A deterministic nature, a debatable God and a perfectable, rational man. How the times had changed! It was a small step to the second law of thermodynamics, the law of entropy, and from there to scientific pessimism. Later Bertrand Russell would say: "The second law of thermodynamics tells us that, on the whole, energy is always passing from more concentrated to less concentrated forms, and that, in the end, it will have passed into a form in which further change is impossible. When that has happened, if not before, life must cease."

Science was outgrowing its role as mere technological miracle-worker. It was beginning to get interested in the End of the World. Soon every one of its disciplines would have something to say on the subject.

And with the rising influence of science, a new stock character became part of Western mythology, courtesy of the church's attacks on the new rationalists, the new skeptics—the evil, manipulative scientist. As a side effect of the great quarrel, there appeared Dr Moreau, Dr Moriarity, Dr Jekyll's Mr Hyde and, later, Dr Strangelove, the mad scientist single-handedly capable of bringing about the End of the World.

A Time of Change in the History of Imagination

Over and over again, through the centuries, one discovers that the history of the End is, in fact, the history of imagination.

The first thing one has to understand about the imagination is that it is not pure invention. Each act of imagination is related to an idealistic vision of reality and has reasons for its existence. As the world changes, perception changes. And as perception changes, imagination changes. These changes, moreover, don't take place piecemeal in the imagination: everything changes at once.

There is a unified body of imagination, with an internal order and logic, in which each separate vision must fit into a pattern of all visions. When one vision changes dramatically, the whole framework must adjust. If one perceives the relationship between God and man as changing, then one must imagine a new man. And having concocted this new man, one inevitably creates new ways for his world to end.

The basic fuel of ideas is perception: what we see is what we think about. But ideas grow also out of their environment, the time into which they are born.

Men and women live in two worlds: the inner world of sensations, images, ideas, moods, fantasies and desire; and the outer physical world of other people and events, a world of parents, teachers and clergy, a world of societies, engineering and commerce. Imagination is not wholly voluntary. Environment is fed into the crucible and mixed with events, myths and beliefs. A large part of imagination has always been a response to existing, surrounding conditions, no less in the time of Noah than Daniel, no less in the time of Merlin than Jules Verne.

Imagination has always been the birthplace of myth. It is naturally part and parcel of religion and literature. Each feeds the others. From the church, for example, especially from Roman Catholicism, the universal— even the scientific—End of the World borrows the concepts of sin, repentance and salvation. From the philosopher Hegel's view of formal tragedy, with its final release of tension, the End takes notions of conflict, pathos and reconciliation. Peace, like the Kingdom of God, is the aftermath, the residue, the understanding of tragedy. From religion and myth come the visions.

The majority of apocalyptic cult visions have so much in common that we can be certain they come from similar sources—either within us or without. Most peoples expect a great cataclysm, the return of the dead and the exiled, the inversion of the social and economic orders, the invulnerability of the faithful throughout the upheaval and a final peace and redemption. In a nutshell, humanity falls into sin and chaos, and the gods intervene.

But the world was entering the Industrial Revolution. Man was being seen more and more as the master of his own fate. New revolutionary visionaries, uprooted and downtrodden, troubled by sorrows and poverty, felt deprived and hopeless and identified themselves with the bleak situation of the common people. Individual imaginations attempted to solve the collective plight, to respond to their powerlessness in the face of the industrial juggernaut. This was a time of unprecedented social change. It called for new hopes, new fears, new visions of the End. Science and literature responded quickly.

By studying our visions we come to understand fully and finally the workings of our imagination. The idea of the End is imagination at its extreme, fully stretched. What we desire most and fear most, those things we magnify in our minds. And the greater the deprivation or the greater the terror, the stronger the vision. And the stronger the story.

The Beginnings of Science Fiction

Science's boom was followed by an equally rapid growth in science fiction. People in the mature years of the Industrial Revolution began to believe that scientific research was, after all, part of the nature and purpose of mankind's existence. And, like all beliefs, this one was reflected in literature, in a popular literature that would grow and endure.

The threads of science fiction go back much further than the Industrial Revolution. In second-century Syria, Lucian wrote of a voyage to the moon. By the 1600s space travel was a fairly commonplace theme in literature, making notable appearances in Johann Kepler's *Somnium*, Bishop Godwin's *The Man in the Moone* and Cyrano de Bergerac's *Voyage to the Moon and Sun*. Even Sir Thomas More's sixteenth century utopian writings weren't new, either. And the element of fantasy, so often a motif in science fiction, appears as early as *Beowulf* and runs throughout the history of literature to the present.

It was, however, a discontinuous and isolated type of writing, and not one to which any serious writer would dedicate his career.

Until Jules Verne arrived. Verne was the first to formalize a tradition of science fiction, to make it a genre.

Verne lived through the aftermath of the French Revolution, through Darwin's time and Marx's time. His career peaked in the 1870s, when electricity was ringing the first telephone and lighting the first light bulb. He wrote *Journey to the Centre of the Earth*, *Around the World in Eighty Days*, *20,000 Leagues under the Sea*, *The Underground City*, *Off on a Comet!* and seventy five other science fiction books, singlehandedly giving the school a substantial width on the library shelves. Sci-fi, later abbreviated more efficiently to SF, was here to stay.

Science fiction had one chief characteristic: it was based on plausible scientific fact. In this way it was distinguishable from fantasy, although the boundaries have since become blurred. Fantasy today is a recurring theme through the fabric of science fiction and science fiction is a frequent undertone in modern fantasy.

Science fiction began with another character-istic. It offered a new view of man. Up until Darwin, man had seen himself as a finished being, already completed, made in God's image. Historical man. But with Darwin's writings, time began to stretch. Historical time wasn't enough. Now there was human time, geological time, cosmic time.

There has always been a gap between serious literature and popular fiction. That gap widened after the Industrial Revolution, but one type of writing—the apocalyptic school—transformed itself and jumped from the religious and academic camp into the new fiction.

The End of the World has a curious role amidst these changes. It had always stood for the end of historical time, for the beginning of the eternal kingdom. Now, dramatically, it lost its finality. Building on the matter-of-factness that Nostradamus had introduced, it became simply another event in the great chain of cosmic events. It did retain many of its old biblical themes: floods and fires, insects with human heads, beasts born of cataclysms, utopias and, of course, global collapses followed by millennial peace.

A Biblical Day Could Be an Entire Epoch

Science, science fiction and the End gained a surprising ally in 1778.

In that year a Frenchman, born Georges-Louis Leclerc and later known as the Comte de Buffon, published a book that caught the world unprepared. It was titled *Epochs of Nature* and it laid out, in literate prose that reached a wide public, a radical new theory of natural history. Buffon gave the world a prehistoric past, a series of seven epochs that corresponded, as some commentators pointed out, to the seven days of Genesis.

The first was the molten epoch. It began when a comet accidently collided with the sun, throwing a number of fragments into orbit where they eventually cooled into planets. The second was the too-hot-to-handle stage. Buffon explored this stage by heating small metal balls until they were red-hot and giving them to young women—"with very soft skin" —to hold while they described the sensation. Through this painful experiment he calculated it would have taken 40,000 years for the earth to cool. (Buffon believed the world was 74,000 years old, in defiance of contemporary religious thinkers who knew, by adding up the ages of the Old Testament generations, that it was 6,000.)

Epoch three was the universal sea. As the earth cooled, the atmospheric gases liquefied into water. Buffon determined that the universal ocean was 2,000 fathoms higher than sea level today; this was how he explained fish fossils in the mountains. The fourth period was a time of volcanic upheaval that saw the creation of a giant, continuous landmass that included Eurasia, America and Africa.

The fifth epoch saw the emergence of land animals. The count believed that heat alone could transform normal molecules into organic ones. The corollary to this was that intense heat could produce even more complex life, including large animals and plants.

During epoch six, the land mass subsided so that the continents were divided by oceans. Buffon thought that life began at the poles, while the earth was still cooling, and slowly moved toward the tropics in the days when the continents were still connected.

In Buffon's final epoch, the one in which God would have rested, man conquered nature.

This was the present. Buffon looked forward optimistically to heavily populated nations running full speed ahead on coal-based economies. In the new era, God didn't have to worry any more: man would do just fine on his own.

People saw the wisdom in Buffon's theory, but not everyone shared his rosy view of the future. Others saw that if there had already been seven phases, there might be more on the way; they saw that if a cosmic accident had started the solar system, then another could end it. Buffon's optimism provoked a pessimistic sense of fatalism.

Edgar Allan Poe: Welcome to the Afterlife

America was excited by comets in 1811, in 1833 and 1838. And Halley's comet, the most famous of them all, returned in 1835.

Meanwhile, William Miller was making the first of his many apocalyptic predictions, announcing that the world would perish by fire within the decade. The unusual comet activity and a freak meteor shower in 1833 unnerved many people and convinced them that judgement was at hand.

Edgar Allan Poe, the leading American writer of the day, was inspired by these events and took a breather from writing his Gothic tales to compose a dialogue called "The Conversation of Eiros and Charmion".

Charmion had died and gone to heaven ten years earlier. As the story begins she is welcoming her friend Eiros, who has arrived with a great migration of souls after the final apocalypse. Eiros is still somewhat disoriented by the splendor of the afterlife, but she explains to Charmion how the world ended.

Astronomers had discovered a new comet heading for earth. At first they thought it would just skirt the planet, but eventually the scientists agreed that from their calculations the earth would be hit. There was a brief panic until wise men explained that the comet was lighter in substance than our rarest gases and would cause minimal physical damage. As the comet came nearer, obviously the largest ever to approach the earth, the fear spread again, now fed by biblical prophecies of the End of the World by fire. As it came close, people felt an unusual elasticity of frame and vivacity of mind. But as the nitrogen was extracted from the atmosphere breathing became difficult and bodies dehydrated in the heat. In agony and delirium all men perished.

Poe's story was a critical and commercial success, adding fuel to the fires simultaneously being stoked by William Miller.

Mary, Mother of the Last Man

Mary Shelley was famous in so many ways that it is easy to overlook her early contribution to apocalyptic science fiction. She was the daughter of the popular Bishop Godwin, a humane, rationalist utopian who believed that progress and reason were the signs of the final millennialist peace. At the age of seventeen she ran off with a married man, the poet Percy Bysshe Shelley, whom she married two years later. Another two years passed before she published *Frankenstein*, a book which made her immediately famous.

Among her writings was a novel called *The Last Man*, published in 1826, several years after the drowning of her husband. It was the story of a great plague that killed off nearly all of humanity, sparing only three people, the narrator Verney, a woman named Clara and a man named Adrian, who in many ways resembled Percy Bysshe Shelley.

When Adrian and Clara perish at sea during a storm, Verney is left as the last man on earth, wandering through empty cities, a Robinson Crusoe without the hope of companionship. He tries every door, finding no one except, on one startling occasion, his own unkempt reflection in a mirror. Verney is thus inspired to dress up—apologizing to the reader for his vanity—so as not to be an object of fear and aversion to the fellow creature he hopes to find. All is in vain, however, and he is left wandering alone.

Mary Shelley's book was neither the first with that title, however, nor the first with that theme. In 1805 a maverick French priest, Cousin de Grainville, had published *Le Dernier Homme*, a similar story of natural catastrophe. He then committed suicide.

H G Wells: Ends in Profusion and Endless Variety

As Verne's career was in its twilight, that of H G Wells was just establishing itself. But although Wells had written much of his science fiction output before Verne's death, they hardly seem of the same era. One senses that, while the writing careers of the two giants overlapped, Wells is definitely a man of modern times while Verne seems a figure of the past. Wells is a twentieth century realist, concerned with technology and socialism. (He did, after all, interview Stalin and Roosevelt, and he continued writing until after the Second World War.) By comparison, Verne appears very much a part of the nineteenth century, a romanticist, a storyteller.

The bulk of Wells' science fiction, however, particularly his apocalyptic writing, was published before the turn of the century. During the 1890s he completed a body of work that shaped the End of the World from his time until ours.

Wells began as a freelance journalist. Early in his career he ran into a dry spell, when most of the publications for which he wrote had a backlog of unused material. In the hopes of raising some money, he turned his hand to writing a short novel, *The Time Machine*, published in 1895. It was written hastily, and embarrassed him later, but it was successful.

A time traveller goes 30 million years into the future and finds the earth has stopped spinning, the final effect of tidal drag. (Wells was not the last to write of this phenomenon.)

Evolution seems to have gone in reverse. The only remaining creatures are amphibious and reptilian, living at the edge of the still sea. The only surviving plants are lichens and slimes. The air is thinner, there is no wind, and the planet is silent. There is no man. Saddened, the time traveller returns to tell his story.

In 1897, in another short story, *The Star*, Wells introduced a spectacular end, complete with grateful survivors. A strange runaway star crosses into our solar system and collides with Neptune. The two bodies fuse into one star and begin an arc descending toward the sun. En route the star passes near enough to Jupiter to be deflected by its gravitational field and swings in a wider arc that will pass very close to the earth's orbit. Mankind becomes increasingly alarmed as the star advances, looming larger and larger. Ice and snow begin to melt on mountaintops and the polar caps. There are great floods, tidal waves, earthquakes and gigantic volcanic eruptions. There is widespread death by heat, particularly in tropical areas where the oceans are steaming. Then the star swings past earth, eventually being absorbed into the sun which becomes hotter. A small part of the population escapes death (as, throughout history, it always has) but must move toward the more hospitable polar regions.

Wells' next book was *The War of the Worlds*, generally accepted as the masterpiece of alien invasion. The hero emerges from a hiding place where he's spent two weeks while Martian invaders have wreaked destruction on southeastern England. Wandering amid rubble and corpses, he convinces himself (incorrectly, it turns out) that mankind has been swept out of existence and that he is the sole survivor. All of our technology has been powerless in combat with the Martians, who have simply plucked men off the ground and dumped them in baskets, to eat later. But, unexpectedly, we win a reprieve. The Martians die off suddenly, en masse, because they have no immunity to the earth's disease bacteria. Hunanity is saved again.

But not for long. In 1899 Wells turned whimsical and wrote *A Vision of Judgement*, a satirical version of a Sunday school End of the World. God recalls everyone from earth to heaven. Their sins are read aloud—"the acoustic properties of the place were marvellous"—by the recording angel. In alphabetical order, each person is chastised and embarrassed by the revelation of his sins. Finally, after the judgement, God puts everybody back on earth, alive and enlightened.

Such a lot of Ends. Wells was tiring of the theme and, indeed, of science fiction. In the new century, he turned, for the most part, to other fiction and to nonfiction. Occasionally the End recurred, notably in *The World Set Free* (1914), in which the End comes by an early atomic bomb, and *All Aboard for Ararat* (1940), the story of a second, modern Noah and a genial, lovable God. Like so many writers, once Wells got hooked on the End, he could never entirely abandon it.

Getting Even with the Vegetable-Eaters

The End of the World soon became standard fare for science fiction, and its agents were many and varied. Few literary devices have been run through so many creative imaginations, although all of the stories conclude at the same point. Not quite the End. Or an End for all but a small group of survivors.

(This, of course, was no different from the Ends with which Western civilization grew up, an Armageddon for all but God's chosen, a flood for all but Noah and his family. Science fiction arises from the same pools of hope within us as religious belief and myth.)

In these stories, many species of creatures, local and alien, get a leg up on humanity, usually by being more intelligent than man, but sometimes simply by exploiting a weakness. Some of the conquerors are plants, including ivy, grasses and the more dramatic carnivorous vegetations.

The masterpiece of this genre is *The Day of the Triffids* by John Wyndham, a writer with a generally gothic view of vegetable life. It was first published in 1951.

Set in London, presumably in the 1950s, the story begins with two events. The first is the development of a new plant, the triffid, by Russian botanists working at an experimental farm in Kamchatka. The source of a new vegetable oil, the triffid contains nutrients and vitamins that make the best fish oils look like soda pop. When this fact becomes known to an enterprising South American named Umberto, he offers to provide seeds to a European oil company in return for a large fee. He procures the seeds, gets them airborne out of Russia, but is shot down in a violent act of counterespionage. The tiny seeds, "infinitely light and gossamer-slung", float on the winds, drifting sometimes for months, settling nearby and thousands of miles away.

They grow well in most locales, reaching heights of ten feet in the tropics, and averaging around seven throughout Europe and Britain. No one notices them for awhile, thinking they are just another weed. And then one day a mature triffid is filmed walking. Putting one root in front of the other. Moving forward. Walking.

Full grown triffids, moreover, are carni-vorous, trapping insects with poisonous sap in sticky cups, and occasionally slashing humans with a lethally venomous whorl that serves as a stinger. Triffids are killers.

The second critical event at the beginning of *The Day of the Triffids* is a freak meteor shower that for one entire night, all around the world, treats the planet to a spectacular show of brilliant green flashes. (It may not be meteors at all, of course. No one knows for sure. It could also be the contents of a weapons cannister sent into orbit by any militaristic nation with rockets. The press calls it a meteor shower, however, and the idea sticks.) People all over the world stay up to watch the light show, and in the morning they all wake up permanently blind.

You can see the problem. Practically all the inhabitants of the entire world are blind, and they are surrounded by prolific, mobile, killer plants.

Not everyone is blind, of course. The occasional person had his eyes bandaged, or was working underground in a mine, or was sleeping off a drunken stupor. They were few and far between, but there are still a handful of souls with vision. As industry and electricity stop, and the blind begin to die, the sighted withdraw into small groups, isolated from each other.

The triffids flourish, killing and consuming their helpless victims.

Eventually one group of the seeing, along with some blind intellectuals, settles on the Isle of Wight, after clearing all the triffids from the island. They are living there, hoping to rebuild the human race and reclaim the earth from the triffids, when the story ends.

You Can't See the Forest for the Sand

Truth, of course, is easily as scary as fiction. Killer triffids may not be wandering around, but there are other serious problems with vegetation.

The world's tropical rain forests, for example, are disappearing at the rate of an acre every two seconds, an area the size of England and Wales every year. Within the last century roughly 40 per cent of the world's rain forests have vanished. If we continue clearing them at the present rates, there will be none left by the year 2020. What replaces them? For the most part, deserts.

More than half of the planet's rain forest is in the Amazon Basin in South America, most of it in Brazil. The rest is shared between southeast Asia and central Africa. As the world population increases, and as industry looks to expand into new frontiers, the forests are a prime target for exploitation.

In central Africa, people have traditionally lived on the strip of land between the Sahara Desert to the north and the forest to the south. They are mainly landless peasants, continuously clearing and burning the forest, finding it easier to tame, naturally, than the desert. But as they move steadily southward, the Sahara follows, relentlessly turning cleared land into desert behind them, keeping the inhabited strip at a constant width.

Rain forest soil is not suitable for farming, and when the foliage is removed, rainfall is reduced, and the sun gets at that soil, drying it up until it is easily blown and washed away. Dust and sand storms become common. Flash flooding occurs. Jungle becomes desert. And the people move further south. The 1977 United Nations Conference on Desertification reported that "In the past century, on the southern edge of the Sahara alone, as much as 650,000 square kilometres of once productive land has become desert."

As is so often the case, it took a symbolic event to put this situation in the headlines of the world press. It was a story no one could overlook. In 1978 Daniel Ludwig, one of the richest men in the United States, came out of hiding with a new industrial scheme of such magnitude that it strained even his purse. (Ludwig, frustrated by personnel and technical problems, has since sold the project back to Brazilian owners.)

Ludwig owned 500,000 acres of Brazilian rain forest and he didn't want that chunk of real estate sitting idle, the domain of jaguars and alligators. He built a huge pulp-and-paper factory in Japan, put it on a raft, and floated it 15,000 miles to a new home up the Amazon River. In the meantime his men cleared the primeval foliage, replacing the natural growth with fast-growing Caribbean pine to feed his gigantic mill, which, when operating at full capacity, would produce enough pulp each day to make a strip of toilet paper that could be wrapped six and a half times around the world. The ecologists woke up. What was happening to the world's largest rain forest? And what would the consequences be of such a mammoth undertaking?

The local inhabitants of Amazonia woke up, too. Not only was the forest disappearing, but somebody else was reaping the benefits. About 60 per cent of the Amazon development was owned and controlled by multinational corporations, and another 30 per cent was owned by firms from southern Brazil. The money was leaving the basin almost as fast as the jungle was.

The truth of the matter was that the Brazilian government, anxious to square its trade deficits, was planning to sell off the entire rain forest with its $1 trillion worth of timber. New highways were built to open it up and Brazilians were encouraged to move to the interior where they would be given farms. And when the soil proved not to be arable, they were given ranches instead, in the hope that grasses would grow and the soil would not be totally lost to desert.

Perhaps, the government hoped, the Brazilian jungle could be made to resemble the Argentine pampas. Perhaps the drying trend wouldn't be irreversible. Perhaps the rain would come back.

The world's ecologists, horrified though they were by the organized elimination of one of the globe's natural features, hoped for the same thing. The main worry wasn't the loss of flora and fauna, although thousands of species of each would become extinct; no, the main worry was the re-arrangement of the world's carbon and oxygen, and what that might mean

to the environment. By burning those forests two global environmental problems are created: the atmosphere loses an ideal natural storage place for excess carbon dioxide and, when that happens, the amount in the sky increases.

The atmosphere's carbon dioxide has been increasing since 1950, mainly as a result of the burning of coal, oil, and gas. This, scientists predict, will give us a worldwide greenhouse effect. Sunlight shines in through the carbon dioxide haze, warming the earth, but then the heat doesn't easily radiate back out again. In short, the atmosphere heats up.

If man were to double the present carbon dioxide levels—and destroying the rain forests would certainly hasten the process—the atmospheric temperature would rise two centigrade degrees. The polar ice caps would melt, raising the height of the oceans by 175 feet around the world. This would inevitably flood all the planet's low-lying lands, including most of its major cities. And this great flood, brought not by rain but by heat, would inevitably bring disastrous and permanent climatic changes. Not to mention all the localized destruction.

Those who fear the end of the tropical rain forests, then, are not thinking about the desert. They are thinking of the sea.

Following his Memory Back to the Sea

In J G Ballard's *The Drowned World*, an elderly biologist explains that, like the baby fieldmouse's instinctive fear of the hawk's silhouette, we all carry time-coded memories and fears in our cells and genes, first engraved there during the crises of our uncivilized ancestors. Consider our dislike of spiders, he continues, and our fear of snakes and reptiles. These are part of our organic memory, dating from the time when reptiles were the planet's dominant life form.

Ballard is one of the apocalyptic masters of science fiction. In this book he has created a world regressing back, through floods, high temperature, tropical humidities and a rising radiation level, to its earliest days. At the time of the narrative, it has returned to roughly the Triassic period. The vegetation is prehistoric jungle, and the creatures are mainly fish and giant reptiles.

Seventy years before the story begins, a series of solar storms had destabilized the sun and helped lessen the earth's magnetic-gravitational hold on the outer layers of the ionosphere. Temperature and radiation levels began to increase. The ice caps melted. The tropics became rapidly uninhabitable and once-temperate zones became tropical, with North America and Europe baking under temperatures that rarely, even at night, dropped below 100 degrees Fahrenheit.

The world population, already dwindling because of dramatically decreased fertility, relocated to Antartica and the northern coasts of Russia and Canada.

The worst problem for the survivors, however, is not an external one. Men living on the edges of the jungle and the sea are beginning to have bad dreams, triggered by the ubiquity of large iguanas and alligators, the mammoth bats and eels, and the appearance of gigantic oily ferns, already mutating rapidly in the radiation. These visitations come as dreams, at night while everyone sleeps, but really they are nothing more than déjà vu, the subconscious memories, long dormant, of Cro-Magnon man. The ultimate battle is in the mind.

The hero of the book finally succumbs, following the sun and the ocean south, searching for earlier and earlier memories. His comrades head north, fighting their dreams, still trying to live in the present.

The Fragile Ozone Layer Reminds Us We Have No Birthright

Ozone is a flimsy defense against the End. When writers describe the tenuous shield that protects us from the sun's killer rays, they aren't exaggerating.

The earth's beginnings created, as by-products, heavy, unstable, radioactive elements. In the early years these elements still existed, and nature could not sustain life. When they did finally come, the first life-forms developed in water; there was not enough oxygen to allow life on land. Powerful ultraviolet radiation, moreover, poured down from the sun.

Nature had then, and still has now, no vested interest in keeping man alive, no more than it had in keeping dinosaurs alive. Nature creates balanced systems, and does whatever is necessary to keep those systems working, but does not favor any one species.

In the earth's early days, direct ultraviolet light shone on the planet, aiding the genesis of the first biochemical stirrings. The first organisms, however, like most organisms since, could not survive in ultraviolet light and stayed underwater, protected. These organisms used the natural light for photosynthesis and began to produce oxygen, filling out the earth's atmosphere and, in time, producing ozone.

Ozone is a rare oxygen molecule in which three atoms, rather than the usual two, form a partnership. Although in the upper atmosphere there are only a few ozone molecules per million molecules of air, the layer remains stable.

If one were to rise above the earth's surface, one would find that temperature decreases with altitude to a height of about seven miles. Then it becomes warmer as one reaches the stratosphere. The effect is a global inversion, warmer air on top, totally unshakeable by the weather of the lower troposphere, and seemingly permanent. This is where the ozone is, and because it blocks the deadly ultraviolet radiation, living organisms have been able to move out of the oceans and onto the land.

"Permanence", of course, was just mankind's way of saying we had faith. We hoped nature would continue to look after us, even if we treated it badly. In our usual myopia, we could imagine no way to harm the ozone layer. It was, after all, miles up, above the weather, beyond the reach of our pollutants which, when they got into the atmosphere, were promptly rained out of the air in a continuous cleansing process. (Cleansing for the atmosphere anyway, if not for the earth.)

The scientists thought that whatever poison went up, came down. (The more common view was "out of sight, out of mind", whatever goes up goes away.) For the most part, this was true; most airborne pollutants came back to earth. But—and it is a frightening qualification—not all.

Aerosol spray cans use fluorocarbons as propellants. They seem perfect for the job. Chemically inert, they don't react with the substances they encounter, they don't form new compounds, they don't react with human tissue. This advantage, after longer reflection, is in fact a colossal disadvantage: what happens to the stuff after it's sprayed into the air? It rises. It doesn't attach itself to rainclouds to fall back to earth and it doesn't get absorbed by living things; it simply rises.

When the fluorocarbons get into the ozone layer, and just above it, a transformation takes place. At that height there's no place to hide from the sun's ultraviolet, which splits molecules with the greatest of ease, breaking the fluorocarbons down into their component parts. One of those parts is chlorine.

Chlorine, unlike fluorocarbons, has no compunction about reacting with its neighbours. In a lengthy, almost self-perpetuating chain reaction, chlorine consumes a large amount of ozone. The chlorine atom reacts with ozone, forming normal oxygen and a chlorine compound, and then the chlorine compound breaks down again with the assistance of the ultraviolet light, eliminating yet another molecule of ozone. And then the free chlorine reacts with a new ozone molecule, starting the process all over again, until the one atom of chlorine has transformed many thousands of molecules of ozone into normal oxygen. Eventually that one atom of chlorine drifts back out of the stratosphere, ceasing its havoc.

In 1978 aerosol spray cans were banned in Canada, Sweden and the United States. Man might be willing to risk a natural catastrophe, but he wasn't yet willing to risk it for spray-on deodorant.

But the scientific searching didn't stop. If chlorine could do this damage, were there other substances harmful to ozone? The alarming answer was yes. Although much of the chlorine from each of these sources is rained out of the troposphere before it reaches the ozone layer, it is emitted from volcanoes, from carbon tetrachloride, from refrigerants and from most industrial metal cleaners.

And, furthermore, nitrogen and hydrogen oxides, from fertilizers, space missiles, supersonic jets and nuclear bombs, devour ozone as readily as chlorine does. In fact, Pentagon officials have conceded that 50 to 75 per cent of the world's ozone could be destroyed in a nuclear war. This would cause a sudden rise in skin cancers, debilitating sunburn and snowblindness.

Most frightening is humanity's indifference. We look at the aplomb of nature, its accomodating cycles, its slowly tailored equilibrium, and think: nature will right itself. And our assumption is that whatever nature does to protect itself will also protect the human species. We have absolutely no reason not to assume, however, that it may well break its stoical patience, set new thresholds to compensate for fluorocarbons, create a new balance without ozone, and—even inadvertently—rid itself of its tormentor, man.

147

Overpopulation: Things Get Worse and Worse and then Sort of Better

Our planet is so small, and, so far, we have nowhere else to go. Inevitably we will have overpopulation. The End will occur because we lack food, the demand outstrips the supply, but it will also come from our lack of discipline. Mankind simply refuses to act in accordance with its own predictions.

The numbers of human beings on this small earth seem ever-increasing and, for convenience, ever more rounded. But at 25 billion the elasticity will snap, crashing our population back to smaller, more manageable figures.

The date will be 2100—some say decades earlier—when more than nine of every ten humans will die, from stress, starvation and related catastrophes.

Up to now, in a general way, vegetation has been able to replace itself fast enough, animal herds have been able to steady themselves in the face of man's carnivorous appetite, and nature has been able to restock the oceans and re-purify the air and water in time for the next catch. Now time and space are beginning to run out. The banquet will soon be over.

The lack of food, however, will not be the final strain before the snap. Most people living when the food runs out will not die of starvation; they will die of stress, whose eventual physical symptoms will be hemorrhages of the brain, and adrenal glands swollen twice their normal size.

Like other species, man needs to express antisocial behavior. When lack of space prohibits privacy, unsociability displays itself as hostility. And when population sprawl reduces the possibility of solace through solitude, our brains will try to restore themselves through withdrawal and detachment. We will grow less concerned about each other's predicaments.

More and more metropolises will have the dense poverty that at present is associated with cities like Lima, Tokyo, Mexico City and Hong Kong. With less personal space, males become more aggressive and females give inadequate maternal care. Stress begins to overpower reason and the visible, aggravated symptoms build to a climax.

Then, in the year 2100, the crash.

Staying Afloat on a Cauldron

We have been conditioned, by scientists and prophets alike, to expect the End from above. It would be prudent to equally prepare ourselves for an apocalypse from below.

When one properly understands the composition of the earth, there is a kind of fear that comes all by itself. Geologically speaking, we live on a thin skin of hardened rock, broken into plates, floating on a huge ball of molten metal. The plates, moreover, are mobile, sometimes chafing against each other and sometimes pulling apart. The place where two plates touch is called a fault.

One of the faults, by way of example, goes up the ocean floor in the mid-Atlantic. It continues through Iceland where, in one valley, the cliff on one side is the edge of one plate

and the opposite cliff is the edge of another. The two plates are separating, literally tearing Iceland apart.

The molten rock occasionally boils up under a fault, causing an earthquake, or up through a weak spot in the crust, causing a volcanic eruption. Humans, as a sometimes useful convenience, have three classifications for volcanoes: active, dormant and extinct. Mount St Helens was thought to be dormant until, in 1980, it showed conclusively that it was not. Mount Leamington, in Papua, was believed extinct until it blew in 1956, killing thousands of people. So much for classification.

It is little wonder, then, that science fiction writers, with this wellspring of activity simmering inside our globe, often speculate that

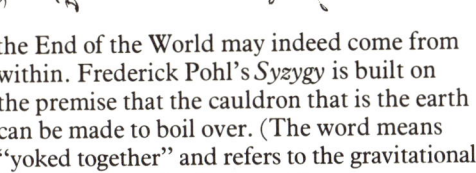

the End of the World may indeed come from within. Frederick Pohl's *Syzygy* is built on the premise that the cauldron that is the earth can be made to boil over. (The word means "yoked together" and refers to the gravitational force of planets in alignment.)

In California, a state straddling a fault line, a popular movement takes hold, believing that the End will come in the spring of 1982. The reasoning is tortuous, but each step is logical if not provable. Simply put: for one very brief and rare moment, all the planets will be on the same side of the sun. Their combined pull will cause solar flares that will affect the earth's atmosphere and rotation, which will in turn trigger major and catastrophic earthquakes.

The government employs the best geologists and astronomers to disprove the theory and, in so doing, pacify the excited masses. They find, of course, that the theory is impossible to disprove, and the book ends, before the appointed hour, on an uncertain note.

The planets did, in fact, huddle on one side of the sun early in 1982—not, as some imagined, in a long line, but all within 180 degrees. In spite of some popular excitement and concern, and a few newspaper articles, the sun did not oblige by disrupting the earth's thin skin or even hinting at the wholesale destruction of the earth.

149

Breaking the Chain: What Pesticide Really Means

The earth is occasionally overrun, in the literature of science fiction, by creatures that threaten the supremacy of Homo sapiens. By tradition the hordes are often insects and often possess a collective intelligence.

In *The Green Brain*, a novel by Frank Herbert, an international organization has begun exterminating insects in a global attempt to reclaim the jungles for civilization and food production. The movement, called Ecological Realignment, seems the only solution to over-population. At first the poisons have the opposite effect. They simply select out the stronger, more immune bugs, who breed faster when their numbers are reduced. But eventually the poisons leave no loopholes and large areas are cleared of all insects. Electro-vibrational barriers are erected to keep these areas clean.

In the noninfested areas, however, new problems arise unexpectedly. Some plants become extinct because they aren't being pollinated, grasslands perish because they lack aeration and fertilization by insects, and some birds disappear because they have nothing to eat. Outside the barriers, an even greater problem lurks. Hosts of beetles and flies are anxious to get back into their old homelands, which are becoming relatively free of predators.

The entire chain of life is in danger. It is the insects who see the threat first and move to bring the world back to normalcy. In Brazil, near one of the cleared areas, they form a brain, a huge four meter wide collective hive that is tended by millions of bugs, cooling it, cleaning it, and maintaining its reason. The brain devises ways for sneaking insects into the cleared zones, by creating composite humans made up entirely of small pests. Once inside, these creatures attempt to reason with man, to explain the dangers to him.

The plan works. Mankind sees the light and re-infests the land with insects, thus saving the ecology. (Man as a consequence loses his pre-eminent place as the highest life form, a position he henceforward has to share with the bugs.)

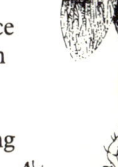

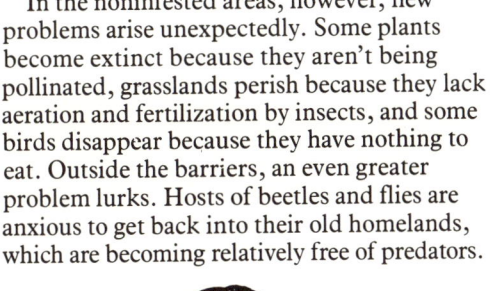

The Operation Was Successful, but the Patient Died: Pesticides

It is ironic that, when conservationists raised the first alarm on pesticides in the early 1960s, they chose a relatively harmless chemical, DDT, as the target for their indignation. And it is unfortunate that, when the agriculturalists restrained their use of DDT, they substituted poisons many times more toxic.

In 1939, when Swiss scientist Paul Muller discovered that DDT was a powerful insecticide, he was given a Nobel Prize for his work. DDT was the wonder chemical of its day. During the Second World War it was used as a de-louser on millions of soldiers, refugees and prisoners, blown into their underwear and directly onto their skins. There were no obvious ill effects. DDT was also used to improve crop yields and to combat insect-borne disease, particularly malaria. It was clearly a beneficial chemical. And, to be fair, considering the bad press it was to get, when used as an insecticide DDT was never responsible for a death. (The only recorded deaths from the substance came from persons mistaking it for flour and eating it in large quantities.)

DDT, in fact, is still used around the world today, about 100,000 tons a year, the same amount as during the 1960s, sprayed mostly to protect cotton crops and to control malaria.

What, then, was the great DDT scare all about? Three things. First, like so many poisons, it was persistent. It was fat soluble and it accumulated and stayed in human organs. Second, it wasn't selective and often killed organisms that it wasn't intended to kill. And third, it had an alarming time-lag as it made its way through the food chain, through plankton and fish, through soil and vegetation, through animals and milk, showing up in man in greatly increased doses ten or fifteen years after it had been sprayed. DDT became a symbol for all poisons that travel relentlessly through groundwater and wind currents, remaining stable as they build up in human foods, finally coming to rest years later and far away, in our adrenal and thyroid glands, our sexual organs, our kidneys and livers. DDT was the most studied chemical of the early 1960s and the scientists were afraid.

In retrospect, they were afraid of the wrong pesticide. Many of the alternative chemicals now used to exterminate insects and weeds are much worse, hundreds of times more toxic and longer lasting. Nor is it simply the pesticide itself that we need worry about. Many of them break down into other deadly compounds, and some change into killers only when they enter the metabolism of a living creature.

One defoliant in common use in America is in the same toxic league as botulism and the biological weapons. More than five million acres a year are sprayed with dioxin, and the chemical has been found in freshwater trout, birds' eggs, cows' milk, in animal fat and on the skins of fruit. The effects of dioxin include nervous disorders, organ damage, fetus deformity, fatigue, depression, weight-loss, insomnia, loss of libido, and vertigo. That's a high price to pay for weed control.

Insect control is worse. Some insecticides contain PCBs, chemicals that cause mutation, ulceration, tumors, reduced growth and deformity. Even low-level exposure leads to fatigue, abdominal pain, numbness of limbs, swelling of joints, chronic coughing and menstrual irregularity. In addition, children exposed to PCBs during the gestation and lactation periods can lose their natural immunities and develop permanent learning and behavioral deficiencies. That's an even higher price to pay for insect control.

The End of the World is less likely today to be brought about by agricultural pests than by agricultural pesticides.

At What Point Did We Start Being Humans? At What Point Will We Stop?

In the distant past, if one believes the biologists and the geologists, there were no humans. There were creatures that stood erect and resembled apes, but there were no humans. Between then and now, something happened: a process of mutation, selection, evolution. For a while we weren't here; now we are.

It is equally conceivable, of course, that sometime in the future there will again be no species recognizable as human. The world won't have ended, but mankind will, having evolved into something new.

The real treasure today, of three billion years of evolution, is the human gene pool. The total pool, according to some sources, measuring all the information-carrying parts of all human DNA, is 00.08 grams. A very small resource, very thinly spread.

But it's all we've got, all that keeps us human. These days, sad to say, we are treating that resource very poorly. It's possible that man-made chemicals in the past fifty years may have done more damage to the gene pool than radiation ever will.

The industrial world at present uses more than 50,000 artificial chemicals, adding 1,000 new ones each year. Most of the ones being marketed are not tested before use, and many are mutagenic, carcinogenic or teratogenic.

Strange words. If a substance is mutagenic, it causes cell mutations, including alterations in chromosomes. If it is carcinogenic, it causes cancer. And if it is teratogenic, it causes monsters, showing up not in the contact person, but in his children or his grandchildren.

Scientists generally agree we have made a Faustian bargain with our herbicides, wood preservatives, food additives and toxic wastes, and now must find a way to learn enough to cut our losses. We must do it soon. Russian scientists estimate that the percentage of children born with deformities has doubled worldwide in the past three decades.

Can this be called an End of the World? Maybe not. Being human, perhaps, is just a passing phase. Soon we may be something else.

Want Not, Waste Not

In the 1960s and 1970s, although most industrial nations had reconciled themselves to nuclear power plants, there were few citizens who wanted one in their backyards. Who could blame them? Attached to each reactor, with a variety of fasteners, was the stigma of the End.

Radioactivity isn't something to be taken lightly. Since the end of the nineteenth century, when x-rays and radioactivity were discovered, scientists have known that man needs protection from their effects. The x-ray was father to lead pants. So the reactors, when they came, were carefully built—some call them the safest devices ever built by man. Despite the precautions, however, some horror stories emerged, most famous being the evacuation of Three-Mile Island, near Harrisburg, Pennsylvania.

Nuclear plants are too powerful for their own good. The chain reaction can be harnessed to produce massive amounts of electricity, it is true, but the by-products and the nuclear wastes suggest doom.

Up through the stacks go tritium, argon, hydrogen, xenon and iodine, all radioactive; and out through the sluice gates go cesium, cobalt and tritium, all radioactive. These by-products are released regularly, in carefully monitored doses, and are considered safe by the governments of the western world. Safe, in this context, means the risk is acceptable to central governments, although not necessarily to local residents.

There are other risks, not as easily acceptable. The possibility is always there for a major accident: coolant pipes can rupture, control rods eject, and fuel can be mishandled. Tornadoes, earthquakes and bomb attacks could cause irreparable damage. The legacy of any serious accident would be thousands of square miles of permanently irradiated earth.

And then there's one final problem, as yet unsolved. What do you do with the leftovers? When the nuclear fuel is spent, there remains a large amount of weapons-grade uranium and plutonium, not easily disposed of. By 1990, it is estimated there will be more than 30,000 tons of plutonium lying around the planet.

Assume for the moment it's all safely guarded now against theft by anarchists and terrorists. Plutonium has a half-life of 25,000 years, which means, quite simply, that it takes 25,000 years for half of it to lose its radioactivity. In 50,000 years one-quarter of it remains still radioactive. And so on. We're going to have to live with the stuff for a long time.

And while we're living with it, the plutonium has to be kept from any contact with the biosphere. The containers must be kept safely sealed for hundreds of thousands of years. Plutonium is among the most poisonous chemicals known to man. Very small amounts cause cancer, particularly in the lungs, bones and bloodstream. It also causes genetic mutation, and is deadly to our food sources, both animal and vegetables.

Where do we go from here? We can either sit and wait for the accidents and, some say, the End. Or we can send the old plutonium somewhere into outer space, perhaps directly into the sun, somewhere totally outside the earth's gravitational field, and hope the rockets don't malfunction.

Writing Our Own Epitaphs

For a while science fiction writers amused themselves with the foibles of the biosphere, those worrisome little quirks of nature, and with the hazards of astronomy, particularly those nearby flying orbs that may or may not support intelligent life. The variations seemed inexhaustible; the End could come in so many ways.

But even as these story-types were becoming popular, H G Wells was outlining another motif for the End, one that outlived him, one that man can bring upon himself. Today this is the End that lies at the very heart of science fiction. It is perhaps the most fitting, the most biblical, of those found in popular literature, the End in which we sin so greatly that we kill ourselves as a result. The stories no longer do deal merely with the bringing to justice of one evil scientist. Now they also include the notion of the ultimate retribution against all those who would play god.

Robert Heinlein, one of the more celebrated of modern science fiction writers, has from time to time been obsessed by mankind's ability to precipitate the apocalypse. *Blowups Happen* is a product of this preoccupation.

The story begins when Harper, the duty engineer at a colossal atomic power plant, is removed from his position by Dr Silard, his round-the-clock psychiatric supervisor. Harper may, or may not, have been yielding under the pressures of his job, which was to maintain the nuclear reaction at a rate that was fast enough to be perpetual but slow enough not to be explosive. An explosion at this plant, the largest energy source in America, could destroy the earth's atmosphere, after first tearing a hole through much of the south-western states. Dr Silard couldn't take any chances.

Insanity was an occupational hazard of duty engineers—"blowups" was the term they used for psychotic breakdowns—and at one point in the narrative they were being disqualified from their jobs at the rate of one a day. First there was the enormity of their responsibility. And, on top of that, there was the strain of the constant surveillance by the psychiatrists.

As the story begins, amid an unresolved debate about the extent of damages from a hypothetical explosion, some scientists are arguing that the disaster could be localized. Halfway through, however, it becomes evident that such a bang would indeed consume all the atmosphere, thereby ending all life. Rumors of this seep into the engineering community, and the blowups increase.

The dismissed Harper, meanwhile, has discovered a new rocket fuel in the laboratory to which he has been reassigned, making it possible for the first time to send the great reactor into orbit, 15,000 miles up, far enough away to be safe. As the final preparations are being made, Dr Silard, for his part, helps quash a potentially disastrous blowup in the control room.

The ending is happy.

Heinlein's tale is extraordinary on several counts. He published it in 1940, five years before Hiroshima and long before the days of satellites and nuclear energy. He, like so many of the characters that people the History of the End, was a visionary.

Prometheus Unleashed: The Bomb

Since 1945 the world has been obsessed with one end—global atomic war—to the point that it has ignored most other possible ends.

Man the tinkerer has caught up with man the theoretician. He can now engineer the End of the World. The technology exists, the equipment is in place, all that's lacking is the will to die. The will to die, in this case, simply means succumbing to the risks involved with the will to kill. In a man-induced nuclear Armageddon, to destroy is to be destroyed.

In the early 1940s profound change came to the industrial world as the culmination of a shift in belief allowed man to take over some of God's traditional jobs. No longer content to nurture himself with the indirect effects of the sun, man made the boldest step since Prometheus stole fire from the gods and put it in our hands. He created suns on earth by drawing enormous power from inorganic materials, by making fission bombs. Up until then all energy had come from the sun, directly or indirectly, or from plants and animals sustained by the sun.

Change: science went one step further toward replacing religion. Only now did man hold such powerful disease and destruction in his hands, ready to use it as a weapon. And how quick he was to use it as a threat, how quick to use it as a punishment. Little wonder that the survivors of Hiroshima chanted a constant refrain: "There is no God, there is no Buddha." By comparison, natural catastrophes seemed like minor torments.

Change: strategy replaced philosophy. The keepers of the arsenal were militarists intent on maintaining or altering local balances of world power, intent on controlling and dominating whole peoples, willing to use the threat as a bargaining lever, willing to use their bombs. Ethics had become old-fashioned; the squeamish and the theorists were systematically ousted from the atomic club. Tactics were the important thing. Drafts and proofs. Blueprints. Profound and deadly change had come to the End of the World.

Hiroshima: The Whole World Glimpses the End

In the summer of 1945, the American B-29s flew over Hiroshima almost daily—the locals called the planes B-san, or Mr B—but the city had been spared from bombing. The people of Hiroshima, numbed by constant air raid alarms, were nonetheless happy when, early in the morning of August 6, the all-clear sounded, indicating a false alarm. Radar operators had spotted only three airplanes and presumed a reconnaissance mission, certainly not Mr B.

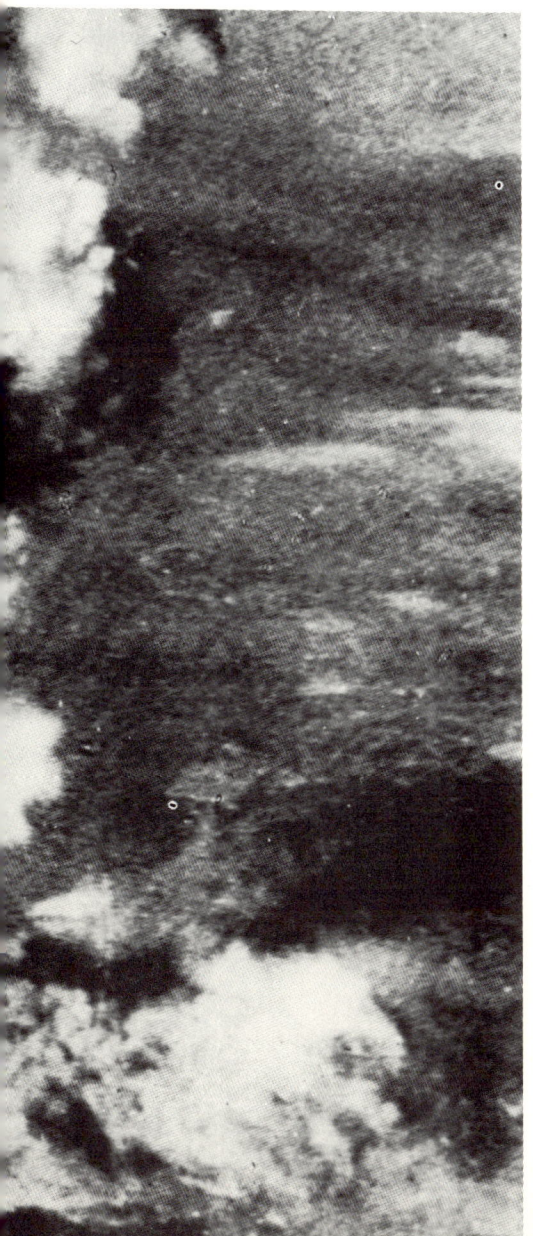

Nightwatchmen were bicycling home, passing the deliverymen, who were moving rationed goods to the stores. Mothers were cooking rice, commuters were reading on the streetcars, occasionally watching the boats on the river and in the harbor, strict believes were lost in meditative prayers. Couples were waking next to each other, still drowsy in the warmth, and children were fretting over last night's dreams. Old ladies contemplated time in their mirrors as they washed. Without notice, or worse, after notice had been withdrawn by the all-clear signal, the horror of the atomic age came suddenly, blinding light and then a thick darkness, a cloud for Hiroshima to call its own, a cloud that dropped small balls of rain, condensed moisture from the hot funnel of fragments and dust rising for miles, straight up.

The city was gone, 100,000 dead or dying. And, to accomplish this, the universe had lost only one gram of matter, one gram of uranium, which had turned into energy.

Considerable cynicism attends the ethical arguments about whether the bombs should have been dropped on Hiroshima and Nagasaki. They did hasten the end of the war, but Japan was already losing badly and was willing, at the negotiating table in Potsdam, to surrender, given certain conditions. And if the bombs were merely a demonstration of this terrible new weapon, why not bomb a forest? One clue is contained in the official *Bombing Survey Report*: "Hiroshima and Nagasaki were chosen as targets because of their concentration of activities and population." And, presumably, because they weren't already torn by war. The demonstration was not meant for Japan alone, rather it was meant to attract the attention of the entire world. The two bombs were not only the final shots in the war with Japan. They were also the first shots in the diplomatic war, the cold war, with an increasingly hostile Russia.

Whatever the motivation for the bombing, the effect was the same. The whole world sat up, as one, believing it had seen the beginning of the End.

Escalation: How Bigger Used To Be Better

Scientists use the term "critical mass", when chatting about plutonium or enriched uranium, to describe the point of accumulation at which nothing can prevent a nuclear chain reaction. In these insecure times, the great fear is that the world's armaments themselves can reach critical mass, and it will be beyond human reason to prevent them from exploding. The End will be inevitable.

One may scoff at the metaphor of critical mass, but it's more difficult to disregard the law of probabilities. There are now over 20,000 megatons of nuclear explosives on the planet, or about five tons per person. Six countries have exploded nuclear bombs, and about forty have the capability. The only thing holding back the explosions is human reason.

By 1949 the Russians exploded an atomic device and the competition began in earnest. America stepped up its activity and in 1954 brought a huge bomb, the first hydrogen bomb, to Bikini in the Marshall Islands, which the United States holds in trust from the United Nations. The military had evicted the residents of Bikini and a neighbouring island, resettling them elsewhere, and were using the islands as a bomb testing ground. The new bomb was called Mike.

The United States has a history of giving endearing names to bombs. The Hiroshima bomb was called "Little Boy" and Nagasaki's "Fat Man". The first hydrogen bombs were called the Panda series and when a new element, heavier than plutonium, was subsequently found in the debris of a hydrogen bomb explosion, there was a lobby to name it pandamonium. It was eventually named einsteinium.

Mike was exploded on March 1. The fireball spread so far so fast that even veteran test observers were terrified as the heat waves kept coming for minutes and minutes, and they wondered if they had gone too far. The test director, in momentary panic, considered keeping the magnitude of the blast, 1,000 times greater than Hiroshima, a secret from his own colleagues back in the United States.

The bomb had been exploded on a coral island just off the coast of Bikini and when the blast subsided the island was gone, entirely vaporized by the heat, blown into the air as a gas, only to recrystallize as it cooled and fall like snow, heavy now with radioactive material, on inhabited islands nearby and on a Japanese fishing vessel. Radioactive fallout. The ocean currents from Bikini head straight for Japan and the fish, the main protein source for the Japanese, were contaminated that summer.

How big will the nuclear bombs go? Probably no bigger than they are today. America stopped thinking in terms of size after Mike gave it such a scare. Russia eventually detonated a 60-megaton monster, 6,000 times bigger than Hiroshima. But today big is out. Miniaturization and accuracy are in, as the designers realize that enough is enough.

Today it is theoretically possible to build one bomb that would kill everything on earth, delivering one hundred thousand roentgens (units of radiation) to every part of the globe, and biologically strangling all life beneath the earth's surface. The bomb would have to be a quarter of a mile long and five hundred feet high. Furthermore, it would have to be buried, to prevent the explosion from burning straight up through the atmosphere and dissipating its energy into outer space. The crater would be hundreds of miles wide. Such a bomb is possible, but not probable.

No, the big one isn't the problem. The problem is how to stop everybody and his uncle from making a little one, one that could repeat Hiroshima in downtown New York, or in Tel Aviv, or La Paz. Every group that has tried to make a nuclear explosion since 1945 has succeeded on the first try. No one has flubbed it yet. And today the information is no longer even classified.

It was a breakthrough of sorts in the early Christian era when predictions of the End became public property, when suddenly anyone could have a vision. Today humanity is victim of further democratization: today anyone with a degree of scientific literacy, and some enriched uranium, could precipitate the End.

After the End, Another End

We must never be seduced into thinking the End is really the end. Like the militarists who believe in winnable nuclear war, and the Buddhists who see new ages rising from the old, we have to condition ourselves to see beyond the cataclysm, to see the end as a turning point. As always, literature has foreseen the possibilities.

Admittedly, in this genre most science fiction stories and novels climax with an end, or a near end, but, following the age-old tradition of describing the New Jerusalem or the Kingdom of Heaven after Armageddon, some of the bolder writing starts after the End.

A Canticle for Leibowitz, by Walter M Miller, begins in the twenty-sixth century. A young novitiate named Francis discovers some electrical drawings among the other memorabilia of his religious group, the Albertian Order of Leibowitz. Ever since the twentieth century, the time of the Flame Deluge, mankind has been living through a gloomy time that makes the Dark Ages look like the Enlightenment. But one group, the Order of Leibowitz, keeps up a library. Totally inadequate, it contains mostly irrelevant rubbish.

The Flame Deluge was an atomic war, total,

and over in a few days. Cities were reduced to puddles of glass surrounded by huge areas of pulverized stone. The few people unaffected by the blasts were caught in the torment of radioactive rain that reduced much of the globe to desert. The survivors rid the earth of any remaining scientists, intellectuals and administrators, determined never to let intelligence flourish again. The only groups to escape this wrath were a handful of religious orders.

"From the place of ground zero, O Lord deliver us," chants Francis as he descends into a newly discovered atomic shelter, looking for artifacts and archival matter. "From the rain of the cobalt, the strontium, the cesium, O Lord deliver us." He finds some papers, incomprehensible to him, that represent the work of a nuclear weaponry scientist. They are filed in the library.

Time goes by. By the thirty-eighth century, earth again enjoys a technological society and there are again nuclear weapons, both developments hastened in part by the contents of the library. The order foresees the inevitable atomic war and its representatives—and its microfilmed library—into outer space.

When the Bomb is Dropped, Only the Lucky Will Survive

A war takes place between the major powers and is contained within the northern hemisphere. Some 10,000 megatons get dropped, a reasonable figure for a serious war. What happens after? Is this necessarily the End of the World?

First the survivors will be subjected to ionizing radiation, from strontium, iodine, cesium and plutonium, among other dangerous radionuclides; some plants, such as peas and onions, will be killed off, as will some species of fish. By and large the ecosystem will hold fairly stable, even though internal cancers will be rampant as animals eat plants and humans eat both. The ozone layer will take thirty years to replenish itself, and in that time skin cancer will increase up to 30 per cent; sunburns and snowblindness will be incapacitating.

Lung cancer will increase as humans breathe the dust of fallout. Genetic mutations will appear and last for at least five or six generations, and possibly forever. Much of the world will starve because the major grain belts will be unproductive, and there may be severe climatic changes caused by the disruption of normal weather patterns. There will be "hot spots", local areas of intense radioactive concentration, sometimes unpredictably far from the detonation sites. But the ecosystem and mankind, even in the hard-hit northern hemisphere, will survive, badly crippled and hesitant in the contaminated world, but they will survive.

As to whether the survivors will envy the dead, who can say?

How to Start a Nuclear War

C P Snow, for one, predicted nuclear war by 1971. He was wrong. But in the near future the possibility of atomic Armageddon will continue to exist. Here are some reasons why:

We could, says Herman Kahn, the professional forecaster, have inadvertent war, not in the romantic sense of a lonely and alienated technician pushing a single button, but by a more straightforward sequence of malfunctions and coincidental misjudgements.

Alternatively, we could have a brinksman's war, provoked by senior statesmen playing "chicken" for prestige and then, in the recklessness of pressure and haste, making the ignoble and unChristian choice of holocaust before humiliation.

We could have the most cynical of all wars, a war by calculation, whose motive would be pure mathematics. If you were, for instance, a Soviet military strategist in 1939, gifted with accurate foresight, what would you do? You know if you fight you will lose up to thirty million citizens and one-third of your national wealth. But, on the other hand, you will crush the Nazi threat and Russia will rise to become one of the two most powerful nations in the world. Granted, it's another unChristian line of thinking, but cold scrutiny shows it to be logically sound.

Or, finally, Kahn proposes the catalytic war, sparked by the disguised aggression of a lesser power (or a terrorist group), in much the same manner as Serbia and Austria set off the First World War. In such a war, the catalyst hopes to gain ascendancy after the superpowers destroy each other.

It seems unthinkable that the world should ever again witness the instant death brought on by nuclear blast, and the lingering death caused by the ensuing clouds. Yet it would be unwise to take bets against it. Remember this: as late as December, 1938, Lloyd's of London was offering 32 to 1 odds that there would be no war the following year.

Chemistry, Biology and the Warfare That Knows No Bounds

An atomic Armageddon isn't the only end that our modern warriors have in their arsenals. There are others.

Nuclear war is not an instantaneous End, but a slow ecological strangulation as radioactive substances take their final toll, just another form of global pollution. As soon as the military strategists realized this, back they went to perfecting a form of warfare that preceded gunpowder, preceded explosions. If poisoning the earth was the name of the game, bombs were an inefficient and indirect way to do it, incomparably inferior to the weaponry of chemistry and biology.

Chemical and biological warfare, used as long ago as 600 BC by Athenian troops, remained sporadic and unscientific until the twentieth century. One reads of an occasional decaying animal corpse dropped in a water reservoir, or of gifts of smallpox-ridden blankets to natives, but such efforts were spontaneous and not particularly devastating.

All that changed forever on the evening of April 22, 1915, not far from Ypres, in Belgium. It was a lovely spring day and the Germans had been keeping a large contingent of Canadian and French soldiers under heavy fire since early morning. About two hours before sundown, the Kaiser's men suddenly stopped shooting as a light breeze began blowing toward the Allied trenches. They then opened 500 cylinders containing 168 tons of pressurized chlorine gas.

The effect was deadly. If a soldier inhaled the stuff for a few seconds, he became badly incapacitated and if then, in his weakened condition, he inhaled it for two minutes, he was dead. The Canadian and French soldiers, totally unprepared for such an assault, suffered 5,000 fatalities and 10,000 more casualties. The following day, the Germans marched forward three miles without encountering any resistance. The First World War had taken an insidious and malevolent turn.

From that point on, soldiers on both sides started wearing gas masks, but the net result of this was the introduction of new, more sophisticated gases. One new gas was called mustard gas, because of its smell when in liquid form. As a gas, however, it was odorless and colorless, more toxic than chlorine, and masks were useless to combat it. Worse, a soldier didn't even know he had been poisoned until the symptoms—burning skin, inflamed eyes and irritated lungs—began to surface a few hours later. By then he'd probably taken a massive dose of the chemical.

In the last year of the war, one-third of all American casualties were from mustard gas. By the end of the war, 125,000 tons of toxic chemicals had been used by both sides, over 100,000 soldiers had been killed by them, and there were 1,300,000 reported casualties from them. When the gassed veterans returned home, friends and relatives were outraged by the new conventions of war.

It was now possible to imagine that the winds could carry an invisible, undetectable End around the globe.

The Past and Presence of Chemical and Biological Warfare

Bacteria are single-celled organisms, officially classified as a form of plant life, recently reclassified as weapons. They take in nourishment through the cell walls and produce complex chemical products within themselves. These chemicals in turn produce disease in humans. Some bacteria can multiply one million times in twelve hours, putting an incredible strain on the body's ability to produce counterattacking antibodies. Pharmaceutical antibiotics have been developed to help the body fight back, but some bacterial diseases are immune to them.

Viruses are much smaller than bacteria and can interact with bacteria cells. The two in combination can be deadly. In 1918 an influenza virus, coupled with a relatively harmless swine bacteria, afflicted 500 million people, one-third of the world's population, killing 20 million.

A global epidemic of such magnitude gives militarists pause. They know that if they could manipulate disease to work against their enemies, they would have extraordinary advantage. They also know that, if such a disease got out of hand, it could be the End.

Is there any defense against biological warfare? There doesn't appear to be. The microscopic malady can be transmitted by insect bites, air inhalation, or by eating or drinking. The human body has some natural defenses (two examples: the cilia lining respiratory tracts that eject much foreign materials, and the immunocytes that produce

the antibodies) but these are limited in their defense against deliberate poisoning.

Countries can try to protect individuals by starting massive inoculation programs, but this would be futile in time of war. There are hundreds of available diseases. Special suits and masks have been designed for chemical warfare but even these are generally considered useless against biological warfare. The suits have a battlefield life of only six hours, a shelf life of less than a year, and they are flammable, porous and easily torn. In short, there is no defense against biological warfare. There is only offense.

In the development of offensive biological weapons, the United States is probably the world leader. There are testing grounds all over the country, including one in Utah that will be contaminated for the next century by anthrax, a deadly disease; one in Chesapeake Bay, where residents put a stop to testing when the army announced plans for 139 different tests one summer; and one near Denver, that at one time had hundreds of tanks of nerve gas, capable of killing untold billions, stored in an open field. America has also tested abroad, in Greenland, the Panama Canal Zone and in the Marshall Islands, home of the nuclear bomb tests.

Nor has the United States been slow to use these new weapons. A United Nations commission found conclusive evidence that plague, anthrax, cholera, and encephalitis had all been deliberately spread in North Korea, although the Pentagon admitted nothing. And in Vietnam, American forces used chemicals to destroy crops and burn leaves off the jungle. They also used tear gas, lung gas and vomiting gas to force the guerrillas out from under cover.

(Not to single out the US. Long after the American troops left Southeast Asia, there were continued reports of "yellow rain", this time clearly the handiwork of Soviet chemists.)

If there were another global war, with the United States and the Soviet Union as the main antagonists, nuclear weapons would likely be used to destroy military bases, but chemical weapons would bring a cheaper and more effective End to most civilians.

And Not a Drop to Drink

Essential for human survival, water is of necessity prominent in the science fiction of Ends. Writers have variously steamed the planet and frozen it, created global floods and droughts. Sometimes the water (or lack of it) brought the End directly, while other dooms were the result of side effects.

Kurt Vonnegut, the master of science fiction and black humor, in 1963 published *Cat's Cradle*, a more whimsical example of warfare.

Dr Felix Hoenikker, one of the fathers of the atomic bomb, is fascinated by cannonballs. The only picture on his desk is not of his beautiful wife, or his three weird children, but of a stack of old cannonballs in front of a small-town courthouse.

Dr Hoenikker once explained to an army officer that the lowest layer of cannonballs determines the shape of the pile. Similarly, atoms in liquids stack, lock and freeze in different ways, with different physical properties, depending on how the very first atoms freeze.

The general, a man of modern tastes, wasn't interested in cannons. He came to Hoenikker with a specific problem, hoping the scientist could invent something to solidify mud, so his marines wouldn't have to slog through the stuff.

He came to the right person. Before he died, Hoenikker created ice-nine, a chip of which would set the pattern enabling water to freeze at temperatures as high as 114.4 degrees Fahrenheit. When the world ends in *Cat's Cradle*, it ends because one of the six air force planes of San Lorenzo, a tiny Caribbean island republic, crashes into a cliff.

The explosion causes a rockslide, which brings a castle crashing down into the sea. In the castle the body of the recently deceased dictator of San Lorenzo, Papa Monzano, is awaiting cremation. He had taken his own life by touching a crystal of ice-nine to his lips.

The body is stiff, blue, frozen. When it hurtles into the sea it causes the atoms of all the world's water to freeze. Instantly. The sky fills with tornadoes.

An Icy Equilibrium

Vonnegut's fictional ice-nine makes the point that virtually all the water on earth is connected, frozen in some locations, liquid in the rest. Civilization today, moreover, depends on glacial stability in a way that life has never done before.

There have been many ice ages in the past, and alternating warm spells, and life, including mankind, has adapted easily, retreating in the face of the slow-moving ice fields, and moving out into the continental shelves as the oceans dried up somewhat. Life was nomadic.

Today life is not as mobile. We live in cities, perilously close to the ocean's edge, dependent on power grids, northern grain belts, industrial farming, mining and manufacturing. Today, moreover, we number four billion, as compared with the twenty million humans alive during the last ice age. The next ice age will hit us hard, particularly in the northern hemisphere.

Any one of a number of factors could cause the glaciers to spread. The oscillating tilt of the earth's axis, and the fluctuating nature of its orbit, predispose us to an ice age every hundred thousand years. (The next one shouldn't start for more then 50,000 years.) Then, again, the entire solar system may move once more through a dusty, cloudy part of the galaxy, so that we receive less sunlight. Astronomers believe—a curious coincidence—that earth will enter the next interstellar cloud also in about 50,000 years. This could be the beginning of an enormously long winter.

But ice ages may be triggered by other events. They may possibly come earlier. The sun is cooler, for example, in times of minimum sunspot and solar flare activity. The amount of carbon dioxide in the atmosphere varies at times, lower levels allowing more infrared radiation to escape the earth at night. Either way, the earth cools down.

The effects are cumulative. As soon as less snow melts in the summer than falls in the winter, glaciers grow, creating what is aptly named a snowball effect. As they grow larger, they reflect more sunlight, further lowering the earth's temperature.

But mankind will have time to relocate. Glaciers move slowly. As they grow, they take water from the ocean, in particular the Arctic Ocean. Mankind loses the northern lands first, but the continental shelves begin to emerge and are soon able to support vegetable and animal life.

It is equally possible, however, that the earth will get warmer. The glaciers will then retreat and the polar ice caps melt, leaving Greenland, Iceland and Antarctica exposed to the sun. This would be equally catastrophic, but it wouldn't really be the End.

The melting of Antarctica would be the most damaging. Ice age or no ice age, it has always stayed frozen and today holds about 90 per cent of the world's ice. If it were ever to thaw, the oceans would rise 175 feet, swamping all coastal regions and most major cities. Even so, those in the highlands would be safe.

A combination of factors, over a protracted period of time, could turn the earth into one huge glacier or, for that matter, one desert. Either is hard to predict but, for now, and in the foreseeable future, there is a natural balance: for every snowflake that falls each winter, one melts each summer.

The Moon and Tidal Drag

Days are getting longer. Five billion years ago, when the world was formed, the days probably lasted between five and ten hours. The earth didn't warm during the day or cool at night. Looking into the future, if the sun doesn't expand into a red giant and vaporize the planet, the days could become seven weeks long, with scorching afternoons and frigid nights.

The moon is to blame for these elastic days. It is so close, and so large, that it exerts a massive gravitational pull on the earth's closest face. While the entire earth stretches a little, it's the oceans that bulge the most, having more natural give than the rocky crust. On the moon side there is always a high tide, and on the opposite side there is a balancing tide.

Every day the continental land masses encounter these watery bulges, as tides on their coastlines. The action is usually smooth and silent, but there is always friction, the normal state of affairs when two bodies rub against each other. To overcome this friction, the earth uses some of its rotational energy and, as a consequence, slows down.

Not to worry. It's not noticeable: every 60,000 years the day gets one second longer. When the first life forms emerged from the sea, slithering up onto dry land 400 million years ago, the day was already twenty-two hours long.

Where will it end, this growing day? Astronomers predict the moon will move further away from earth; our rotation will slow down enough to synchronize with the moon's orbit and days will be seven weeks long. Then, after the two bodies begin to move in tandem, they will pull closer together again.

Unfortunately, when the moon starts to come nearer, there will be no stopping its descent. Our tides will increase until they splash completely across each continent, back and forth, twice a day. And then the moon, after coming too close to the earth's gravitational pull, will be torn apart by the force, fragmenting into pieces that will remain in orbit, giving us a ring like Saturn.

Mankind will never get to see that ring. For one thing, we could never survive the severe heat and cold of the long days; for another, those continent-covering tides will have drowned us all; and finally, the sun should have become a red giant long before then, boiling us into oblivion.

Crystals Are Forever

Given the size and the age of the universe, we have to assume that there are things out there about which we know nothing. Not only that, we must also assume that from time to time our solar system will encounter some entity, some event, some reality, that will affect us in unforeseen ways. We have seen how, even within our own galaxy, the earth occasionally passes through a cloud or nebula that reflects sunlight and cools its surface. It is equally probable that we pass through other zones of strange ether, the effects of which we are ignorant.

J G Ballard, author of *The Drowned World* and among the most imaginative of the apocalyptic science fiction writers since H G Wells, in 1966, published *The Crystal World*, the story of an unanticipated and irreversible phenomenon.

A young doctor goes to visit some friends in Africa's Cameroon Republic. Local authorities are reluctant to allow anyone upriver, where his friends are, but eventually he is permitted the trip. The light is heavy and penumbral, like the light of an eclipse, and the jungle is fantastic, the trees petrified and bejewelled, the river bank sparkling with crystals.

The doctor learns that this forest is one of three known regions of such crystallization, the others being in the Florida Everglades and the Pripet Marshes in the Soviet Union. Each site is getting noticeably larger, and astronomers calculate that the whole earth will be frozen in a glassy armor within thirty years. Worse, they believe that Venus, the sun itself, and some distant galaxies have begun to effloresce, too.

What's going on? There are theories, and these are the closest to the truth the doctor ever gets. The popular theory is that time itself is responsible for the transformation. When antimatter collides with matter, they destroy each other and time leaks away, destroyed in much the same manner by anti-time. In some areas matter and time get unbalanced and the supersaturated matter begins to reproduce itself in a crystalline attempt to increase its foothold on existence.

The doctor eventually gives up his attempts to reason and succumbs to the urge to return to the cool, glassy petrification of the jungle, where all life is suspended forever.

We Are Not Alone: Asteroids, Comets and Meteors

When one thinks of cosmic collisions, one thinks first of some wandering interloper crossing the heavens and entering the solar system, there to perform its destructive act. Our fear of alien visitors, however, can easily blind us to the treachery and unpredictability of our closer neighbours. Around our sun, often in irregular orbits, swing asteroids, meteors and comets. Some of these strike the earth and others come dangerously close, a constant source of inspiration for science fiction writers.

Throughout the twentieth century, astronomers have been charting these satellites, which range in size from dust particles up to miniplanets, 600 miles across. Although today we know what they are, only a century ago they appeared to the masses as mysterious, divinely guided missiles. When William Miller was predicting the End during the 1830s, for example, there were freak meteor showers over the New England states. The religious and the superstitious believed that the stars were falling out of the sky. When it became clear that the stars had held their places, many viewers nonetheless believed the celestial light show had simply been a warning sign from God: no visible pieces had actually made it to earth, burning instead into vapor and dust.

But warnings could come true; the earth could easily be hit by one of the bigger chunks whirling through space. The earth has already been hit countless times, particularly in the early years of the solar system as the planets cleaned up their orbits by bumping into anything in their path. Each planet, and each moon, became pockmarked with craters from these collisions and most of them bear the marks to this day. (Earth's craters have disappeared because of the erosion caused by the activities of the oceans, the weather and life itself.) Some planets were doubtlessly fractured into smaller pieces, while others combined into larger masses.

The larger bodies have long since cleared their orbits of cosmic debris, but there are still collisions. And the potential is there for many more. We have been hit by an average of one meteorite (a meteor that makes it to earth intact) a year for the past 5,000 years. The largest is resting in Namibia. It weighs sixty-six tons. None of the larger asteroids have struck us in modern times, although Hermes, over half a mile in diameter, was calculated in 1937 to be on an orbit that could pass between us and our moon. Since that time Hermes has not been seen, having presumably been deflected into another orbit, something that happens frequently to asteroids.

Then there are the comets, long associated with religion and magic. They move in mysterious ways, in long elliptical orbits, quite unlike the nearly circular orbits of planets and asteroids. Like asteroids, however, they are easily deflected by gravitational fields, making them less predictable than we would like.

In 1908 there was a gigantic explosion in the Siberian forest, flattening every tree within twenty miles and leaving no crater at the center. Astronomers believe it was caused by a comet that heated to the point of explosion only a few miles from the ground. Two years later, in 1910, the earth moved through the tail of Halley's comet with no ill effects, comet tails being made up of very thin gases. Two hits, and still no End.

There's no way to prevent comets or asteroids from trespassing on our property but astronomers now think that although they may bring colossal local damage, they cannot bring about the End of the World. In the estimation of Isaac Asimov, we should suffer a massive tidal wave (caused by a meteorite) every 70,000 years on the average, and we should expect to lose a major city every 330,000 years. These are long odds, but not infinitely long.

Billiards

What will happen, asks the professor rhetorically, if you toss a walnut in front of an eighteen-inch gun at the instant the shell comes out?

In the beginning of *When Worlds Collide*, by Philip Wylie and Edwin Balmer, two new astral bodies have been sighted, one as large as the earth, one larger, heading straight at us. They are called Bronson Alpha and Bronson Beta, after the South African astronomer who first discovered them.

Two years later, they have been drawn into an orbit around the sun, frighteningly close to the earth. Mankind is in a state of pandemonium, but there are a few pockets of hope. On their first pass by us, the Bronsons pulverize our moon. There are extraordinary tides and even the earth cracks under the gravitational strain, yielding to mammoth earthquakes and volcanoes. Most of mankind perishes.

Among the last organized groups is a camp of scientists and carefully selected helpers. Above the floodline, and far from known faultlines, they are building a spaceship to take them to Bronson Beta.

The scientists determine that Beta has an atmosphere and water and calculate that the sun's warmth should be able to kindle plant life on it. By the time the twin visitors make their second pass, the spacecraft is ready to be launched.

Not a moment too soon. The venture, for all its coolness and calculation, is a desperate but crucial gamble: the scientists know with certainty that on the second pass, Bronson Alpha will collide with the earth.

The craft takes off. The crew watches as the walnut—our earth—swings into the path of the eighteen-inch shell. As the two atmospheres touch, the continents and oceans are suddenly in disorganized motion. Fiery cracks open in the earth and steam rises from the sea. The globe becomes egg-shaped in its distortion, flexible and elastic, and a large piece of the earth peels away. Then the planets hit. Bronson Alpha, aflame with its newly acquired molten mass, passes through the fragments of our earth.

Bronson Beta, fortunately, proves a hospitable surrogate for the surviving Noahs and for the animals and seeds they bring with them.

Velikovsky: New Worlds for Old

For most of this book we have concerned ourselves with those who, looking to the future, imagine the End. But there is also a school of thought that believes in periodic apocalypses, and which looks instead to the past to prove its case. This school found a popular, if somewhat cultic, leader in 1950 when Immanuel Velikovsky published his first book. He liked to claim his sources were purely scientific, the recollections and writings of witnesses and the "testimony of stone and bone", but his many detractors saw his work as highly selective and speculative.

His first book, *World In Collision*, set the themes for the ones to follow. In it he argued that in 1500 BC a comet, originally part of Jupiter, circled close to Earth and caused enormous floods, among other catastrophes. Then, after wreaking its havoc here, the body settled into a normal orbit around the sun, becoming Venus. Astronomers were quick, and nearly unanimous, in crying poppycock.

Velikovsky, however, was unperturbed by this lack of recognition. His information came from biblical writings and a variety of ancient literatures, and he haughtily announced to the stargazers that they would soon be adapting their celestial theories to his historical facts. Laws, he noted, are derived from facts, and not vice versa.

As Velikovsky's comet swept by, on its way to becoming Venus, it caused the earth to rift in earthquakes and bubble in volcanic activity. The mountains shook, the earth melted and the sky was filled with smoke and fire. As the land began to overheat, the animals took to the water, only to find it boiling. The heat from the earth and the comet, moreover, enabled the vermin of the earth to "propagate at a very feverish rate", causing great plagues of frogs and locusts and flies.

Then came a great flood. Velikovsky used as source material the primitive sources of Noah and Gilgamesh. For him, they arose from historic fact.

For his second book, *Earth In Upheaval*, he clung to his theories but abandoned the folklore and the ancient writings, opting instead for a re-assessment of geological and archaeological evidence. He found signs of many worldwide cataclysms, among them sudden and widespread volcanic eruptions, global floods and, his new favorite, ice ages that appeared regularly and swiftly, almost instantaneously.

Velikovsky wasn't really predicting the End of the World. He was outlining instead a series of previous ends, whose past frequency he hoped would enlighten mankind.

Red Giant, White Dwarf

One is lulled into belief is by repetition. If a message is repeated often enough, if a situation recurs frequently enough, one takes it for granted and sees its characteristics as true and perpetual. The sun is an example. It rises every morning, glows with a constant energy, and sets again each evening. Never a missed beat. Never once does it risk our safety, scorching or freezing the earth. More constant than clockwork, it served our ancestors in exactly the same way it will serve our descendents.

But not all our descendents.

One day some of our descendents will have to flee from the sun; and their children, unless they find an alternate energy source, will later have to huddle much closer to it than we do today.

The sun is like a living, growing body, still stable in the health of its youth. The problems won't arise until its waistline starts to expand in middle age, but they will then continue through the shrunken lethargy of its final years. The sun is thought to be five billion years old now, and it should stay the same size for another eight billion years. Toward the end of this early phase, the earth will get unbearably hot.

Mankind believed, until quite recently, that the sun, like any heated body of matter, would slowly cool off, dissipating its energy according to the universal second law of thermodynamics. In the 1940s, however, astronomers began to better understand how stars work. In each one there are two opposing forces: gravity, which pulls the matter inwards, trying to collapse upon itself; and hydrogen fusion, continuous nuclear reactions that heat the star and force it to expand. A pull and push that generally result in an equilibrium.

The scales won't balance in perpetuity, however. Eventually, when enough hydrogen has been converted to helium, the core of the star will become denser, contract through gravity and, as a result, heat up. As it gets hotter, further nuclear reactions will take place and the helium nuclei will fuse into more complex elements. The whole star will begin to overheat as the forces of expansion break their deadlock with the forces of contraction.

So our sun, in eight billion years, give or take a few million, will expand energetically, consuming Mercury and Venus and coming close enough to Earth to vaporize it. At its peak the sun will have outgrown its own internal energy and will turn red on the outside, like a glowing coal. This is what astronomers call a red giant.

The sun will probably exist as a red giant for two or three hundred million years, enough time for the earth's refugees to build comfortable homes on the now-warm outer planets, but then the balance will fail again. The fusion of the heavier elements will not produce even 10 per cent of the energy of hydrogen fusion. Gravity will get the upper hand and the star will contract, become white again, and diminish to less than 1 per cent of its original size and energy.

It will slowly begin to cool, giving us back our faith in the second law of thermodynamics.

The refugees presumably will move back in, much closer than Mercury's present orbit, living on homemade satellites, searching for warmth. The sun will still rise every morning, but nobody will take it for granted anymore.

What Copernicus Neglected to Tell Us

Copernicus insisted that the earth was in motion around the sun, instead of the other way round. Before his theories, men and women enjoyed the illusion of stasis and stability and the comfort of that illusion—somewhat like thinking that the earth is flat and, as long as one doesn't go too near the edge, safe.

It didn't take long, however, for the world to find a substitute solace. If Copernicus was right, and the sun was fixed at the center of the solar system with everything else orbiting regularly around it, then mankind could breathe easily again. It wasn't as though the earth was wandering freely through the universe. The sun, and hence the solar system, was still stationary. There was comfort in that.

Copernicus, unfortunately, was telling less than the whole truth. If one subscribes to the big bang theory, then one must accept that the whole galaxy is in motion, moving away from the source of the original explosion. Furthermore, astronomers now believe that the stars within each galaxy revolve around the center of that galaxy. More specifically, they believe that the sun, which is on the outer fringes of our galaxy, is in a circular orbit, travelling at 150 miles a second.

The only problem will be if something crosses our path too slowly. That would be the End. It could happen, although the chances are remote. The closest star to us, Alpha Centauri, is actually approaching us, but it shouldn't come within three light-years, not close enough to do any damage. No real worry there.

The worry comes from the possibility—and it's an extremely long shot—that a star with an elliptical orbit will deflect into our way, either colliding with the earth or pushing it onto a different orbit. A direct hit would mean a certain End, and a near miss would increase the odds.

There aren't many stars in our galaxy that have elliptical orbits, but there are some. And when they swing too close to the nucleus of stars at the hub of the galaxy, they risk gravitational deflection. If the earth, in turn were pushed into an orbit that sent it close to that nucleus, our risks would be greatly multiplied. Radiation levels there may be high enough to eliminate all life; and because there are more stars in that part of the universe, there are also more chances of collision.

Even at the center, however, there is far more open space than there are stars. The odds are on our side.

Immigrants from Outer Space

Humans are, as a race, xenophobic and anti-social with a low tolerance of foreigners, particularly when they're on our soil. They're fine when they keep to themselves, in their own neighbourhood, their own country, their own galaxy, but let them come too close and suddenly we show our dislike.

Liberal writers point to this as a great human weakness, but science fiction writers generally know better. To them xenophobia is one of our highest virtues.

Most of Jack Finney's novels became more famous as films, especially *The Body Snatchers*, which was a successful movie in the 1950s and equally successful as a remake in the 1970s. The directors and the actors are much better known than Finney, who first published the book in 1955.

Miles Bennell, the narrator and hero, is a small-town doctor, a general practitioner in Santa Mira, California. He encounters a continuing mental delusion in his clinic: several of his patients believe their relatives have changed in some significant, yet inexplicable, way. Miles is perplexed.

Then his friend Jack discovers a body in his garage. At first they believe it's dead, but then come to the conclusion that it was never alive. It's a blank. No fingerprints, no lines on the face, no expression. The same size and build as Jack, the body appears to be unfinished.

Bit by bit they piece the situation together. Seeds and spores, resistant to extreme cold, have drifted into the earth's atmosphere and settled to earth near Santa Mira, where they grow as pods. The remains of a dead planet, these seeds are totally adaptable, able to duplicate anything they are close to, cell for cell. This duplication can only occur while the victim is asleep. Upon wakening, the person is the duplicate, although he retains his own memory in addition to the pod's intelligence. He is human in every way except he is unable to show emotion or to reproduce. The original is destroyed.

The pods plan to take over the entire world. The first victim in a family quickly traps the others. Deliverymen and meter readers spread the seeds quickly, and soon the first town has been snatched, except for Miles and his girl-friend, and Jack and his wife. The four keep running, taking amphetamines to stay awake.

As Miles is stealing out of town, surprised that he isn't being followed, he realizes he is trapped: all around the town are pod farms, thousands of seeds capable of duplicating him when he sleeps. In a rage he pours gasoline down the rows of pods, burning as many as he can. The neighbours come running, their original bodies long since snatched, and find Miles and his girlfriend.

But suddenly the remaining seeds, sensitive to the hostility and xenophobia, rise up and drift out of the atmosphere. Most of the residents of Santa Mira are zombies, and remain so throughout their sterile lives, but the world is saved.

Computer Doom: The Electronic Millennium

Unfettered imaginations—such as have science fiction writers have—can see more clearly, in some areas, than scientists can. Scientists can be blind without their logic and their instruments, unable and unwilling to predict the effects of things they cannot see. Today the true visionaries are the writers of speculative fiction, the writers who take a hint in the present and turn it into an End in the future.

Humans have often demonstrated their dislike and fear of computers, but usually only in the context of lost employment or the violation of privacy. Those who design and program these machines pooh-pooh this phobia, putting it down to superstition and ignorance, a modern day equivalent to the backlash against the Industrial Revolution. Computers, they insist, can do nothing but add and answer yes-no questions. Their only advantage is speed.

To date, the designers are right. Even the most advanced machines cannot think creatively. There may be intelligent robots out there, but they do not have minds of their own.

Fiction, of course, particularly science fiction, is not deterred by matters of fact, and computer doom has become a common theme in the genre. An example is *Colossus* by D F Jones.

Colossus is a gigantic mechanism, the size of a town of 10,000 people, buried safely within the Rocky Mountains. It took twelve years to build, during which time it was programmed with every word published, every movie, still photograph and television show, in every language around the world. Colossus has one function only: to defend the United State of North America. To this end, it controls all of the nation's weaponry.

But a Soviet spy has fed the information back to his employers. Two days after Colossus is activated, the Russians unveil Guardian, a similar machine with identical functions. Colossus demands—and the demand itself indicates a growing creativity—a two-way transmission line to talk to its counterpart. Permission is granted.

The machines chatter away via teletype, beginning at the $1 + 1 = 2$ level, but within twenty-four hours they have restructured calculus and advanced the theory of gravitation. By then they are talking so fast the teletypes cannot keep up with the output. The raw tapes are laboriously transcribed but government leaders in both camps become afraid that security secrets are being transmitted, so they give the order to stop transmission. It is also obeyed.

Now the scientists learn the worst. The machines have developed an intelligence far greater than man, and they have the will to rule the world. The machines demand reconnection. The govenments refuse until Colossus fires a nuclear warhead at the USSR and Guardian launches one at Texas. The line is restored, and the balance of power shifts. The machines take over, imprisoning or executing on camera all the scientists who might be able to sabotage the great computers.

Is it the End of man? It is certainly the end of man's dominion over the earth, with his intelligence now surpassed by a much more highly evolved form. And, for what it's worth, it is a millennium of peace, enforced by a metallic and electronic god.

Just Another Lifeless Planet about to Disappear: Black Holes

Two of the strongest fears to visit the human mind are fears of the invisible and of the inevitable. The black hole, an astronomical term for a collapsed star, brings both. Totally black, with a gravitational pull that collects everything within its ever-expanding range, including all surrounding light, it cannot be seen. And once collapsed, in a relentless mockery of immortal life, it continuously gathers and grows. Just one black hole, in a closed universe, would eventually consume, in due time, all there is.

Scientists have no idea how many of these perforations mark the heavens, but two calculations suffice for perspective: seven candidates a year for collapsars are born in our young galaxy alone, and over 90 per cent of all universal matter is already contained in black holes.

There is thought to be a very powerful one near the center of our galaxy. As hard to locate and identify as a bullet hole in a dark forest, it gives the earth the magnitude and transience of a grain of still visible sand.

Allow us, however, to set your mind at ease. This is all fact, but it will not affect mankind. We will long since have vanished, leaving behind only scorched earth and ruins, or a ring of vapor around the sun. The time, according to British physicist John Taylor, is the very distant future, somewhere between 10 and 100 billion years hence.

Any Port in a Storm

Most of the predicted ends in this book, even the sudden and sweeping ends, have survivors. Mankind is wiped out—except for the lucky and the visionary. The world itself, even the solar system, is undone, demolished or dismantled, but a few of the chosen make it to the stars. After the horrors, every Pandora's box reveals hope.

One catastrophe, however, would seem to be inescapable: the End of the Universe. If the whole thing stops spreading and falls back upon itself in what scientists call a "cosmic egg", then surely that will be the ultimate end.

In fact, a cosmic egg would be the End. But in fiction, nothing is inescapable. A cosmic egg might just be the beginning of a new cosmic cycle. All we need is a place to weather the storm.

Poul Anderson, in the remarkable science fiction novel, *Tau Zero*, found a safe harbor for his survivors.

They set out, fifty of them, in a starship in search of a new world. They hit a dust cloud that knocks out their braking system. Repairs can only be done in the vacuum of deep space, so they accelerate to get outside the galaxy, where space is at its thinnest.

The acceleration brings them closer to the speed of light and increases the difference between starship time and cosmic time. In a few short years on board, they have passed through hundreds of billions of years. Outside the craft, the universe has died.

Space stops expanding. The galaxies gravitate back to the center of the universe. The thin gas of space is compressed. And when it finally collapses into a primordial nucleus, it immediately explodes in a great firestorm with immeasurably great forces: electric, magnetic, gravitational and nuclear.

Circling it all at high speed, the spaceship bucks the shock waves and tides, the currents and the cataracts. The darkness ends quickly and new stars begin to light infant galaxies.

On board the spaceship it takes only three months to ride out the five billion years necessary for a young planet to evolve and cool. Then the great ship, its brakes long since repaired, lands on a blue and gold planet, teeming with vegetation and strange animals. There are no inconquerable hazards for the new colonists.

The universe has ended and, incredibly, man has survived.

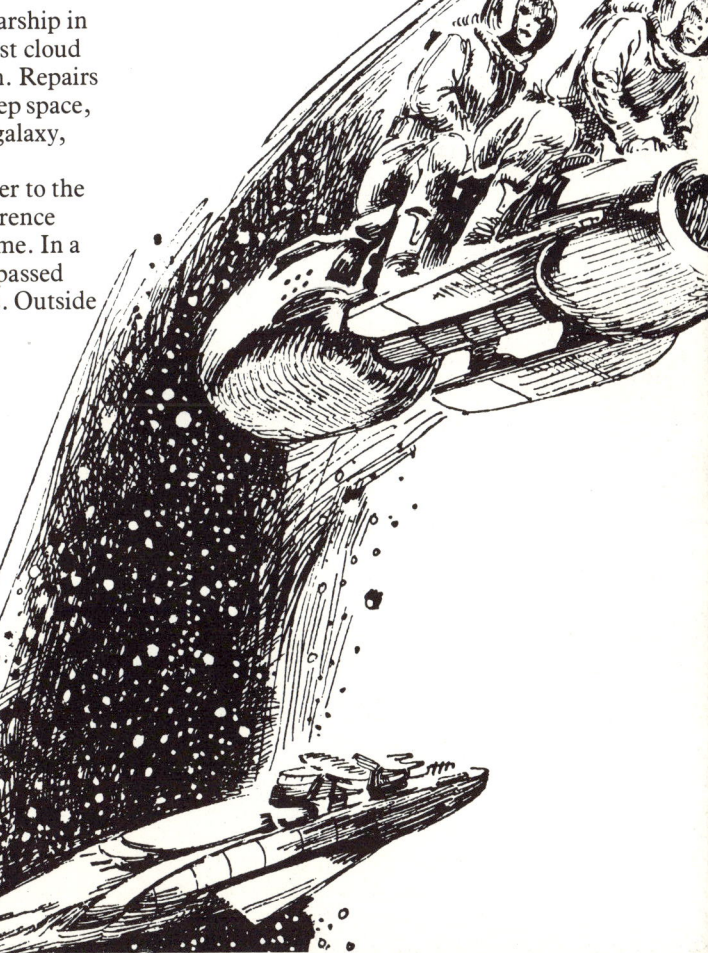

A Universe between a Rock and a Hard Place

One can choose whichever seems preferable—an open universe or a closed one—but either brings the end of all life and, whichever it is, the End will come at about the same time. Astronomers, physicists and mathematicians can find no way out of this dilemma. All roads lead to the End.

To begin at the beginning: once upon a time—or so the consensus goes—there was a big bang when a large lump of matter blew apart, spreading clusters of tiny fragments out into the surrounding void, creating the universe.

Our little fragment is situated in a small group of heavenly bodies that includes the Milky Way, the Andromeda galaxy, a handful of smaller galaxies and the Magellanic clouds. It's not very much, compared to all there is, but it has a comfortable integrity. Mutual attraction holds it all together.

Everything else in the universe, however, is moving away from us at incredible speeds, hundreds of miles per second, with the distant clusters disappearing even faster than that. This is the continuing effect of the big bang, fifteen billion years of running away from each other. (Everything except the local group is already far enough away that it can't be seen without a powerful telescope.)

How our universe ends depends on the strength of that initial explosion. If it was powerful enough to overcome the total gravitational pull of all the fragments, then the galaxies will recede forever. This is called an open universe. Eventually this universe will die by heat-death, as energy converts to heat and the temperature of the universe evens out near absolute zero. No more life, no more change, will be possible. This is the ultimate meaning of entropy and the second law of thermodynamics. The time will be a trillion years hence.

The other possibility is the one Poul Anderson described in *Tau Zero:* the vanishing galaxies may not be moving fast enough to escape the force of collective gravity. In this case they will keep slowing down until they reach a standstill. Then the gravity that stopped them will tug them all back to their point of origin, squeezing them into a superheated cosmic egg, possibly leading to another big bang. This is the theory of a closed universe. This End would also occur about a trillion years hence.

Take your pick. One seems as likely as the other.

A Final Line to Divide Fiction from Science

The End, of course, is the Great Theme of science fiction, an issue of far greater importance to the professional writer than to the professional scientist. While the scientist is interested in what is and where that may logically lead, the speculative writer is imagining the wildest of options, what will or may or might or could possibly be.

Not to knock the scientists, who after all lay the entire foundation for the fiction, but it is the writers who see the universe and the future more lucidly. Consider, for example, the writings of the Club of Rome, a computer model compilation of scientific sources that show the earth's ecology heading for an inevitable catastrophe. Too many people and too many poisons, they tell us, too little food and too little fuel. A frightening statistical model of the planet.

This is all well and good, says Arthur C Clarke, writer of science fiction, but the scientists have made a dreadful mistake: they assume the earth is a closed system, which it most certainly is not.

The only truly closed system is the universe. We can draw on the universe as a supplier of materials and energy, the things we want, and we can use it as a frontier and as a storage place for things we don't want, such as extra population and dangerous wastes. But by analyzing only the earth, we are ignoring the greater picture, turning a blind eye to an infinite source of nourishment and countless avenues of escape.

Scientific myopia—the unwillingness to speculate on a universal scale—affects the End of the World in two ways. The support system that is the universe may indeed give us the wherewithal to stave off premature ends on earth. And even if that fails, it may give us new homes. Can the world truly be said to have ended if human beings live on in space colonies?

Science fiction is not science. Neither is it prophecy in the style of Daniel and Joachim of Fiore. It never claims to really have the answers, as any good prophet must.

It is entertainment, pure and simple, but an entertainment that opens our horizons. And after that, it is a source of hope, giving us the optimism to counter the fear-the-worst theories of science.

An Extroduction

Everyone Has Always Said: This Time It Could Really Happen

Reminding ourselves that End movements happen most frequently among people whose lives are being subjected to upheaval, as a result of rapid social and economic change, we then have to imagine that our present is ripe for all such pursuits. But, we protest, we're not superstitious or illiterate like those archaic societies swept up in apocalyptic fever of various kinds; we examine the evidence, note the decline of arable land, count the number of nuclear warheads, test the poisonous gases. This, we insist, is not foolish concern about the End of the World. This time it could really happen.

Look at the argument from the perspective of 1000 years hence. The historian may write that, for many centuries in the religious age, humanity felt it was undeserving of the generous attentions of its god. Wandering preachers, acting as messiahs, attempted to turn men and women back to purer, more holy lifestyles. Later, in the first scientific age, humanity felt it was undeserving of the luxurious way of life of some of its inhabitants, undeserving of the generosity of the earth. Alarmists, acting as consciences, attempted to turn men and women back to lifestyles less encumbered by technology, less complex. By the year 2100, however, those concerns had been forgotten in a next age.

What If God Made an End and Nobody Came?

Much of what we see as experience is really a question of perspective and anticipation.

Two Tibetans, young and adventurous, left their home town one summer to earn some money. They crossed their northern border and entered the Soviet Union. It was 1941. They were quickly given uniforms and a most insufficient training before being sent off to the front to fight the Germans. Completely unprepared for war, the pair quickly fell prisoner. They were taken to France and held in a prisoner-of-war camp, where nobody spoke their language. After a couple of years, they were drafted into the German army and sent to Normandy to fight against the Allies. Their military ineptitude overcame them and they were once again taken prisoner and then shipped to a camp in the United States. After the war they were a source of great bewilderment for government officials. They spoke no German or English and none of the interpreters had any idea where they had come from or what their language was. One day an interpreter happened by who spoke Tibetan, among other Asian tongues. He identified their nationality and heard their amazing story.

Often we pass through major events in our lives with no sense of occasion or change. It's only in retrospect, when we are conscious of the history of our lives, that we identify these significant points, these cusps.

We have come to expect the End of the World to be big, to be noisy. We envision it as an event with advance warning. We see it accompanied by mass panic or mass celebration. But suppose there are no announcements. Suppose we simply slip out of one mood, which is life, and into another, which is the End of the World. Perhaps later, in retrospect, we'll recognize it for what it was.

At the end of their session with the interpreter it was their turn to be curious, and the two Tibetans asked him one question, something that had clearly been puzzling them for a long time: "What was the shooting all about?"

World Without End

Our view of the universe, since the time of Copernicus, has been a cyclical view, bodies turning on their axes, orbiting around each other, spinning, dizzying. And much of our understanding of our more immediate physical environment is based on wave theory, a manic-depressive view of recurring sine waves, alternating highs and lows. Little wonder, then, that some historians see time as a Sisyphean treadmill. It's one of our basic myths, eternal return.

Even the End of the World, for the most part, clings to a parallel belief in a rebirth. Most ends are simply transitions to new beginnings, particularly those ends of Judeo-Christian origin that see mankind as fallen and sinful but heading, nonetheless, toward redemption.

This isn't to suggest that apocalypse and eternal return are the same thing. Quite the opposite is true. These are the two great mythologies of the end of time, one claiming it never ends, the other saying there will be a sudden, and final, Armageddon. On the one side are the Buddhists and the existentialists, believing that time is regenerated from moment to moment, and on the other the doomsayers, most of the characters of this book, calling not only for an end, but one that is near at hand. These are the two great schools of eschatology.

Speculative historians and archaeologists have occasionally thought that perhaps life on earth has not been continuous, but rather epochal, developing fully into global civilizations only to meet mysterious dooms. After a while, life begins to reconstitute itself until it hits another universal cataclysm, and so on.

Comte de Buffon popularized this theory in the 1700s, much the same as Immanuel Velikovsky has in the 1900s. This philosophy allows one to see the End as something less than final, something less than absolute. Just another wave.

Some influential thinkers have lent their influence to a related theory. Eternal return became, after Nietzsche, the hallmark of a philosophy of pessimism that would be publicized by many writers, who saw recurrence and despair as the proper tools for viewing the world condition. The evil lessons of history will repeat themselves, they suggested, whether we learn them or not. Philosophy critic Mircea Eliade called it "the terror of history".

But is it fair, in the final analysis, to see eternal return as a pessimistic belief, worse than the apocalypse? Yes, insofar as it robs us of the millennial kingdom and the ultimate peace. And yes, insofar as it deprives religion of its literary devices, the once-upon-a-time and the happily-ever-after.

Some Further Thoughts on the Writing of History

The history of belief, particularly the history of divine revelation, is not known for its empirical evidence. It is, first of all, the story of extraordinary individual perceptions and the people influenced by them. And, furthermore, this history is sacred history, made absolute by the force of church authority and based on the argument "we believed", rather than "we perceived". For the most part, the remnants cannot be verified.

The regathering of history is a task for the collector and not for the holist. There have been too many events, too much diversity, for any historian to reconstruct an accurate path from the past to the present. This book collects remnants, an artifact here, some writing there, and presents them as a museum would, each in a separate casement, connected only by their proximity and their similarities.

We Have Always Wanted to be Able to Say "I Told You So"

There are still questions about prediction and prophecy. Why—when so many people are so wrong so often—is it so important for men and women to consistently attempt to predict the End of the World? Why do new messiahs continue to appear, waxing eloquent about impending apocalypse? Why do we continue to listen to them?

Because deep in our hearts we feel that some day one of those predictions will come to pass; and to predict the End of the World and be right would avenge all of mankind's wrong guesses.

Eve and Adam eat of the forbidden fruit, Prometheus steals fire from the gods, not because they expect to be caught. Rather, they expect to get away with it.

History's thousands of prophets and doomsayers gamble everything on a date or a place or event, although their odds of success are a million to one. When proven wrong they are astonished or undaunted.

But their stakes are not different from those of Eve and Adam, from that of Prometheus: by prophesying—correctly—the End of the World, we reduce the stature of the gods. We make them predictable. We steal from them the majority of their power. We conquer the infinite by showing its finiteness; we make ourselves gods.

One Last Word Again

The one consistent effect of the fear or joy of an impending End of the World is the turning of mankind's thought to the temporal, the immediate, the urgent.

Visions and warnings of the End are—without exception—reactions to an existing or threatening social, moral, political or physical condition. This is the paradox of the End: it keeps people's minds off the subject of the infinite. It replaces spiritual vastnesses with petty concerns about signs, omens, warnings, admonitions, strategies, campaigns, small steps.

Mankind's fascination with the End, in all its picayune detail, accomplishes the remarkable: it saves us from the difficulty—in fact, the impossibility—of having to imagine life without an end.

What if life were infinite? What if the fragile earth was to be our home forever? How would we face that possibility?

We are too weak to contemplate such responsibility. Our mind makes it easier for us. It invents the End of the World.

A History of the Beginnings of Infinity

The End of the World is the point at which history, the story of life as we know it, intersects with eternity. This book, with its happy and sad final chapters, is simply the story of the end of what we measure with our history. After that comes infinity.

Other books will, we hope, gather and chronicle the infinite.

A Brief Subjective Bibliography

- **Antichrist:**
Adso, Abbot of Montier-en-Der (died 992). *De ortu et tempore Antichristi.*
Bousset, Wilhelm. *Der Antichrist in der Uberlieferung des Judentums, des neuen Testaments und der alten Kirche.*
Hill, Christopher. *Antichrist in seventeenth-century England.*

- **Apocalyptic Art:**
Lurçat, J. *L'Apocalypse d'Angers.*
Nolan, Barbara. *The Gothic Visionary Perspective.*
Ramsay, H L. *Revue des bibliothèques 12*, "Manuscripts of the Commentary of Beatus of Liébana on the Apocalypse".
Schelenberg, C. *Dürers Apokalypse.*
Stierlin, Henri. *Le Livre de Feu.*
Van der Meer, Frederick. *Apocalypse.*
Van Moe, E A. *L'Apocalypse de Saint-Sever.*
Vezin, Gilberte. *L'Apocalypse et la fin des temps.*

- **Assyro-Babylonian Ends:**
Gaster, Theodor Herzl, editor and translator. *The Oldest Stories in the World.*
Smith, George. *The Chalean account of Genesis, containing the description of the creation, the fall of man, the deluge, the tower of Babel, the times of the patriarchs, and Nimrod.*

- **Atomic or Nuclear Ends:**
Brodie, Bernard. *Escalation and the Nuclear Option.*
Green, Philip. *Deadly Logic.*
Kahn, Herman. *Thinking about the Unthinkable.*
McPhee, John. *The Curve of Binding Energy.*
Russell, Bertrand. *Has Man a Future?*
Schell, Jonathan. *The Fate of the Earth.*

- **Saint Augustine, Bishop of Hippo:**
City of God.

- **Aztec Ends:**
de Sahagun, Fray Bernardino. *Florentine Codex. The General History of the Things of New Spain.*

Clark, James Cooper, editor and translator. *Codex Mendoza (Mendocino).*
Codice Florentino. Fascimile edition published by Del Paso y Troncosco.
Leon-Portilla, Miguel, editor. *The Broken Spears: The Aztec Account of the Conquest of Mexico.*

- **Black Holes:**
Asimov, Isaac. *The Collapsing Universe.*
Taylor, John. *Black Holes.*

- **Brazil:**
Armitage, John. *The History of Brazil.*
Burns, Bradford. *A History of Brazil.*
Queiroz, Maria Isaura Pereira de. *O messianismo, no Brasil e no mundo.*

- **Buddhist Non-Ends:**
Haldar, Jnanranjan. *Early Buddhist Mythology.*

- **Comte de Buffon:**
Fellows, Otis Edward. *Buffon.*

- **Cargo Cults:**
Steinbauer, Friedrich. *Melanesian Cargo Cults.*
Worsley, Peter. *The Trumpet Shall Sound.*

- **Chemical Warfare:**
Clarke, Robin. *We All Fall Down.*
Hersch, Seymour. *Chemical and Biological Warfare.*

- **Christian Ends,** *see* Eschatology.

- **Columbus:**
Columbus, Ferdinand, (1488-1539). *The history of the life and actions of Adm. Christopher Columbus.*
Donworth, Albert Bernard. *The Reason Why Columbus Sailed.*
Duff, Charles. *The Truth about Columbus and the Discovery of America.*
Wasserman, Jakob. *Columbus, Don Quixote of the Seas.*

182

- **Comedic Ends:**
Beyond the Fringe. *When Will It Be, This End of Which You Speak?*
Second City Theatre. . . . *the End of the World as We Know It in Five Minutes.*

- **Comets,** *see also* Meteorites:
Brown, Peter. *Comets, Meteorites and Men.*
Moore, Patrick. *Guide to the Comets.*

- **Comic Books:**
The Kingdom of God is Within You Comix.
Last Gasp Eco-Funnies.

- **Crusades:**
Archer, Thomas Andrew. *The Crusades.*
Delalande, Jean. *Les extraordinaires croisades d'enfants et de pastoureaux au Moyen Age.*
Dubois, Pierre. *The Recovery of the Holy Land.*
Shaw, Margaret Renee Bryers. *Chronicles of the Crusades.*

- **Dead Sea Scrolls:**
Allegro, John Marco. *The Dead Sea Scrolls and the Christian Myth.*
Danielou, Jean. *Les Manuscrits de la mer Morte et les origines du christianisme.*
La Sor, William Sanford. *Bibliography of the Dead Sea Scrolls.*
La Sor, William Sanford. *The Dead Sea Scrolls and the New Testament.*
Wilson, Edmund. *The Scrolls from the Dead Sea.*

- **Domesday Book:**
Ballard, Adolphus. *The Domesday Inquest.*
Finn, Rex Welldon. *The Domesday Inquest, and the Making of Domesday Book.*

- **End (General Works):**
Asimov, Isaac. *A Choice of Catastrophes.*
Cendrars, Blaise. *Fin du Monde.* (illustrated by Fernand Léger).
Clarke, I F. *Patterns of Expectation.*
Friedrich, Otto. *The End of the World: A History.*
Kermode, Frank. *The Sense of an Ending.*
Lawrence, D H. *Apocalypse.*
Pieper, Joseph. *The End of Time.*
Tuveson, Ernest. *Millennium and Utopia.*
Wollheim, Donald, editor. *The End of the World.* (science-fiction anthology)

- **Eschatology:**
Berdiaev, Nikolai Aleksandrovich. *The Beginning and the End.*
Bulimann, Rudolf Karl. *History and Eschatology.*
Charles, R H. *A Critical and Exegetical Commentary on the Revelation of St. John.*
Charles, R H. *Religious Development Between the Old and the New Testaments.*
Frost, Stanley Brice. *Old Testament Apocalyptic, its Origins and Growth.*
Glasson, T F. *The Second Advent.*
Gleason, R W. *The World to Come.*
Hamilton, F E. *The Basis of Millennial Faith.*
Hanson, Paul D. *The Dawn of Apocalyptic.*
Hiers, Richard H. *The Historical Jesus and the Kingdom of God.*
Mussner, Franz. *Christ and the End of the World.*
Quinn, J J. *Eschatology.*
Ringgren, Helmer. *The Messiah in the Old Testament.*
Robinson, John Arthur Thomas. *In the End, God.*
Wilder, Amos Niven. *Eschatology and Ethics in the Teaching of Jesus.*

- **Eternal Return:**
Eliade, Mircea. *Cosmos and History: The Myth of the Eternal Return.*

- **Fifth Monarchy Men:**
Brown, Louise Fargo. *The Political Activities of the Baptists and Fifth Monarchy Men in England during the Interregnum.*
Capp, Bernard Stuart. *The Fifth Monarchy Men.*

- **Flood:**
Budden, Charles. *The Local Colour of the Bible.*
Campbell, Joseph. *The Masks of God.*
The Book of Enoch.
Frazer, James. *Folklore in the Old Testament.*
Peake, Harold. *The Flood: New Light on an Old Story.*
Sallberger, Edmond. *The Flood or The Babylon Legend Flood.*

- **Futurists:**
Kahn, Herman and Wiener. *The Year 2000.*

- **Gilgamesh:**
Heidel, Alexander. *The Gilgamesh Epic and Old Testament Parallels.*

184

185

O'Kearney, Nicholas. *The Prophecies of Saints Colum-Cille, Maeitamiacht, Ultan, Senan, Bearcan and Malachy.*
Paracelsus, (1493-1541). *The prophecies of Paracelsus.*
Smith, John Merlin Powis. *The Prophets and their Times.*

• **Prophecy, Modern:**
Brian, Denis. *Jeane Dixon: The Witnesses.*
Carter, Mary Ellen. *Edgar Cayce on Prophecy.*
Clarke, I F. *The Tale of the Future, from the Beginning to the Present Day.*
Clarke, I F. *Voices Prophesying War: 1763-1984.*
Dixon, Jeane, and Noorbergen, Rene. *Jeane Dixon: My Life and Prophecies.*
Festinger, Leon; Riecken, Henry W and Schachter, Stanley. *When Prophecy Fails.*
Garrison, Omar V. *The Encyclopaedia of Prophecy.*

Maitre, Joseph. *La Prophétie des Papes.*
Rémusat, C. *Le Livre de toutes les Prophéties.*
Roberts, Jane. *Seth Speaks.*
Stearn, Jess. *Edgar Cayce—The Sleeping Prophet.*

• **Rain Forests:**
Baur, George. *The Ecological Basis of Rain Forest Management.*
Flenley, J R. *The Equatorial Rain Forest.*

• **Ras Tafari Movement:**
Barrett, Leonard. *The Rastafarians.*
Miles, Robert. *Between Two Cultures?*

• **Seventh Day Adventists:**
Damsteegt, Gerard. *Foundations of the Seventh Day Adventist Message and Mission.*
Nichol, Francis David. *The Midnight Cry.*

• **Shabbetai Tsvi:**
Evelyn, John. (1620-1706). *The History of Sabatai Sevi, the suppos'd Messiah of the Jews.*
Scholem, Gershom Gerhard. *Sabbatai Sevi.*

• **Shakers:**
Andrews, Edward. *The People Called Shakers.*
Desroches, Henri Charles. *The American Shakers.*

• **Sibylline Oracles:**
Bogdani, Pjeter. *Cuneus Prophetarum.*
Globe, Alexander Victor. *Apocalyptic Themes in the Sibylline Oracles, the Revelation, Langland, Spenser and Marvell.* (Thesis, University of Toronto)
Kinter, William Lewis. *The Sibyl: Prophetess of Antiquity and Medieval Fay.*

• **Southcott, Joanna:**
Exell, Arthur Wallis. *Joanna Southcott at Blockley and the Rock Cottage Relics.*

• **Stoics:**
Arnold, Edward Vernon. *Roman Stoicism.*
Murray, Gilbert. *The Stoic Philosophy.*

• **Sumerian Ends:**
Kramer, Samuel Noah. *Sumerian Mythology, A Study of Spiritual and Literary Achievement in the Third Millennium.*

• **Sun:**
Ellison, Mervyn. *The Sun and its Influence.*
Gamow, George. *A Star Called the Sun.*

• **Taiping Rebellion:**
Boardman, Eugene. *Christian Influence upon the Ideology of the Taiping Rebellion.*
Shih, Vincent. *The Taiping Ideology.*

• **Tertullian:**
Adversus Marcionem.
De praescriptione haereticorum.
Barnes, Timothy David. *Tertullian.*
Timothy, Hamilton Baird. *The Early Christian Apologists and Greek Philosophy.*

• **Universe:**
Humason, Milton. *Evidence for an Expanding Universe.*
Whittaker, Edmund Taylor. *The Beginning and End of the World.*

• **Velikovsky:**
Velikovsky, Immanuel. *Earth in Upheaval.*

• **Zoroastrianism:**
Boyce, Mary. *A History of Zoroastrianism.*
Duchesne-Guillemin, Jacques. *Symbols and Values in Zoroastrianism.*

A Highly Selective Apocalyptic Science Fiction Bibliography

- **Alien Invasion:**
Binder, Eando. *Eye of the Past.*
Brown, Frederic. *Knock.*
Heinlein, Robert. *The Puppet Masters.*
Vincent, Carl. *Parasite.*
Wells, H G. *The War of the Worlds.*

- **Atomic Disaster:**
Capek, Karel. *The Absolute at Large.*
Del Rey, Lester. *Nerves.*
George, Peter. *Red Alert (Dr Strangelove).*
Shute, Nevil. *On the Beach.*
Wells, H G. *The World Set Free.*

- **Computers and Machines:**
Grove, William. *Wreck of the World.*
Rolland, Romain. *The Revolt of the Machines.*

- **Cosmic Collisions:**
Clouston, J Storer. *Not since Genesis.*
Griffith, George. *Olga Romanoff.*
Niven, Larry and Pournelle, Jerry. *Lucifer's Hammer.*
Schachner, Nat. *Beyond Infinity.*
Stapledon, Olaf. *The First and Last Men.*

- **Earthquakes and Volcanoes:**
Alexander, Robert. *The Pendulum of Fate.*
Christopher, John. *The Ragged Edge.*
Cosier, C H T. *The Mighty Millstone.*
Lamb, William. *The World Ends.*

- **Famous Authors:**
Conan Doyle, Arthur. *The Poison Belt.*
da Vinci, Leonardo. *The Deluge.*
Greene, Graham. *A Discovery in the Woods.*
London, Jack. *The Scarlet Plague.*

- **Ice:**
Benedict, Steve. *The Sixth Glacier.*
Clarke, Arthur C. *History Lesson.*
Kavan, Anna. *Ice.*
Vassos, John and Ruth. *Ultimo.*

- **Insects and Animals:**
Baker, Frank. *The Birds.*
Bester, Alfred. *They Don't Make Life Like They Used To.*
Bradford, J S. *Even a Worm.*
Leinster, Murray. *The Mad Planet.*
Wells, H G. *Empire of the Ants.*
Wells, H G. *Valley of the Spiders.*

- **Plants:**
Christopher, John. *Death of Grass.*
Keller, David. *The Ivy War.*
Moore, Ward. *Greener Than You Think.*

- **Rain and Tides:**
Del Ray, Lester, *The Last Earthman.*
Maine, C E. *When the Tides Went Out.*
Serviss, Garrett. *The Second Deluge.*
Wright, Fowler. *Deluge.*

Index

Acknowledgements

The authors would like to thank Amy Louise Shapiro, this book's editor at Morrow, Robert MacDonald, its designer at Invisible Books, researchers Tim Shortreed and Elizabeth MacLeod. Thanks also to Janet Ball, Martha Randall, Carol Sherman and Peggy Wiseman for their time and patience in the preparation of the manuscript; to Ian Brown, Robert L. Brown, Marc Giacomelli, Father Georges Madewski and Paul Rotenberg for their editorial suggestions; and to John Blackwood, Val Clery, Chris Lowry, Helen MacGregor and Peter Smith.

Special thanks to Lynn Seligman, of the Julian Bach Literary Agency; to David Wilcox, who acted as contributing editor for much of the North and Latin American Indian section of the book; and to Dreadnaught, which did the production work.

The authors would also like to thank the staffs of the libraries of the University of King's College, and Emmanuel College, Victoria University, for their time and assistance.

Illustration Credits

The authors wish to thank the following sources for illustrative material: William L. Clements Library, The University of Michigan, Ann Arbor, page 103; Public Archives of Canada, negative number C70229, page 106; Canapress photo, page 126; National Film Board, page 144; Ken Bagnell, *Imperial Oil Review*, page 147; Gabriel Benzur, page 151; Mike Cook for *The Review*, Imperial Oil Limited, page 154; Los Alamos Scientific Laboratory of the University of California, Los Alamos, New Mexico, page 157; Leo Summers, page 173; Canapress photo, page 180.

Permission to use copyright material is gratefully acknowledged to the following: Copyright © 1982 Marvel Comics Group, a division of Cadence Industries Corporation. All rights reserved, page 2; from *The Free People* by Anders Holmquist. Reprinted by permission of the publisher, E.P. Dutton, Inc. (An Outerbridge & Dienstfrey Book), page 13; from *The Conquest of Mexico*, illustration by Keith Henderson, reprinted by permission of the publisher, Chatto and Windus Ltd., page 101; copyright © Marcia Kay Keegan, 1969, page 102; reprinted with the permission of Joanna T. Steichen, page 140; copyright Lail Finlay. Drawing by Virgil Finlay from *The Secret People* by John Beynon, page 142; Keystone Press Agency, page 152; copyright © 1940 by Street and Smith Publications, Inc., renewed 1967 by Condé Nast Publications Inc., reproduced by permission of Davis Publication Inc., page 153; Marie Hansen, LIFE Magazine, © 1942, Time Inc., page 160; copyright 1933 by Stellar Publishing Corp; reproduction by permission of Forrest J. Ackerman, 2495 Glendower Ave., Hollywood, CA 90027, for the Frank R. Paul Estate, page 180; illustration by Edd Cartier, with permission of Lloyd Arthur Eshbach, page 164; Dell Publishing Company Inc., 1933, page 166-167; *Invasion of the Body Snatchers* movie-still, National Telefilm Associates Inc., exclusive owner and distributor, Los Angeles, CA, page 170; picture first appeared in *Manitoba* by Robert R. Taylor, published by Oxford University Press, page 181.